MW01063464

THE BEST PRESIDENT THE NATION NEVER HAD

MERCER UNIVERSITY PRESS

Endowed by

TOM WATSON BROWN
and
THE WATSON-BROWN FOUNDATION, INC.

THE BEST PRESIDENT THE NATION NEVER HAD

A Memoir of Working with Sam Nunn

Roland McElroy

Mercer University Press
Macon, Georgia
2017

MUP/ H940

Published by Mercer University Press
1501 Mercer University Drive
Macon, Georgia 31207

9 8 7 6 5 4 3 2 1

Books published by Mercer University Press are printed on acid-free paper that meets the requirements of the American National Standard for Information Sciences—Permanence of Paper for Printed Library Materials.

ISBN 978-0-88146-628-7
Cataloging-in-Publication Data is available from the Library of Congress

Contents

Preface	vii
Foreword by Sam Nunn	xi
Prologue	1
1: That Was Then	4
2: The Word Never Spoken	15
3: Definitely Interested	19
4: Christmas Eve without Santa	34
5: And So It Began	38
6: St. Patrick's Day in the Waffle House	56
7: All the Difference	78
8: On Capitol Hill	110
9: Ramrod Straight	137
10: "You think this job is funny?"	147
11: 1978 Reelection Preparation	152
12: Avoid Alcohol, Sex and Personal Attacks	158
13: Consistent, Cautious, Exhaustive	167
14: A Legacy of Landmark Accomplishments	179
15: That Vision Thing	186
16: Running for President?	194
17: A Confiscated Label	205
Epilogue	217
Appendix: Bipartisan Victories	221

1972 Election Results 224
1972 Campaign Staff 226
Bibliography 231
About the Author 235
Acknowledgments 237
Index 239

Preface

If you were born in Quitman, Georgia, as I was in 1944, you were already about as far South as you could be without stepping into Florida. Quitman was named in honor of General John A. Quitman, a New York native and West Point graduate, who moved south to Natchez, Mississippi, in 1821, bought a plantation, and put down roots. Mississippians thought Quitman's military service in the Mexican-American War exemplary and showed their appreciation by making him their governor—twice. When Quitman died in 1858, no less than five communities across the South took his name, including my hometown in South Georgia. General Quitman might have been born a Yankee, but somewhere along the way, the honeysuckle vines of Mississippi worked their magic and made him a strong convert to the "cause."

One hundred years after General Quitman's death, his South Georgia namesake hadn't changed much, and neither had attitudes about the merits of the "cause." Quitman, as I remember it, was a small farming community surrounded by tobacco barns and watermelon fields, with cotton and peanut acreage sprinkled here and there. Just about anything you could think of grew well in the black, sandy loam of Brooks County. It wasn't known as the "Breadbasket of the Confederacy" for nothing. Beyond the carefully tilled farmland, the acres withered away into wild scuppernong vines and gallberry bushes, black-water ponds and mosquito-infested swamps. And everywhere there was kudzu, sometimes growing three feet in a single night, while constantly searching for something—anything—to strangle in its ever-tightening grip. Cows, of course, weren't allowed to eat kudzu because it made their milk bitter. That's what I was told.

My dad, Frank H. McElroy, was pastor of Quitman's First Presbyterian Church at the time of my birth. "Preacher McElroy," as he was known around town, owned a cow named Judy that he kept on Wilson's farm. Twice a day, Dad milked Judy and made sure to never miss a milking. On a preacher's pay, it would be hard to feed nine children without help from Judy, and she did her part, producing eighteen quarts a day. The preacher was counting on Judy's only calf, Buttercup, to help meet future demand. After all, he had decided to go for an even dozen children. Buttercup, unfortunately, was stung by a honeybee one day and raced around the manse in panicked circles until she dropped dead.

Dad also raised bees in forty-four hives set along the banks of the Okapilco Creek just outside of town. About the time he was making enough money from honey sales to pay the college tuition of his first daughter, the bees were swept away by the Great Flood of 1948. The waters destroyed the hives and put the bridge that spanned nearby US Highway 84 under three feet of Okapilco Creek water.

Such was life in the land of milk and honey.

Washington, DC, was never mentioned around Quitman unless someone was telling a story about the day President Roosevelt died at Warm Springs in north Georgia and was taken away by train back to Washington. They could tell you every detail of that day, although it's doubtful any actually witnessed it. Occasionally, locals bragged about how much Roosevelt's New Deal had improved their lives and helped a struggling nation regain its financial footing after the Hoover Crash of 1929. Republicans weren't good for much in those days, so the Great Depression was often spoken of as the Hoover Crash.

When farmers gathered around potbelly stoves at the closest general store, they talked about the good old days when Gene Talmadge was governor of the state, back in the 1930s and again in the 1940s. It was rumored that Talmadge declared, "The poor dirt farmer ain't got but three friends: God Almighty, Sears Roebuck, and Gene Talmadge." Farmers had no way of knowing whether or not he actually said it, but they didn't care. They believed it.[1]

[1] In an interview for the Southern Oral History Program Collection, journalist Jack Nelson asked Senator Herman Talmadge about this quote. Talmadge responded, "He [Gene Talmadge] never made that statement. Some individual, introducing him to an audience once, made that statement, and it was attributed to my father from then on." Interview A-0331-1, Washington, DC (15 July 1975).

Growing up in South Georgia in the 1950s, nothing in my life allowed me to dream that one day I might work under Brumidi's famous fresco, painted on the canopy of the US Capitol dome in Washington, DC. There was a better chance that another young man, Sam Nunn, born in Perry in 1938, might wind up there, perhaps even serve in Congress. Nunn's blood already ran red, white, and blue. His father was directly involved in the success of a generation of Georgia Democrats. In addition, young Sam was the grand-nephew of Rep. Carl Vinson, a member of the United States Congress from Milledgeville since 1914. Nunn's political lineage and genetic inheritance practically assured he would be taken seriously if he were ever to pursue a political career. He just needed a pathway when the time was right to put him in Washington.

For young Sam, success in just about everything had come easily—in the classroom, on the basketball court, in the courtroom, even as a freshman legislator in the Georgia House of Representatives. But a race for the US Senate? "Foolhardy," said most of his friends, but not his basketball coach, not his teachers, and, of course, not his mother. None of them could imagine *how* he was going to win, but they knew if Sam Nunn ran it was likely that he *would* win.

Nunn wasn't sure how he would win either, but he knew he wanted to serve in Congress more than anything he had ever wanted. With total naiveté about all things political, I joined him and pledged to help him earn the trust of enough Georgians to assure his election in November of 1972. Georgia voters, to their credit, were able to discern the essential qualities of public service in Sam Nunn that were necessary to earn their trust: intellectual honesty, moral and ethical behavior, and a nonpartisan approach to solving problems. They sent the gifted young man from Houston County to Washington, where, for a generation, he influenced the quality and substance of debate on a wide range of issues of national import.

Folks looking to see "what really makes Sam tick" will enjoy this nuanced and richly detailed portrait of how Nunn's political accomplishments were shaped by his ramrod-straight commitment to ethics and his selfless approach to consensus-building on thorny issues. *The Best President the Nation Never Had* offers the reader an intimate understanding of the man through my personal recollections of Sam Nunn's journey from unknown backbench Georgia legislator to his role as one of the most influential senators to ever serve. Majority Leader Robert C. Byrd (D-WV) fittingly said, upon Senator Nunn's retirement, "[Sam Nunn] would have been an outstanding senator at any time in the history of the Republic."[2] Few, if any, Georgians would disagree.

[2] Robert C. Byrd, "Tribute to Senator Sam Nunn," *Congressional Record* 142/136 (27 September 1996).

Foreword

By Sam Nunn
US Senator (D-GA) 1972–1996

Very few people gave my candidacy much notice when I announced my intention to run for the US Senate in March 1972. Even fewer thought that I had a chance to win. The campaign had almost no money, and hardly anyone outside of Middle Georgia knew who I was. If that wasn't challenging enough, only four and a half months remained before the Democratic primary. I was the darkest of dark-horse candidates. Many friends were afraid I was going to hurt my reputation and perhaps destroy any chance for a shot at higher office later. They didn't understand that I was singularly focused on a run for the US Senate seat formerly held by the legendary Richard B. Russell of Winder and no other office.

Roland McElroy was with me from the very beginning as my key communications strategist and spokesperson. He became an invaluable advisor and confidant and played an indispensable role in both my 1972 campaign and my Senate career. I am pleased that he captures the difficult early days of the 1972 campaign as well as the risky decisions made in the heat of battle that helped separate me from 15 other candidates. Since I am no longer running for office, I can afford to be "ruined with praise rather than saved by criticism," and Roland's flattering memories more than meet that criteria. I am grateful for his kind words, but, most importantly, for our longstanding friendship, which goes back to our work together on the "Goals for Georgia" program when Jimmy Carter was governor.

Both Roland and I got off to a rocky start in March of 1972 when I launched my campaign in my home county with hundreds of friends and supporters in attendance. We were feeling pretty good until we read Bill

Shipp's column the next day in the Atlanta newspaper labeling my announcement as the "least significant political event of the year."

Every day of the 1972 campaign presented a new set of challenges, each with the potential to sink the entire enterprise, and there were plenty of days when it appeared Bill Shipp and the other early doubters would be proven right. Success was little more than an elusive dream until the actual votes were counted.

My election occurred when Georgia was on the cusp of a major political transition—from a reliably Democratic electorate to reliably Republican. Of course, it didn't happen overnight. The transition began in 1964 when Georgians supported Republican Senator Barry Goldwater for president. 1964 marked the first time Georgia had given the nod to a Republican presidential candidate—ever. Four years later, American Party candidate George Wallace won the state, and in 1972, Georgia voters were second only to Mississippians in the percentage of their vote given to Republican Richard Nixon. (In the eleven presidential contests since 1972, Georgia has voted Democratic only three times—twice for Jimmy Carter and once for Bill Clinton.) "The National Democratic Party left us," supporters reminded me repeatedly even as they continued to support this Georgia Democrat with their split vote.

My challenge in 1972 was to find a way to earn the trust of "the doubter" while not alienating loyal Democrats who considered themselves a lot more "progressive." Some in the media labeled my supporters "a strange coalition" because they ranged from civil rights leaders Julian Bond and Leroy Johnson to segregationist Lester Maddox. My perception of our "coalition" was that all of them were in search of the same candidate—someone willing to listen to their views, study the issues carefully, give them honest opinions, and cast a vote that served the best interests of Georgia and the nation.

This is the model I tried to follow during my twenty-four years in the Senate. I did my best to find a path forward for our state and nation that would preserve civility and involve leaders from both political parties. I also tried to instill in young people—by word and by example—the understanding and belief that it remains possible to be involved in the "rough and tumble" of the political process while committed to both intellectual honesty and ethical behavior. In the final analysis, this may be the single most important responsibility of public service. Roland was always there to remind me of that obligation.

I am hopeful that a potential young leader considering his or her first statewide race, as I did in 1972, will read this book and find useful lessons to guide their path. He or she will be very fortunate if they have a friend and partner like Roland McElroy.

Prologue

August 1938. The air was still and thick as swamp water as US Sen. Walter George mounted the makeshift stage on the Perry Courthouse grounds. Mayor Sam Nunn followed him closely. "Mr. Sam," as he was affectionately known in those parts, was about to introduce Senator George to the waiting crowd. As he stepped onto the stage, the mayor cast a wary eye toward the now darkening southwestern horizon. From a vest pocket, he pulled out his watch and leaned toward Senator George. "A little after two," he whispered and nodded toward the horizon. "Early for a shower, but if we start now, we might finish before that thing breaks open."

Senator George didn't care. "It'll be what it has to be." He'd spoken to crowds in just about every type of inclement weather known to man. "God knows what he is doing, and I'll be fine with whatever he sends our way."

A slight breeze started, but the humidity it carried offered no relief from the 90-degree temperature. Around Perry, as in most towns of South Georgia, summer weather patterns dictates when one gets up, when one goes to bed, and all activities in between. Folks adjusted their lives accordingly.

When politicians came to town, it was big news, and, therefore, generally not difficult to attract a good crowd. With enough advance notice, even the country folk who rarely came to town any day but Saturday stopped their chores and came to hear the latest from those who governed or had dreams of governing. The most successful among them were able to tell a good story or two, usually about "those lying Atlanta newspapers" or some "liberal foreigner" (a non-Georgian). Public address systems were expensive and unreliable, and, therefore, seldom used. The strength of a speaker's voice determined whether or not he was able to hold the crowd's attention. And so it would be on this August day.

Jostling for a better viewing position, the gathered throng pushed closer to the stage, which was nothing more formal than a flatbed truck used by farmers most days of the week to haul hay, but disguised on this occasion in red, white, and blue bunting.

From the podium, Senator George estimated more than 800 citizens had come out to hear him. With one third of the town's total population in attendance, he knew it would be a good day. And he needed a good day. George had served sixteen years in the US Senate, but this year, he faced his first serious opposition. His challengers in the Democratic primary were former governor Eugene Talmadge and US District Attorney Lawrence Camp. Due to Georgia's overwhelming Democratic majority, the winner of the primary was virtually assured of becoming the next US senator.

Some in the crowd wondered what "Mr. Sam" would say in support of their senior senator, especially in light of the news that President Roosevelt had endorsed the candidacy of Lawrence Camp. George supported most of Roosevelt's New Deal but he opposed the minimum wage provision in the Wages and Hours Act and Roosevelt's plan to enlarge the Supreme Court. The president was not happy that Senator George was out of step with his goals.[1]

Roosevelt, in separate speeches in Athens and Barnesville earlier in 1938, had launched a particularly pointed attack against Senator George. "I differ heartily and sincerely on the principles and policies of how the government of the United States ought to be run," said Roosevelt, "and if I were able to vote in the September primaries in this state, I most assuredly should cast my ballot for Lawrence Camp."[2]

When "Mr. Sam" took the podium, there was more than the usual interest in the substance of his remarks. His relatively new bride of three years, the now pregnant Mary Elizabeth Cannon, beamed from her seat next to his.

---

[1] Roosevelt had called Senator Russell to the White House to ask for his help in ousting Walter George, but Russell refused. Senator George opposed FDR's effort to "pack" the Supreme Court by adding an additional justice on the court for each justice who did not retire after reaching 70 years of age. No more than six justices could be added, limiting the total to fifteen, under FDR's proposal.

[2] Franklin D. Roosevelt, speech opening the nation's first electric membership cooperative, Lamar EMC, Barnesville, GA (11 March 1938).

Mayor Sam Nunn, a gifted and successful lawyer, was respected throughout Middle Georgia for his considerable intellect and impeccable character. "His code of ethics was stricter than the Code of Georgia or the Canons of the American Bar Association," was the often-heard description from family friend J. M. "Buddy" Tolleson.

A few in the crowd blew gnats away with gentle bursts of air, alternating from side to side through lips tightly pursed just so. But even that activity stopped as "Mr. Sam" spoke. The somber cadence of his delivery and the authority imbued in each word had all nodding as he spoke:

> Georgia has been accustomed, in the long years of her history, to send to represent her in the Senate of the United States, men of vision, men of character, men of ability, men who are capable of thinking for themselves, men who are capable of forming their independent judgment on matters affecting our state, our section and our nation. It has never been regarded in Georgia as a place to be filled by weak men, subservient men, nor by men who would blindly follow the leadership of even a President of the United States, in whatever direction he might choose to lead them.[3]

Cries of "Amen, brother" could be heard as the crowd voiced approval for all they had heard. Georgians didn't "cotton" to anyone, even a popular president, coming down to tell them how to vote. "Mr. Sam" had sent the president a message, there was no doubt about that.

And the rain held off on that exceptional day.

A month later, Sen. Walter George easily defeated his opponents, including Roosevelt's personal choice, US District Attorney Lawrence Camp.

A few days later, on September 8, 1938, Samuel Augustus Nunn Jr. was born to Sam and Elizabeth Cannon Nunn. And a new chapter in Georgia's political history was about to be written.

---

[3] "Perry Welcomes Senator George," *Houston Home Journal* (1938): 1.

Chapter 1

That Was Then[1]

Five years after Sam Nunn's 1938 arrival, I was born—the sixth child in a sequence that would not end until there were nine—in Quitman, a small town deep in rural Georgia, a bit more than a two-hour drive south of Perry. The two towns were similar in many respects. Quitman's population was slightly more than 4,000 citizens, and Perry counted about 3,000. If you spent any time at all in either town, you would soon know all you needed to know about every small town in Georgia. My father once said, "You could take all the small towns in Georgia, throw them in a barrel, pull them out one at a time, place them at random anywhere on the map of Georgia, and hardly anyone would notice."

The little towns were dominated by Protestants attending Baptist and Methodist churches, mostly, with a sprinkling of Presbyterian, Episcopal, and Church of Christ thrown in. Sunday-night worship services were important to almost all those rural churches, that is, until television sets became ubiquitous in the mid-1950s. It was a commonly held belief that *The Ed Sullivan Variety Show* singlehandedly killed off Sunday-night worship services throughout the South.

---

[1] I am often asked how I know so much about Nunn's early life since I grew up 140 miles farther south. Most of Nunn's early biography was told to me by his mother and a host of proud Perryans, including his basketball coach, minister, teachers, friends, and colleagues. Over the years, they shared generously with me their own recollections of his youth. The result was a rich tableau of the life of a gifted young man from whom great things were expected. Bobby Branch, longtime editor of the *Houston Home Journal*, once told me Sam Nunn was "the best bet Middle Georgia has had in years to get somebody in a high office in Atlanta." Branch had no idea that Nunn intended to skip Atlanta and head straight for Washington.

The social calendar of Quitman and Perry revolved around the basketball and football schedules of the high school sports teams. Very few youth were involved in organized baseball, and as far as most locals were concerned, soccer was still to be invented.

There was always a café or diner near the center of town where the locals gathered to share gossip and, sometimes, real news. In Quitman, the most popular spot was the Royal Café, where the breakfast favorite was creamed chipped beef on a slice of toasted Wonder Bread. It may be the favorite at the Royal still.

In Perry, "snowbirds" driving south for the winter often stayed at the New Perry Hotel. The legendary hotel could be counted on for all the simple amenities of life—a clean, quiet place to sleep and good Southern cooking served at tables covered with starched white cloths. Bobbe Nelson, Houston County historian, said travelers "in the know" also knew to stop at Cooper Jones' Pecan Shop. "He had a variety of pecans and pecan sweets to offer," Nelson said, "as well as a full repertoire of zany stories for every occasion." Long before the interstate highway was completed nearby, there was a good chance that people driving down from Ohio and Michigan on their way to Florida knew more about Perry than most Georgians.

In his preteen days, young Sam Nunn often rode his pony bareback down Main Street. "Nothing unusual, just 'Little Sam' and Cricket, his pony." That's all anyone might say if they bothered to look up at all.

And you'd be hard-pressed to find anyone in Perry or Quitman who felt the need for locked doors. Most people knew each other by first name, and if a stranger showed up in town, everyone would know in about fifteen minutes. The "picture show" didn't open on Sundays because everybody knew the Sabbath was a day of rest. Most other businesses were closed, too. The preacher might drop by Sunday afternoon, so Nunn's mother wore her Sunday best most of the day.

In Quitman, my father was that preacher, but he usually remained at the manse to host anyone who might drop by. "During the war years," he told me, "most of the 'drop-bys' were mothers or sweethearts seeking help in getting their husband, son, or beau an early release from military service." Dad wrote many letters on their behalf to the War Department and to our congressman, Stephen Pace.

Perry was no *Mayberry RFD* filled with caricatures of Southern life. This vibrant and proud county seat was one of many small towns in our nation that are capable of nurturing and shaping a young life until it is ready to assume the mantle of leadership in whatever field of endeavor he or she may choose. Perry had already produced the likes of four-star general Courtney H. Hodges, commander of the US First Army and a senior advisor to Gen. Dwight Eisenhower during World War II. The educational environment created by Perry and the principled example of his parents guided young Sam toward a career in public service that was grounded in faith, integrity, and a strong sense of duty.

It didn't hurt that he was imbued with a pounding thirst for knowledge.

Some people can name a few of their teachers from grade school through senior year of high school, but Nunn can name them all and remind you of how each one influenced his life. At the 1996 dedication of the Sam Nunn Museum in Perry, Nunn ticked off the entire list of his teachers, many of whom were present for the occasion. "Malissa Tucker, the junior high principal, was the tough disciplinarian. If you misbehaved, the ruler in her hand showed no mercy." He gave a whack to his knuckles with an invisible ruler as the audience applauded. And then he spotted Florence Harrison in the crowd. "Florence Harrison, our English and speech teacher, was my favorite. She brought this shy young man out of his shell [and] enabled me to gain enormous self-confidence. Of course, the threshold for improvement was already so low that any influence at all was bound to be profound."[2]

When I interviewed Mrs. Harrison for a film on Sam Nunn's Perry years, she described how she brought Nunn out of his crippling shyness. "I asked all the students to prepare a speech for class," she said. "Sam was so shy I thought he would never do it. I finally got the idea to have him talk about golf, his favorite sport. His eyes brightened. He even asked me if he could be first." She laughed as she recalled the day. "I really think he

[2] Sam Nunn, speech, dedication of the Houston County Board of Education complex, and Sam Nunn exhibit, September 8, 1996, from author's personal file.

wanted to get it over as soon as possible. But the other students loved it, and kept asking questions. It was a long time before he sat down." She paused and then looked away from the camera as she thought of another event involving the usually serious Sam Nunn. "I even put him in one-act plays." She looked at me for reaction. "Can you believe that?"[3]

"No, I can't. Are you sure you're remembering *our* Sam Nunn?" I wanted to get more of this story on film.

"Well, yes, of course. He played Donny Miller, a young Romeo in our senior class play, *Eighteen in June*...but he was still shy." She laughed again. "Don't put that in your movie."[4]

Some years later, I was working with Nunn on a speech draft when he recalled Mrs. Harrison's attempts to help him shed his shyness. "She was good, but not entirely successful," he said. "I was forced to overcome public-speaking fears while at Georgia Tech, and again while studying at Emory Law School." Nunn put down his pen and shook his head. "The first year in law school was agony. A five-minute talk was tough. I could get through it, but...it was just...agony." I could tell from the look on his face that reliving those moments wasn't any fun either. He claimed his fear of public speaking went away entirely when he started practicing law.

If only that were true. He suppressed his fears well, but they managed to reemerge several times over the course of his political career, which will become clear as this story unfolds.

"Wouldn't concede a putt to his own mother"

Sam Nunn never pretended to be another William Jennings Bryan[5], but he had other gifts that enabled him to succeed in nearly every interest he decided to pursue. For one thing, he had a competitive streak that bordered on the obsessive. When I asked Ed Beckham, close friend and teammate from Nunn's basketball years, about his competitive streak,

---

[3] Florence Harrison, videotaped interview with author, July 18, 1996.

[4] Ibid.

[5] Bryan was an American orator in the late nineteenth century who sought the presidency three times as the nominee of the Democratic Party. He was a gifted speaker of worldwide renown.

Beckham leaned toward me in mock imitation of one disclosing some great family secret. "Sam's natural coordination was such that he couldn't drive a nail with a hammer, but whatever sport he took up, he kept practicing, and soon he was beating everybody."

"But what about golf?" I asked. "That's a gentleman's sport. Surely, he would cut some slack for friends there?"

Beckham shook his head. "The gentleman we're talking about wouldn't concede a putt to his own mother if a dollar was one the line."

Sam Nunn's competitive nature was never more evident than when he took to the basketball court as a member of the Perry High School Panthers. Their coach was the stocky, cigar-chewing Eric Staples, known as the "winningest" coach in Georgia high school basketball. When Staples retired at the end of thirty-four years of coaching, his record was 926 wins and only 198 losses. Among the wins were four state championships. Thus, it was not surprising that Nunn always spoke of Coach Staples in the most reverential tones. "'Fessor Staples, as we students knew him, taught us how to play well, but he also taught us how to live our lives well. My experience with 'fessor Staples taught me that a student studies, an athlete trains—and both condition themselves for success in life."

When asked to comment on how his student, Sam Nunn, became successful in politics, Coach Staples talked of an ambition he spotted years earlier. "Since Sam was a small boy, as soon as he decided what his objective was going to be, he was always willing to pay the price to obtain that objective. He was never deterred for any reason whatsoever."[6] When the Perry Panthers played for the state championship in 1956, Nunn played guard and was team captain. At the buzzer, Nunn had scored twenty-seven points, eighteen in the second half, including the go-ahead basket.

Nunn was short for someone who envisioned success in basketball, and he had weak ankles. His mother once told me that she wrapped his ankles every day for basketball practice. She didn't mind because she knew how much he loved the game, and more important, how much he

---

[6] Coach Eric Staples, audiotape, recorded prior to 1971 (location unknown).

loved to win. He was twice named to the Georgia All-State Class B basketball team. In the 1956 North-South All-Star game, the South came up short, but he led the South in scoring with fifteen points.

"We were behind by five points at the half," recalled Ed Beckham. "Our coach knew how to win, no doubt about it, but it was Sam who gave us the half-time pep talk."[7]

What Did You Miss?

Coaches and teachers were an important influence on young Sam Nunn, but no one played a more significant role in shaping the future United States senator than his father.

"Mr. Sam" was well known in Georgia political circles, having begun his career in 1915 when first elected to represent Houston County in the general assembly. In 1926, he managed the successful gubernatorial campaign of Dr. Lamartine G. Hardman. Fresh from that victory, the senior Nunn was chosen as a delegate to the 1928 National Democratic Convention. And he was chairman of the Georgia delegation in 1932 when Franklin Roosevelt was nominated in Chicago. Several local admirers once tried to persuade him to run for the US House of Representatives, but he declined.

The senior Nunn was one of the most respected, if not beloved, citizens of his community. At the Methodist Church, he was a Bible teacher and dedicated lay leader. Among Houston County farmers, he was admired as a devoted practitioner of soil conservation.

"Mr. Sam" was 51 at "Little Sam's" birth in 1938. Perhaps it was the age difference that kept the two of them from developing a tight father-son relationship. There were no fishing or hunting trips scheduled for bonding experiences.

"We had a strong student-protégé relationship," Nunn said, "and he had high expectations. That was made pretty clear." If Nunn didn't bring home an A in a particular subject, his father's only comment would be a dry, "What did you miss?"

[7] Michael Kramer, "Smart, Dull and Very Powerful," *Time* (13 March 1989): 28.

"Marvelous" Lady from Cordele

Sam Nunn's mother, Mary Elizabeth Cannon, grew up in Cordele, about 38 miles south of Perry. When she graduated from Wesleyan College in Macon, she began a teaching career in Canton. Later, she moved back to Cordele and joined the faculty at the O'Neal School. While Nunn's father was the guiding force who laid down the principles upon which Nunn was expected to conduct his personal behavior, his mother was the daily constant in his life, managing expectations, making sure homework was done, reviewing questions before a test, and recording every step of his progress toward a coveted Eagle Scout award. I was going through a family scrapbook with her in the days preceding Nunn's 1972 campaign announcement when she pointed to a photo of her husband and said, "Sam is very much like his father, from his devotion to work to his compulsion to read, to his ability to study carefully before making decisions." She was proud of her son and wanted me to understand as much as I could about the extraordinary young man she had raised.

I have fond memories of breakfasts with Mrs. Nunn during the 1972 campaign—sitting at a table for two in the breezeway between the kitchen and Nunn's bedroom at the back of the house. Such occasions usually followed a short night's sleep. I preferred to call it a short night rather than a four-hour break in the campaign. On my first overnight stay at the Nunn residence, I arrived around midnight, and as I pulled into the driveway of 1105 Gilmer Street, I caught a glimpse of a figure silhouetted against a lamp in the library.

I told her not to wait up.

Before I could stop my car, Mrs. Nunn was standing at the side door waving me in. She was doing what she had always done for her son. I soon learned not to worry about being an imposition at such times. She welcomed my visits at any hour if for no other reason than she could find out what was really happening in the campaign from a source other than her son, who told her only good things.

Nunn's mother was a devout Christian, and a lay leader in the Perry Methodist Church. At one of our breakfasts together, she asked about my father, a former pastor of the Presbyterian Church in Quitman.

"My father insisted that each of his nine children should memorize a Bible verse for each letter in the alphabet." I began reciting as many of the twenty-six verses assigned to me as I could remember.

"What a marvelous gift," she said. She loved the word, "marvelous." If she described a biscuit as "marvelous," you needn't bother putting butter on it. Whenever I happened to be at her home for breakfast, I tried to come with at least one new Bible verse to share. She always had more to share than I did.

Uncle Carl

Between his parents and his maternal grand-uncle Carl Vinson, Sam Nunn's grasp of politics matured quickly. Grand-uncle Carl's influence was, indeed, profound, and it started early. Young Sam would sit quietly and listen to his father and Uncle Carl as they sat around the dinner table, usually at Thanksgiving, discussing world events and local politics.

Thanksgiving dinners in Perry with Carl Vinson sitting at one end of the table afforded "Little Sam" an opportunity to learn about defense and foreign policy from the legendary legislator himself. "A nation can maintain peace only if its defenses are strong, and preparedness is a non-partisan issue" was a sentiment often expressed as conversations continued in the library following dinner.

Carl Vinson was born in Milledgeville in 1883 and sworn into the US House of Representatives in 1914, at the age of 31. Fifty years later, he retired from Congress. Near the end of brief retirement remarks to his colleagues, Vinson said, "My service literally began with the Springfield Rifle and was ending with the Polaris submarine and intercontinental ballistic missile."[8] Vinson received many honors for his leadership in Congress, but none higher than when President Nixon traveled to Georgia's Mercer University in 1973 and used the occasion of Vinson's 90th birthday to announce the naming of the next nuclear-powered aircraft carrier. The ship would be known as the USS Carl Vinson, CVN-70. US Rep. Phil Landrum, dean of the Georgia delegation, introduced Mr.

[8] James F. Cook, *Carl Vinson: Patriarch of the Armed Forces* (Macon, GA: Mercer University Press, 2004) 2.

Vinson on that occasion and described him, to a standing ovation, as "the composer, conductor and maestro of the greatest legislative symphony ever written."[9]

I remember a day, not long after the 1972 Democratic primary was settled, when Mr. Vinson accompanied Nunn to Washington to meet some of the leadership in the House and Senate. As we walked into a hearing of the House Armed Services Committee, the chair, Rep. Eddie Hébert of New Orleans, spied Vinson attempting to slip unnoticed into a back-row seat. Congressman Hébert immediately gaveled the hearing to silence. "I see 'Mr. Chairman' in the back of the room, *the* chairman of this committee, and I call an immediate recess in order that each of us might greet him appropriately." The recess lasted the rest of the day. Indeed, wherever he appeared on that trip to Washington, all business came to a complete halt out of respect for the legendary Vinson.

On our last day in Washington, I stood in the back of the House chamber with Mr. Vinson, listening to the debate. After a few minutes, Vinson, ignoring the proceedings, whispered in my ear, "You see that," and he pointed to an elderly member of the House being assisted by two young pages, one on each side, guiding the member to his seat. "That's why I retired after fifty years. I didn't want anyone pointing at me, saying, 'There goes Vinson, that doddering old fool.'" Mr. Vinson turned, looked straight at me, and in a serious tone said, "There is a time to come and a time to go, and it takes a smart man to know when his time to go has come."

Carl Vinson served for fifty years. With his good health, he could have served another decade, perhaps more, but he was smart enough to recognize when it was his time to step off the stage.

"Take that ball back"

In the 1940s and 1950s, Perry was a place where nearly anyone could put a child "on report," as adults called those occasions when a parent had to be called about some unacceptable behavior that had been witnessed. Today, most of those incidents would be described as "nor-

[9] Author's personal notes on Landrum's remarks.

mal" adolescent behavior. I suspect young Sam found himself "on report" only rarely.

But there was that one time. He had volunteered to be the batboy for a group of older boys playing baseball in a vacant lot not far from his home. A foul ball, hit hard, soared over the street behind him and into the bushes. He went to retrieve it but instead pushed the ball farther back into the bushes where no one could find it.

"I wanted that ball for myself," he said, recalling the incident to me years later.

The other boys searched a while, but never found his hiding place. When the last of the boys finally went home, young Sam reached under the bush where he had hidden the ball, picked it up, and headed home. As Nunn stepped into the house, his father, who had been reading in the library, put his book down, pulled his cigar out of his mouth, and said, "Sam, you are going to take that ball back in the morning, aren't you?"[10]

The National Security Agency's most sophisticated data-collection network may never equal the speed of information gathered and disseminated by the citizens of Perry in those days when parents had a "need to know."

Some ethical missteps didn't always need a network to reveal them. "I tried to steal some eggs from a neighbor who kept chickens," he told me. "Just once."

"Really? You?"

"Don't act so surprised," Nunn said. "I said it was 'once.' Ed Beckham was in on it, too."

"But eggs?" I found the whole story hard to believe. "What were you going to do with eggs?"

"Extra cash, that's all I wanted; I planned to sell them, but not right away. I decided the best course of action would be to store them until they could be sold without raising suspicion. So, I stored them in the attic."

"How hot does it get in your attic?" I pinched the tip of my nose.

"I never realized they'd rot. It was a theft without a profit."

---

[10] Sam Nunn, conversation with author (17 January 2016).

Days passed before his mother got all the rotten smell out of the house.

Shaped by Little Choices

I thought about those rotten eggs in 2006, a full decade after Senator Nunn left the Senate, when he addressed the question of how leaders are formed at the inaugural Jim Blanchard Leadership Forum at Columbus State University. He quoted remarks made by President Ronald Reagan after he left office: "Character...is determined by all the little choices of years past—by all those times when the voice of conscience was at war with the voice of temptation."[11] Senator Nunn then added this deeply held personal belief: "Character and integrity are not qualities that can be switched on when needed. They have to be built and practiced, day to day, hour to hour, week to week, and year to year."[12]

Lessons from Perry were never forgotten. I'm sure Senator Nunn also heard his father's voice from time to time, echoing sentiments the senior Nunn expressed that summer day in 1938 when he endorsed Sen. Walter George for reelection: *Be a young man of character and ability, someone who does not follow blindly the leadership of others, someone who is capable of forming independent judgments and articulating his views in a way that every listener will recognize and value.* Of such elements are Nunn's character made. Those who followed his career closely witnessed those essential qualities practiced daily.

---

[11] Sam Nunn, Cunningham Center for Leadership Development, Columbus State University, Columbus GA (29 August 2006).

[12] Ibid.

Chapter 2

The Word Never Spoken[1]

Race. It was a word I seldom heard growing up, that is, until the US Supreme Court handed down its landmark decision in *Brown v. Board of Education* in 1954. Fourth graders knew nothing of the decision's import at the time. I knew one thing: adults in Quitman were quite upset about it. People with deep furrowed brows were declaring in the most somber tones, "Well, it'll never happen around here." I didn't know what "it" was, but it didn't sound good. My fourth grade teacher, Harriet Hewett, never mentioned "it" to her students.

I knew there was some sort of trouble brewing when I heard that the black nanny for one of the town's most prominent citizens had been fired when it was discovered that she had joined the NAACP. I was too young to know anything about the NAACP, but I was told she had not made a good decision.

When I was nine years old, I was hired as a "yard boy" to take care of the grounds at the residence of a couple of the grand dames of the community. The two sisters, Miss Willie and Miss Alma, as they were known, shared an elegant antebellum home on North Court Street. I was the first white yard boy they'd ever had, and they were delighted. "We know you'll be reliable," Miss Willie said on my first day. After a pause, she added, "Not like all the darkies we've had over the years."

I'd heard the word "darky" a few times. Such language was common in those days and indicative of the insidious way in which racism was

---

[1] I include reflections on racism in this memoir for two reasons: to give the reader insight into the culture in which Sam Nunn and I grew up, and to provide a basis for understanding the role it continued to play in shaping Georgia's culture during the twenty-four years of Nunn's service in the United States Senate.

handed down from generation to generation. But the language of our Southern culture was not the only way generations were taught racist leanings.

In the spring of 1954, as was the custom at our elementary school, I marched with my fourth grade class to the West End Cemetery with a jar of fresh flowers in hand to put on the grave of a Confederate soldier. The march always took place on April 26, Confederate Memorial Day. Mrs. Hewett, our teacher, said we could distinguish Confederate graves from all the rest because they'd be the ones adorned with a small Confederate flag. My friends and I didn't care. We were just glad to enjoy half a day out of class. We didn't realize at the time that we were also being taught to respect the Confederate flag.

A year later, my class again marched to the same cemetery, and on that beautiful spring day in April, the United Daughters of the Confederacy awarded me two silver dollars for writing the best essay in the fifth grade on the life of Confederate general Nathan Bedford Forest.

In the South of the 1950s, segregation was accepted and ingrained in our culture as if ordained by God. Indeed, some preachers told their congregations slavery was an ordinance of God, and they cited references in the Bible as proof.

By 1958, I was a freshman in high school with a part-time job spinning 45-rpm records after school and Saturdays on Quitman's only radio station, WSFB. The gubernatorial race of 1958 was raging, and it seemed to me that candidates were everywhere. No one warned me that sometimes candidates would drop by the radio station, expecting to be interviewed on the air.

One Saturday afternoon, the door to the control room burst open, and in popped a guy with hand outstretched. "I'm Bill Bodenhamer, running for governor." Except that when he spoke, his thick Southern drawl collapsed the sentence into one word: "BillBodenhamerrunningforgovernor." It reminded me of the way Chuck Berry delivered the opening line in Johnny B. Goode: "DeepdowninLouisiana'crossfromNewOrleans." That was all one word too.

I didn't know anything about interviewing political candidates, so I said, "Why don't you just talk for a couple of minutes while I go to the restroom. It's been a long day."

"Don't worry, son," he said, with a wide grin. "Ah'll take care of everythin'."

I gave him a quick introduction on the air. "Mr. Bodenhamer is going to tell us something about his platform for governor." With that I let him sit down at the mike while I took off. By the time I got to the restroom, he had called the *Brown* decision a "judicial monstrosity" and his opponent, Ernest Vandiver, a "red-faced communist."

I ran back to the control room, all the time giving Bodenhamer a slashing motion across my neck. Something told me his comments had gone too far. "Cut! Cut!"

Thankfully, Bodenhamer stopped in midsentence, and closed with, "Thank-ya, my friends. Vote for Boden-HAMMER." When he got up to leave, his only comment to me was, "Uh...your fly, son, your fly."

Damn.

A couple of minutes after the candidate departed, the station's owner arrived—he'd been listening in his car downtown—and came directly to the control room. "I don't know what that was—or who—but don't do it again," he said, tapping the top of the control console for emphasis. "Ever."

I didn't.

A few weeks later, we aired a speech by Lt. Gov. Ernest Vandiver, Bodenhamer's so-called "communist" opponent. Vandiver's campaign had paid for airtime on just about every radio station in South Georgia that day. The lieutenant governor was different from the firebrand Bodenhamer, I was told, but on the day I heard him, they sounded just alike. "When I'm your governor," Vandiver said, "none of my children or any of yours will ever attend a racially mixed school in the state of Georgia." Over the course of the next several weeks, I heard Vandiver pledge several times, "If elected, there will be no mixed schools or college classrooms in this State—no, not a single one."[2]

Such language heartened legislative leaders from rural parts of Georgia. The General Assembly had passed a law in 1956 forbidding coeducation of blacks and whites, with a provision to cut off funds to any

---

[2] Harold Paulk Henderson, *Ernest Vandiver, Governor of Georgia* (Athens: University of Georgia Press, 2008) 81.

school that was desegregated. Most segregationists didn't want anyone to even talk about changing that law.

Bodenhamer lost by a wide margin but claimed credit for prodding Vandiver to make his infamous "No, not one" pledge.

Vandiver was elected, but soon, to the dismay of conservative Democrats, did an about-face on segregation. He presided over the successful integration of the University of Georgia in the fall of 1961 when Charlayne Hunter and Hamilton Holmes enrolled amid significant objection from students, alumni, and members of the legislature. Vandiver later said his "No, not one" pledge was a mistake and that he always believed in the inevitability of desegregation. Some political observers believe Vandiver also wanted to avoid the spectacle of another Southern governor standing in front of a schoolhouse door, like Orval Faubus of Arkansas and George Wallace of Alabama had done. His courageous stand in 1961 ushered in what many hoped would truly be an enlightened new day for Georgia.

In the spring of 1962, the county-unit system that enabled rural counties of Georgia to disproportionately dominate state government was ruled unconstitutional by the Supreme Court. Georgia was about to take a giant step, albeit a forced step, into a difficult period of cultural transition. The resistance was stiff. The courts had spoken, but traditions molded by generations seemed to be in no danger of disappearing.

Not everyone was thinking about race relations in 1962. I waited one week after high school graduation before enrolling in the University of Georgia's summer school program. Most of my contemporaries chose the more accepted path of matriculating in the fall, but I was in a hurry to start the next chapter in my life. Sam Nunn had just finished law school in 1962 and was headed to Washington, hoping to join the staff of the House Armed Services Committee. I was 18; Nunn was 24.

Chapter 3

Definitely Interested

Sam Nunn's position as part of the House Armed Services Committee staff had never been certain. Committee chair Carl Vinson made that clear. "Sam, you'll be hired only if you pass the bar exam," Vinson had told him, and he meant it. Nunn also had to win the approval of staff director John J. Courtney

"Uncle Carl sent Courtney down to Emory to interview three of my law professors, and only then did Courtney hire me," Nunn said, smiling. "Three!" Vinson didn't want to make a mistake, but more than anything else, he didn't want to give anyone a reason to accuse him of nepotism in hiring a member of his extended family.

In October 1962, Nunn was asked by Courtney to join a congressional delegation on a fact-finding mission to Europe. As a result, he happened to be in Paris in late October when the Cuban Missile Crisis developed. "My participation in the CODEL [the Congressional Delegation] was unknown to Uncle Carl, who was out of town during the October congressional recess." Nunn said. "I think he had promised my mother that he would keep an eye on me."

Khrushchev Blinked

When the standoff between the Soviet Union and the United States began, Sam Nunn was at Ramstein Air Base in Germany attending a dinner with the head of the United States Air Force Europe. As the four-star general sat before an array of state-of-the-art communications gear, he made this chilling revelation: since his men were the closest of American forces to the Soviet Union, they would be the first to deliver their weapons, and they also would be the first targets of the Soviets. "My men are thirty minutes away and our bombers would come several hours later," the general said. "My pilots are sitting on the tarmac next to their planes right now, but they would have about one minute to get into the air before Soviet jets took them out on the ground."

That kind of news would shake anyone, and the young attorney, Sam Nunn, was definitely shaken.

A tense week passed before Premier Nikita Khrushchev agreed to remove his missiles from Cuba. By that time, Nunn and the rest of the delegation had been to Norway and were departing Oslo for a return visit to Paris.

"That was my introduction to the possibility of nuclear war," Nunn said years later when asked to reflect on events of that October and the impact on his life. "I made a decision that if I ever had an opportunity to help reduce nuclear dangers and raise the nuclear threshold so that everybody would have more time before they undertook this kind of God-awful, almost planet-ending kind of military response and action, I would try to do it."[1]

The night after the Cuban missile crisis was brought to a close, Sam Nunn had another life-changing encounter: he was introduced to Colleen Ann O'Brien, a Washington State native and CIA employee currently assigned to the Paris embassy. Their courtship began in Paris the night they met and continued upon her return to America one year later. Their marriage in 1965 took place in Perry, where they settled down quickly. Nunn soon took over management of the family's cattle farm and joined his father's law firm.

If there was to be a political career, it would surely start from the most ordinary of beginnings.

Troubled Summers of 1964 and 1965

Atlanta attorney Carl Sanders, a moderate, as the term was defined in those days, was elected governor in the fall of 1962. He followed Ernest Vandiver, who had overseen the integration of the University of Georgia. By the time Sanders was elected, Georgia had returned to rela-

[1] First "Robert S. McNamara Lecture on War and Peace," delivered at John F. Kennedy Jr. Forum of the Institute of Politics, Harvard University (17 October 2008).

tive calm on the racial front. I remember a press conference Sanders held not long after his election in which he expressed the view that the worst of Georgia's race problems were over.

Governor Sanders—just as Governor Vandiver before him—was wrong.

Both Sam Nunn and I were drawn into separate encounters with individuals who were determined to keep racial discord an integral part of the state's social fabric.

"Nightriders," as members of the Ku Klux Klan were known in those days, murdered a black US Army Reserve officer on a back road outside of Athens in the early morning of July 11, 1964. At trial, their defense was they couldn't have committed the crime because they were having breakfast at the Open House Café in Athens at 5:00 A.M., the estimated time of the murder. They insisted that they were at the Open House Café from 4:30 until well after 6:00 A.M. Witnesses would swear to it, most notably the café's owner, Clyde Harper. When the FBI found out I was also at the Open House Café that morning, I received a visit from two men in black suits.

I was a 20-year-old student at the university, working at WGAU radio station and engaged to marry Ginny Sears later that summer of 1964. I didn't need any extra excitement in my life. When the FBI greeted me at the door of my apartment, I thought I was going to have a heart attack.

"How can you be so sure the accused were not at the Open House Café on the morning of July 11?" they asked, as we settled around my kitchen table.

These guys don't smile at all, and they're taking down every word I utter. Coffee will help—but damn.

"Well, I've seen them there on many occasions. We never spoke, but I can tell you they were *not* in the café while I was there."

"When, exactly, were you there?"

"I arrived at 4:18 A.M. and left at 4:38 A.M."

"That's fairly precise," one said, in a clearly skeptical tone.

I think I detected a slight smile.

"Yes, how can you be that precise?" the other asked. He didn't smile the entire time they were in my apartment.

"Because it was my daily routine. I opened the radio station every morning and had to get the station on the air by five o'clock, or 4:58, to be precise. So, my daily ritual was defined, you might say, by the eight's."

They ARE writing everything down.

I cleared my throat. "Here's how that morning unfolded: I arrived at the café at 4:18. Clyde saw me get out my car and broke two eggs over a frying pan. I had the same thing every morning—two eggs over light, two strips of bacon, a small orange juice, and he knew—" I stopped abruptly.

Why do I feel like I'm in an old Dragnet *skit?*

"And?" one said, with a bit of irritation in his voice.

"I ate breakfast and left at 4:38. A ten-minute drive put me at the station at 4:48. I switched on the transmitter, and while it warmed up, I turned on the coffee and grabbed the latest wire copy for the day's first newscast. I hit the transmit button at 4:58 A.M. and started the national anthem. By the time the anthem finished, I had coffee in hand and sat down at exactly 5:00 A.M. to go on the air with the news."

Suddenly, they seemed very excited. I could see it in their faces as they exchanged knowing glances. "Are you absolutely sure?"

"I am. I arrived at the Open House at 4:18 and left at 4:38, and I can tell you those guys were not there during that twenty minutes. I never met them, but I knew their faces. They were not there on the morning of the murder...not when I was there."

This was big news. If the defendants were not at the café when they said they were, the prosecutor would have an easier time convincing the jury they were, instead, committing murder.

I received a subpoena the next morning with a date to show up and testify at the trial, already underway. On the day I was to testify, prosecutors put me in a room where witnesses were held until they were needed in the courtroom one flight of stairs below. I had been sitting alone in the room for hours when I began to question whether or not this whole testifying thing was a good idea.

Those guys downstairs...don't care for people who get in their way...and they have long memories. Those guys play for keeps. I could leave right now. The prosecutors don't need me. Surely, they would have called me by now if—

The door suddenly popped open and a deputy motioned frantically for me to follow.

Too late. Gotta go through with it.

As I entered the courtroom and was walking to the witness stand, I spotted Clyde Harper, the café owner. He had a front-row seat behind the defendants and was suddenly leaning across the rail, whispering something into the ear of the defense attorney. I'm confident he wasn't asking for the time of day. I imagined he was saying something like, "I forgot about that guy. He came in every morning. He's gonna say these boys weren't there when the murder took place." The defense attorney called for an immediate recess. It was already after six o'clock. I was just steps from the witness stand when the judge recessed the trial until the following day.

I assumed I would be first to testify the next morning, but, to my great relief, I was never called. Overnight, attorneys for the defense agreed to stipulate that their clients arrived on the morning of the murder a minute or two after McElroy left. That would, at least, put the defendants in the café at the estimated time of the murder—five o'clock. No need to allow young McElroy to place any doubt in the minds of the jury, not that my testimony would have made any difference. The jury of twelve white, Protestant men acquitted the two defendants.[2] And I never again ate breakfast in the Open House Café.

Despite Governor Sanders's belief that the worst racial problems were behind us, Georgia continued to be a hotbed of racial unrest. Americus, in particular, was a chronic problem area until civic leaders assembled a biracial committee in hopes of cooling things off. It worked...for a while.

In this atmosphere, Perry's mayor, Richard Ray,[3] approached Nunn in the summer of 1965 about forming a biracial committee to address

---

[2] The full account of Colonel Penn's murder is contained in *Murder at Broad River Bridge*, Bill Shipp (Atlanta: Peachtree Publishers, 1981).

[3] Richard Ray became Senator Nunn's first administrative assistant (title later changed to chief of staff); Ray also served the Third Congressional District in the US House of Representatives from 1983 to 1993.

Perry's unrest. Nunn was the 27-year-old president of the local chamber and about to meet his first political test.

Mayor Ray knew he had to cool racial tensions or he would have a bigger problem on his hands. "At first, we didn't call it a biracial committee," Ray said when recalling that summer. "Biracial was a red flag with many whites; they wanted us to call it a coordinating committee."[4] Who better than Sam Nunn, political scion of one of the most respected families in Middle Georgia, to assist him?

Nunn and Ray were aware of the considerable personal and political risk they were taking with such an initiative. Both believed that dialogue and communication were the only means of preserving peace and promoting a greater understanding between the races. "Being president of the chamber of commerce, I felt an even more acute responsibility not to let the situation blow up,"[5] Nunn said.

Nunn has talked publicly about the first meeting of the Perry biracial committee many times. I included details of that first meeting when I prepared Nunn's biographical sketch in 1971 for the Georgia Jaycees, who named him one of the Five Outstanding Young Men in Georgia that year.

"The biracial committee met in my office," Nunn said, "while law enforcement officers circled the block. That's how much tension there was in the air. No one knew how it would end." Nunn asked the two sides to begin talking to each other, and as he listened, he was grateful for relative calm during the discussion. "The blacks in that meeting weren't demanding anything unreasonable or unattainable," Nunn said. "They were local citizens interested only in being treated fairly."[6] The meeting ended amicably, with both sides agreeing to continue to meet and work together to solve mutual problems.

---

[4] Richard Ray, Sam Nunn Oral History, Washington, DC (30 September 1996).

[5] Steve Coll, interview of 22 January 1986, transcribed for "Sam Nunn, Insider from the Deep Southland," *The Washington Post* (19 February 1986): B1.

[6] Sam Nunn, Sam Nunn Oral History, Washington, DC (30 September 1996).

But a few hotheads in the community would not let the issue be resolved so peaceably. Over the next four to six months, racial tensions flared frequently in Perry despite the best efforts of Sam Nunn and Richard Ray. "Sixty percent of my exterminating business disappeared over one weekend,"[7] Mayor Ray said. The economic impact was fairly easy for local businessmen to measure.

Mayor Ray persisted even as some wanted to see him impeached. At one city council meeting, someone shouted, "Impeach, yes! Why not? Who's going to support you?"[8]

Sam Nunn stood up in the back of the room. "I am."[9]

Nunn and Mayor Ray stood together, remained calm and their action, in turn, encouraged others to do the same. Perry never had the serious problems that Americus and other Southern towns experienced that year. Before the summer was over, Nunn convinced one of the white landowners to set aside enough acreage in a certain black neighborhood for a swimming pool and a recreation center that the city helped fund. "That really took the heat off," Nunn said.[10]

Nunn's participation and leadership skills displayed in the summer of 1965 convinced locals they could trust him to represent their interests in the state legislature. He was virtually unopposed when he ran for the Georgia House of Representatives in 1968 and again in 1970. It took only one term in the state legislature to get locals excited about his chances for advancement to higher office. Bobby Branch, editor of the *Houston Home Journal*, wrote, "I suspect his political ambitions for the future are focused on an office higher than that of state Representative.... It's probably a while off [but] we think the name of Sam Nunn will become familiar in Georgia political circles during the next decade."[11]

---

[7] Richard Ray, Sam Nunn Oral History, Washington, DC (30 September 1996) 43.

[8] Ibid.

[9] Sam Nunn, Sam Nunn Oral History, Washington, DC (30 September 1996).

[10] Ibid., Nunn, 44.

[11] Bobby Branch, "Out on a Branch," *Houston Home Journal* (1 May 1969): 2.

If Mr. Branch had known the level of ambition for higher office that already pushed Sam Nunn forward, he might have written a more decisive editorial conclusion.

In the five years that passed after Nunn's return to Perry from his Washington job in the House of Representatives, he held several key posts in local civic affairs: president of the Perry Chamber of Commerce, chair of the Middle Georgia Area Planning Commission, and a member of the Georgia House of Representatives—all by the tender age of 30. Sam Nunn's political career was on the move.

Goals for Georgia

May 10, 1971. I was just 27 years old when I walked into Jody Powell's office in the state capitol. Powell, press secretary to Governor Carter, was a year older and a chain-smoker whose cigarette ash never quite made it into the ashtray on his desk. The ash always fell off before he could find the proper receptacle somewhere under a sea of newspapers. At one point, I started to search for the tray, too, but stopped when I spotted a small string of smoke rising from under the newspapers. Powell saw the smoke and waved me away with no sense of urgency at all.

I don't know why he can't find the ashtray. Follow the smoke!

Governor Carter was five months into a four-year term and in a hurry to launch a couple of the projects he had promised voters, zero-based budgeting and reorganization of state government chief among them. But another idea had caught the governor's attention, and this one was proposed by Sam Nunn, president of the Georgia Planning Association. By 1971, Nunn's fresh face was beginning to impress leaders in the General Assembly. He had also been an early supporter of the new governor. Nunn suggested to Governor Carter that he create a "Goals for Georgia" program and let the seventeen Area Planning and Development Commissions coordinate the effort in their regions. Nunn thought it a good idea to engage the people in setting state government priorities for the present and well into the future.

When Powell called me, there was an unmistakable urgency in his voice. "I gotta find someone to run the public relations aspect of the governor's Goals for Georgia program, and I need to find that person today. Are you available?"

"Sure," I said. I didn't know anything about Goals for Georgia, but I needed the client. I didn't know Jody Powell, or anyone in the Jimmy Carter political world for that matter, but when a potential client asks if you are available to do a job, the answer is always "Yes."

When Jody finally uncovered his ashtray, it was filled with cigarette butts, some still smoldering. In one continuous motion, he emptied ashes and butts into the bucket of sand behind his desk, pulled out another cigarette, lit it, puffed hard several times, and never stopped talking. "Dr. Fanning speaks mighty highly of you, and that's good enough for me."

Ah, so that's how he got my name.

Dr. J. W. Fanning was vice president for services at the University of Georgia at that time, and a remarkable man who, in his own quiet way, influenced the lives of all he met, and always for the better. I met Dr. Fanning on several occasions during my undergraduate days, but was surprised that he recalled my name at the moment Jody called. Perhaps Dr. Fanning had seen my work during the two years I hosted a program for the Agricultural Extension Service on the Georgia ETV network. Dr. Fanning had a deep interest in agriculture, and I interviewed nearly every professor from the agriculture school on that program. Years later, I thanked Dr. Fanning for introducing me to Jody Powell, and, typically, he deflected any credit. "Oh no, I didn't do anything; you didn't need my help." But I knew better. He was doing for me what he did countless times every day: assisting UGA graduates in need of a hand to get their careers started.

We agreed to meet in Jody's office as soon as I could drive the 62 miles between Athens and Atlanta. By noon, we were discussing terms of an eight-month contract when another young man walked in unannounced. Jody put his cigarette down just long enough to introduce us. "Shake hands with Sam Nunn. He's a state representative from Houston County, you know, Perry."

He looks younger than me.

"He's also president of the Georgia Planning Association. He'll be in charge of the Goals program." Nunn and I shook hands for the first time. "And you'll be working for him."

"I think I saw something about the Goals program on the news the other day," I said to Nunn as I searched for words to express some interest in a program I knew nothing about.

Powell lit another cigarette. "It's supposed to be 'an exercise in participatory democracy,' according to the governor." Powell smiled on his last words.

Nunn started to pace as if irritated by the idle chatter.

Powell, for the first time, placed his latest cigarette safely on the lip of the ashtray and sat down. He leaned back so far I thought his chair would surely go over any second. "Roland's going to help you, Sam, get some media attention for the Goals program; we just signed a contract."

Nunn stopped pacing. "Good, can you start today? I've got a list of things for you to do." Thus began a working relationship that continued into three of his four terms in the United States Senate. I recalled this story recently for Cathy Gwin, a former Nunn press secretary and current senior director of communications at the Nuclear Threat Initiative. "He's never changed," she said. "Forty-four years later, he always has a list of things to be done."

Our first meeting in Jody Powell's office taught me that I would be associated with a man whose mind was always working on long-range solutions to problems that vex government at all levels—and he was always impatient to get started on those problems. I have never met anyone who could match his computer-like ability to listen carefully, analyze quickly, and devise solutions that work and are eminently fair to all parties concerned.

What the People Said

The Goals program excited Nunn because it offered an opportunity for participants to join him in looking toward possibilities that exist beyond the horizon. Most people aren't very good at looking over the horizon, and that may be why it was difficult to get others excited about the Goals program. Media interest was practically nonexistent. Nevertheless, we engaged Georgia's seventeen Area Planning and Development Commissions (APDCs) in the project. For the entire summer of 1971, Sam Nunn and I traveled to meetings hosted by the APDCs—fifty-one meetings in all, including seventeen regional conferences. Participation was excellent everywhere even if media coverage was scant, and by end of the year, Nunn was able to present Governor Carter with a credible blueprint titled *What the People Said.*

One of those regional conferences in the late summer of 1971 became a life-changing event for me.

"You can beat this guy"

It was the last of seventeen scheduled stops on our Goals tour. The site was Dublin High School, and the day was stultifyingly hot. Nunn and the appointed US senator, David Gambrell, found themselves at the same table in the school cafeteria.

Organizers had tried to keep each conference as apolitical as possible but felt they had no choice but to put Gambrell on the program when he showed up. It was the governor's program, after all, and Carter knew Senator Gambrell needed all the public exposure he could get if he was to win the US Senate seat on his own merits. Prior to his appointment to the Senate, David Gambrell had been treasurer of Carter's gubernatorial campaign. That was the sum total of his political experience. I was more than a little excited to observe both men simultaneously, in the same venue, before the same audience. Would there be a contrast worth noting?

I stood in the back of the room as first Nunn and then Gambrell addressed the crowd. Nunn's attempt at humor as he began his remarks came across as stilted and rehearsed.

Why does every politician think you have to start with a joke? In his favor, Nunn spoke extemporaneously from an outline he had prepared on a yellow legal pad. The outline enabled him to maintain eye contact with the audience throughout his time at the podium. But it was his command of the facts that had people sitting up as he laid out the major challenges Georgia faced in the near term. Gambrell's remarks, on the other hand, were almost narcoleptic. He read his speech like an academic who wished he had chosen some other line of work. Both speakers scored "zero" on charisma, in my view, but Nunn clearly won on substance. My first thought was, "If there is to be a game, we're in it already!" My blood was racing now.

Nunn finished and drifted to the back of the room where I was standing. He waited until Gambrell finished answering questions before he looked, expectantly, in my direction.

He wants me to say something. After a moment's hesitation, I whispered, "You can beat this guy."

"What are you talking about?" He acted like he'd never thought of such a thing.

"If you decide to run for the Senate, you can beat this guy," I repeated.

I know he's thinking about it.

"No, I'm not interested in that." He looked perturbed. After a long pause, he added, "What makes you say that?"

"I'm not saying that you *ought* to run, but if you did"—I turned to face him—"I think you could beat the appointed senator—that man." I nodded in the direction of David Gambrell.

"Why? What makes you think that?" He seemed genuinely surprised that I would make such an observation.

"You're a much better speaker, that's all. Anybody can see that."

"No, not interested; forget it." He gave me a dismissive wave and walked to the other side of the room.

His blood is pumping, too. I can see it in his eyes. Holy cow!

"Have you ever had campaign experience?"

The Dublin Goals for Georgia conference broke up around 4:30 P.M. that August afternoon. As the participants departed Dublin High School, Nunn caught up with me. I was about to get into my car for the drive back to Athens. "Do you really think I'd have a chance in a race against him?"

For some reason, he doesn't want to mention Gambrell by name. "Based on what I've seen today, yes, I do."

"Have you ever had campaign experience?" Nunn asked. His expression told me he was quite serious.

He really wants to know. I shook my head. "No, none."

"But you know the press." It sounded like a question, so I nodded.

"Well, what would you say are the key things I—or anybody—would have to do to get his message out?" There was no smile, no change in demeanor, just a very serious expression, so I gave it equally serious attention. We soon found ourselves sitting on the curb outside Dublin High School talking until the sun went down about something he had assured me he was not interested in doing.

"Who else might be in the race?" I asked.

"It'll be crowded," Nunn said. "Probably Bill Stuckey, Lester Maddox, and Carl Sanders—those three are very likely."

Two governors and a congressman? "That's some tall cotton, but I still think you can do it. You have something they don't."

"What?" He was genuinely curious.

"Inexperience." I said, struggling to keep a straight face.

Nunn nodded. "You know, in a strange way, my inexperience might actually work to our advantage."

He thought I was serious. I was just trying to keep the conversation light.

"The others are well known. All have track records and all have their own baggage." He paused. "But it wouldn't be a cakewalk, no matter how confident you might be right now."

"I know.... I know." Our conversation continued for another hour.

He's definitely interested. I finally started up my little Dodge Dart and pulled out onto the main highway. All the way back to Athens, I reviewed our conversation several times. *He's more than interested; I think he's going to do it.*

I had no way of knowing that Nunn's interest was already focused on a seat in the US House of Representatives, a seat that did *not* exist—and was not yet focused on Gambrell's seat.

No District for Nunn

By September 1971, the census numbers from 1970 were in. Tension was already building among legislators when Governor Carter called them into a special session to consider redistricting House and Senate offices and reapportioning congressional districts. For the first time, their finished product would be submitted to the Justice Department for review under provisions of the Voting Rights Act of 1965. A difficult and controversial special session lay ahead.

Houston County, which included Nunn's hometown, was in the Third Congressional District, represented by Nunn's friend Jack Brinkley of Columbus. Nunn made clear he did not wish to take on Brinkley. His only path to Congress, it seemed, depended upon creating a new Middle Georgia district. Somehow Nunn found a way to persuade Governor Carter to appoint him to the reapportionment committee, and from that position, it began to look like the task of carving out a new district in Middle Georgia might be possible. He aligned himself with a couple of urban colleagues, Representatives Frank Pinkston of Macon and Jimmy Mason of Gwinnett County. Together, they created a plan that would put Perry and Macon in a Middle Georgia district, but not Columbus. The so-called Nunn plan passed the House by a comfortable margin.

"It wasn't the first plan to pass the house," Nunn said "It was the second."[12] He thought Governor Carter might support his plan, especially given Nunn's support for Carter's election in 1966 and again in 1970. "I thought he might put in a friendly word or at least be neutral, but he and his administration opposed it rather vigorously in the state senate."[13]

Years later, when President Carter was asked about the Mason-Pinkston plan for creating a Middle Georgia district, he told an interviewer, "I don't recall any details about it."[14] Obviously, Nunn's 1971 plan did not make a lasting impression on the governor.

Both chambers of the Georgia legislature continued to work on other plans. "We kept batting them back and forth,"[15] Nunn said. The Senate seemed to be focused on drawing new lines for the Fourth and Fifth

---

[12] Sam Nunn, Sam Nunn Oral History, Washington, DC (30 September 1996).

[13] Ibid.

[14] Jimmy Carter, July 16, 1997. Sam Nunn Oral History Collection, 1996–1997, Manuscript, Archives and Rare Book Library, Emory University.

[15] Sam Nunn, Sam Nunn Oral History, Washington, DC (30 September 1996).

Congressional Districts. Their unstated goal was to divide the black population into three segments and put them in Districts 4, 5, and 6, a not-so-subtle attempt to make sure the fifth district remained majority-white.

Nine months earlier, Governor Carter had declared in his inaugural address that "the time for racial discrimination is over."[16] Perhaps some members of the legislature weren't paying attention. When the Georgia legislature submitted its plan to the Justice Department in late fall of 1971, not surprisingly, the attorney general rejected it as being discriminatory and sent it back to the Georgia legislature for reconsideration.

The action of the 1971 special session left Sam Nunn with two choices: wait for another time to run for the House of Representatives or run for the US Senate. He certainly wouldn't have the luxury of waiting for the legislature to comply with the Justice Department's instructions. Whatever the outcome of the reapportionment debate in 1972, it would come too late for him to mount a serious candidacy for the House. If he was destined for Washington, it would have to include a run for the US Senate.

Bobby Branch, editor of the *Houston Home Journal*, once asked Nunn's childhood friend Ed Beckham if he thought Nunn would run for the Senate. "Not a chance," Beckham replied. "Shoot, Sam's too cautious to do something as reckless as that."

[16] Inaugural address, Governor Jimmy Carter (12 January 1971).

Chapter 4

Christmas Eve without Santa

We continued to work on the Goals program for the rest of 1971 and didn't discuss the possibility of a Senate campaign again until late November, when, by sheer chance, I ran into Nunn on the sidewalk directly in front of Georgia's capitol.

"I've made up my mind," he said, as I approached.

His grin told me all I needed to know. "You're going to run for the US Senate." It was by now the worst kept secret in the entire state. One only had to mention "US Senate" in Nunn's presence to see how it quickened his speech and brightened his eyes. I heard from several sources that he'd been having conversations with his closest friends about a possible campaign but wanted to keep those talks confidential.

"Who told you?" he asked, as we walked the circle around the capitol.

He'd completely forgotten about our conversation curbside at Dublin High School back in the summer. "Remember Dublin?" I said, "Curbside?" He was still blank. "After the Goals conference?" *He doesn't remember our conversation at all.*

"Sure, sure, I remember," he said. "Well, I've given it even more thought since then, and I'm definitely considering a run." We stopped walking, and he looked me in the eye.

"Are you willing to help?" he asked, "because—"

"Absolutely!" I didn't need to think about it. "You're talking to a 27-year-old who spent the second night of his honeymoon soaking up every word of Senator Pastore's keynote address at the 1964 Democratic Convention. I watched every sweating, eye-blinking second of the Kennedy-Nixon TV debate in 1960. Heck, I even remember the Huntley-Brinkley coverage of a bland Adlai Stevenson at the Democratic Convention in 1956."

"Is that a 'yes'?" Nunn asked.

"Of course, let's do it. I'll help any way I can," I made no attempt to hide my enthusiasm. I probably wouldn't have been so excited if I had known how difficult his statewide campaign would be.

We were well into December 1971 when Nunn called my home in Athens with an invitation to attend a private Christmas Eve meeting at Ben Porter's Macon radio station. The purpose of the meeting was to answer any remaining questions his close friends might have and secure commitments, mostly financial, for the campaign. "The results of the meeting," he assured me, "will determine when—or even if—I'm going to make my intentions public."

When I hung up the phone, I turned to face Ginny, my wife, hands on her hips, glaring. "Did I hear you say Christmas Eve? You're going to a meeting on Christmas Eve?"

"It's the one time when all of the participants can be present without impinging upon other obligations," I said. "No need to worry, the meeting will be over by two o'clock, no later, and I'll be home a couple of hours after that."

Ginny rolled her eyes. Clearly, she didn't believe it.

In addition to Ben Porter, owner of Macon's WCRY, Nunn invited Malcolm Reese, a savings and loan association executive and current mayor of Perry; Richard Ray, former mayor; Bill Thompson, Macon architect; Bibb County attorneys Rudolph Patterson and Charlie Adams; and Roland McElroy, Athens public relations consultant.

Porter was tall and thoughtful; Reese, portly and contemplative; Ray, a bit overweight, too, but supremely loyal; Thompson, fidgety, a realist with a short attention span; Patterson, young and enthusiastic; Charlie Adams, graying and analytical—and McElroy, green as a watermelon, but eager.

The meeting began around 11:00 A.M., later than I had hoped it would, and the questions came quickly from every corner of the room. Where would the money come from? Would there be enough time to develop and implement a strategy for winning? Who would support this relative unknown candidate? How would he convince the voters to support him? Would we need polling? What if Lt. Gov. Lester Maddox and former governor Carl Sanders decided to run? What impact would their presence have on the outcome of the race?

Architect Bill Thompson, sitting on the edge of Ben Porter's desk, was swinging his legs back and forth, trying to get up the nerve to ask the one question on the mind of nearly everyone in the room. Thompson hadn't said much until that moment. He mostly listened. Everyone turned to him when they heard him clear his throat.

"Now, Sam, here's my question. It requires a simple 'yes' or 'no.' I don't want to hear any of that attorney-qualified language—whereas and wherefore. Your answer will determine my level of support for you." The room was quiet except for the sound of carols from the broadcast studio next to us. All eyes were on Thompson. "Right here in Middle Georgia, there is a rumor that you like to play golf at the Houston Lake Country Club. This is bound to be a tough race, requiring all of your time. So, here's my 'yes' or 'no' question. Are you willing to give up golf for the next eleven months? Don't give me anything but a 'yes' or 'no' answer."

Everyone laughed. All knew Nunn was pretty much addicted to golf. There was a long pause, then a firm, "Yes." No one said a word. Several people with firsthand knowledge of Nunn's passion for golf raised their eyebrows and gave each other questioning looks.

"Are you sure?" one asked.

"Yes," Nunn said, with some finality in his voice. Nunn played golf at a championship level in high school and college, and to give it up for nearly a year would be difficult for him and, perhaps, emotionally painful. I took his comment as a sign that he was deadly serious about a run for the Senate.

"That's good enough for me," Thompson said. "I'm in." His legs, which had been swinging slowly, now jerked back under the edge of the desk and froze in place as if waiting for marching orders.

As Christmas carols continued to play in the background, accompanied by the occasional ding-ding-dinging of the bell from the UPI news machine in the next room, Nunn convinced our small group that he was prepared to run and possessed the requisite commitment to the goal. "For years," he said, "I've read the *Congregational Quarterly*, cover to cover, every issue, and I've learned something about the federal process.

Most important, I believe I have some very real answers to the problems that plague our nation." He walked over to the punch bowl, filled his cup with a thick, green liquid, heavy enough to support floating strawberries, and took a sip. "When all things are considered, I don't think there will be a better time for me." He paused, took another sip, and lowered his voice. "This *is* my time."

That seemed to be enough for the cadre of amateurs in the room. It would have to be. As the sun sank lower and lower on that short December afternoon, nearly all were beginning to feel the tug of family obligations for the eve of Christmas. The phone in Porter's office was ringing with wives on the other end wondering what was delaying the fathers of their children.

As I left WCRY, I wondered, *Is that all it takes? Read the* Congressional Quarterly *regularly, and you can run for the US Senate? Surely, there's more to it.*

By the time I reached State Highway 83 and headed toward Monticello, another thought occurred to me. *Any man who will ask you to meet on Christmas Eve to plan a political campaign might ask you to sacrifice a lot more of your life for him...and...maybe you'll tell yourself...this day was worth it.*

Maybe.

Chapter 5

And So It Began

On the first day of January 1972, Bill Shipp, political editor for *The Atlanta Constitution*, wrote a column about the ten most "insignificant" news stories of 1971. He listed Sam Nunn's "plan to break with Jimmy Carter and run for the US Senate"[1] only slightly more significant than the Atlanta police report that cops had "confiscated half a million dollars in hashish that turned out to be pure ragweed worth nothing."[2]

Ten days later, Hal Gulliver, editor of the *Constitution,* encountered Nunn at an Atlanta reception for state legislators. "You're crazy as hell," Hal said, "to think you can defeat the Carter-appointed senator and his well-oiled political machine."

What Gulliver didn't know was that Sam Nunn was committed to the task and not about to be deterred by an extraneous comment at a reception or political commentary in a statewide newspaper. Actually, Hal Gulliver calling the idea "crazy" was closer to a compliment than an insult. The idea was "crazy" in that we had no idea how to make the outcome a reality, but we knew of Nunn's passion for the race.

By early 1972, I wanted to see how this story turned out. By his own admission, Nunn's entry into the Senate race did not pass the "yellow pad test." On the night he made his decision to run, only Colleen was part of the conversation in their little A-frame home on the family farm. Nunn took out one of those yellow pads he was known to employ whenever there was a major decision to be made, and he started to list the pros and cons of the decision. The "cons" were easy, as he quickly listed fifteen or twenty reasons not to run. His list of "pros," however, was not very long.

---

[1] Bill Shipp, "'71 Big on Little News," *The Atlanta Constitution* (1 January 1972): 2a.

[2] Ibid.

The yellow-pad analysis did not yield the answer he hoped for, but he told Colleen, "I've got two choices: one is to run and find out what will happen; the other is to *not* run and sit back and be haunted by it for the rest of my life." He was ready to face all odds, to do the impossible in the view of many of his friends, and perhaps risk his entire political career on this one "crazy" race.

I'd been up close with such a risk-taking visionary only once before in my life. It had nothing to do with politics, but the risk was great and so was the passion to succeed.

In the late 1940s, my father said he had something exciting to show the family. He piled his eight children into his 1940 Plymouth Sedan and drove to the outskirts of town. (The ninth child was not yet born.) Mother held the youngest, Frank Jr., in her arms while one of the toddlers sat on the seat between her and Dad. The six remaining children spread out across the back seat, alternating sitting positions. "Some of you sit back," Dad said, "and some sit forward." We knew exactly what his instructions meant. Such an arrangement was the only way all of us could fit in the car.

Not far from the city limits, Dad pointed to a large worn-out piece of abandoned land, mostly covered in sagebrush, sugarcane, and kudzu vines. A few pecan trees peeked above it all, with a regularity that indicated someone once had high hopes for an orchard. Sagebrush and blackberry briars kept most trespassers away, and I suspect rattlesnakes took care of the rest.

"Salute The Presbyterian Home!" Dad commanded. With that, he offered a quick salute as all of his children roared with laughter.

We saw nothing; Dad saw everything. His vision included a residential development that provided continuous health-care services to a retirement community of more than 200 residents. He could see the completed Presbyterian Home as clearly as he could see us laughing in the back seat of that old Plymouth.

When Sam Nunn made his commitment to seek a seat in the United States Senate, I felt the excitement Dad must have felt the day he had us saluting his vision, and I wanted to witness that kind of passion at work once more. To see a "foolhardy, doesn't have a chance" vision become a reality must surely be one of the most exhilarating experiences of life.

And so it began.

Meanwhile, the nation was watching closely as President Nixon and Secretary of State Henry Kissinger attempted to wind down the Vietnam War. At the beginning of 1972, fighting still raged in Vietnam, even as President Nixon announced a further withdrawal of American troops. "Peace with honor" was the best citizens could hope for, and that's what Nixon promised as his campaign for reelection unfolded. Vietnam hung over every contested race that year. Federal spending was a popular topic, and questioners often talked of government excess, especially since President Nixon's budget included the highest peacetime deficit ever considered.

Other factors would have an unknown impact on Nunn's campaign. Most significant, perhaps, was the shooting of Alabama governor George Wallace while he was campaigning for the presidency in Maryland, May 15, 1972. Wallace had many followers around the nation, and he was especially popular in Georgia. Nunn was fully aware of the impact a Wallace endorsement could have on his campaign, and while that endorsement would be welcome if it came, the bigger question was whether Wallace would be well enough to endorse any of the Democrats running for Senate in the South. Nunn's race was almost over before he got the answer to that one.

Most of these external issues evolved on a broader political stage, but they became hot topics in every Georgia community Nunn visited. Critical to his success would be the way he handled them. However, before the Nunn campaign could begin, far more fundamental political issues had to be addressed.

Apart from the 1971 Christmas Eve commitment of that small group of friends, not everyone in Perry was on board, not because they didn't support Nunn unequivocally, but rather because they preferred to have him choose a more risk-free path to victory. Among the ten or twelve locals who attended a meeting in Nunn's law office to discuss a possible run was another attorney, Larry Walker. When Nunn asked for advice, Walker urged caution. "Sam, you ought to wait until Carl Sanders and Lester Maddox make up their minds."

"I've heard others say the same thing," Nunn said. "About ninety percent of advice—"

"Well, there's a reason for that," Walker interrupted. "It makes political sense. These days you've either got to have lots of money or you've got to have a gimmick, and you're not a gimmick-type person. And, what's more, you're not well known anywhere except right here in Perry." Walker's Southern drawl was such that it took about two minutes for him to get all that out.

The others quietly nodded their agreement.

"You've got Lester Maddox with the ax handles, or pick handles, *and* he's the lieutenant governor," Walker continued. Maddox was known for refusing to serve black citizens in his restaurant The Pickrick. He chased away black customers with ax handles and later closed his restaurant rather than integrate.

"You've got Carl Sanders, former governor, and very well regarded," Walker said. "If Maddox or Sanders gets in, it's highly problematic whether you could make a runoff, and that, after all, is what we're talking about, isn't it?" That much took about three minutes for him to say.

Nunn walked from behind his desk and pulled up a chair near his circle of close friends. "I hear you, and I agree that I'm not well known beyond the Perry city limits. But if I wait for Maddox and Sanders to decide, it'll be too late."[3] His political instincts told him it was going to be a steep uphill climb all the way, no matter when he started.

Sanders and Maddox were not the only major variables that might be introduced before the qualifying deadline passed on June 14. Several sitting congressmen were giving the race genuine consideration. Rep. Jack Brinkley (D-3rd) of Columbus was thinking about it, and so were Representatives Bill Stuckey (D-8th) of Eastman and Dawson Mathis (D-2nd) of Albany. I'm sure they didn't give much thought to Sam Nunn's chances while they were mulling over a decision. Later, as they witnessed his success, there was plenty of "if only" envy.

---

[3] Carl Sanders did not officially take himself out of consideration until the day of the qualifying deadline. If Sam Nunn had waited until Sanders made his decision, as many friends advised him, only fifty-four days would remain before the primary vote.

Sam Nunn was cautious by nature, as many in Perry understood, but even his closest confidants were unaware that he had been preparing for a run at a federal office since his days as a staff attorney for the House Armed Services Committee in 1962—a full decade past. His decision seemed completely out of character with the person they knew to give long and serious thought to every big decision he had ever made. But in Nunn's view, he'd been thinking about this one long enough. To borrow a phrase from President Theodore Roosevelt, Sam Nunn was ready to "dare greatly." Other souls, more timid than he, were not.

In late January 1972, we opened a campaign office of sorts in a one-bedroom apartment on the eighteenth floor of the Landmark apartment building in downtown Atlanta. The cramped quarters, borrowed from architect Bill Thompson, provided temporary accommodations for us. Joie Laroe, a student assistant at Georgia State University, volunteered to help with typing requirements.

Joe Sheehan of the Sibley/Sheehan Public Relations firm was hired to manage the campaign. Sheehan was a former president of the Georgia Jaycees and was said to have contacts throughout the state, although for the short time he was with us, I never saw any evidence of those contacts.

The little Landmark apartment was also where ad agency executives Tom Little and Mike McDonald presented their ideas for an advertising campaign. I wondered what words they would choose to capture the breadth of Nunn's candidacy, to address all the problems associated with his youth and inexperience, and still be short enough to fit on a bumper sticker. They came up with what might be the longest political bumper sticker slogan of all time: "*Get Tough in Washington, Put Sam Nunn in the Senate.*"

Nunn had many questions, including, "Why so long? Who's going to remember it?"

Right on point, I thought.

"'Get tough' says you're going to say what needs to be said and let the chips fall where they may," Little said, walking over to the poster board where he had thumb-tacked the slogan. "Get tough." He started to underline each word in the slogan. "Where? In Washington." He underlined Washington twice. "It's a variation on George Wallace's 'Send them a message' slogan, but it also says you're not running for the state senate; you aim to go to Washington. In the second line, it doesn't say 'vote' for Sam Nunn; we use the action verb 'put' so that people will know we want them to do something beyond casting their one vote. We want them to tell their friends to 'Put Sam Nunn in the Senate.'"

It was long, but Nunn liked it. Maybe not from the start, but it quickly grew on him. I was skeptical and worried that it might get lost in the advertising milieu that surrounds campaigns. Up to that point, the longest slogan I ever encountered was "Winston tastes good like a cigarette should." They taught us in marketing classes at UGA that "brief and memorable" were the best criteria for measuring successful advertising slogans. There was no rhythm, no rhyme, in this one, and it was certainly not "Good to the last drop."

As Nunn and I stepped on the elevator later, I told him what I thought of the slogan. "Ten words? Not brief at all. Memorable? I don't know; I hope so."

He looked at me. "At least it's not 'Nunn's the One.'"

I laughed as I thought of those awful "Nixon's the One" posters displayed by the Nixon-Agnew team in 1968. They were supposed to attract the youth vote.

With a slogan in hand, an ad agency hired, a campaign manager, a secretary, and me—a committed jack-of-all-trades political junkie—we were off and running...well, walking fast, for sure. Just forty-five days remained until the scheduled announcement on his family's Houston County farm. We had a lot of work to do.

Press releases were sent out, barbecue was ordered, and invitations mailed to every major dignitary in the state. Governor Jimmy Carter declined his invitation with a handwritten note, which said in part, "I know this will be a big day for you. Good luck! I'll be at Cumberland on the 15th of March."[4] Governor Carter had his own horse in the race, so his response was not a surprise. But was it necessary, for the record, to reveal that he would be taking a day off enjoying the beaches of Cumberland Island? Carter's note had a distinctly dismissive tone to it.

In addition to Carter's rejection, all signs from the media indicated little interest as well. From the beginning, the media viewed Nunn as

---

[4] Governor Jimmy Carter to Sam Nunn (9 March 1972).

someone they would place in the "also ran" category when the race was over. With the hope that offering free transportation to Perry and back would make the trip from Atlanta more enticing for the media, the campaign arranged for a bus to pick up reporters at the capitol, drive to Perry some 90 miles away, and bring them back when the event concluded. I didn't think the bus was a good idea at all, but Joe Sheehan, campaign manager, insisted. Sheehan was certain the media would accept a free ride to a free barbecue. I was assigned to accompany the bus from Atlanta to Perry. The bus and I waited in front of the capitol for nearly an hour before I got out and went inside to check with Associated Press reporter Dick Pettys. "Nobody's going; it's not news," Pettys told me. "Sam's not going anywhere. Besides—a bus? Are you kidding me?"

"Well, if we shoot a photo of the event and bring it to you, will you put it on the wire?" I knew Sheehan wouldn't be satisfied with that, but I needed something to tell him when I got to Perry.

"Bring it to AP downtown and we'll see," Pettys said.

I think that means he'll think about it.

I canceled the bus, jumped in my Dart, and drove to Perry as fast as the law allowed. When I showed up without the bus, without the media, I thought Sheehan was going to have a heart attack. "Where's the bus?" he shouted. "Where's the bus?"

This guy is going to be no help to this campaign at all.

"Look, as I told you when we discussed the bus the first time, reporters don't need transportation to cover a newsworthy event; in fact, they're offended if it's offered."

"Are you saying—"

"That's right," I said. "This event doesn't meet their test. At this moment, in their view, this event is not newsworthy." So far, the campaign was not off to a good start.

I was too inexperienced to understand that the Atlanta newspapers had already concluded the ultimate winner was going to be the appointed senator David Gambrell or the former governor Ernest Vandiver. The only crack in their crystal-ball-gazing might occur if Lester Maddox or Carl Sanders got into the race. If that should happen, the Atlanta papers would deal with it in good time. Editors were probably sitting around the newsroom the day of Nunn's announcement saying, "We're not going to waste ink on someone who isn't going to scratch in this contest." I'm glad I didn't know that.

"$250,000 was more realistic"

More than 3,000 local supporters came out for the announcement on the Nunn family farm, and while they enjoyed free barbecue, Nunn pledged, "We can, we will, and we must restore our pride in this great nation." And he laid out his approach for doing just that with a platform that reflected the conservative views of most Georgians at that time.

Before Nunn sat down, the mayor presented him with a check for $50,000, the total amount raised by the Houston County community to get his race started. Many of his closest supporters thought naively that the check might be all he would require. Others, claiming to have experience in such things, speculated that $250,000 was more realistic. A few hedged their bets. "Even $250,000 will be hard to come by," said Buddy Tolleson, longtime family friend and a key fundraiser for the campaign. Not one of us realized just how hard it would be to raise the required funds, and no one, including the candidate, could have guessed that the campaign would cost $750,000 before the election was over.

That first $50,000 was as easy to raise as the remaining $700,000 was difficult. From the beginning, the campaign never had enough money in the bank. Indeed, there were several occasions when payday for the staff was in question. Bill Pope, the only member of our staff at that moment with campaign experience, attempted to buck us up with such statements as, "Just wait until Sam wins the primary, the money will start to pour in." It didn't. "Just wait until Sam wins the runoff and becomes the nominee, funds will come from many sources including the national party." It didn't. "Well, just wait until he wins the general election, lobbyists will be clamoring to help erase his deficit." They didn't. In fact, when the campaign wrapped up in November, the Nunn for Senate campaign had a debt of about $140,000, and it took another eighteen months to pay it off.

But that day was a long way off. First, we had to make an announcement.

Retired Rep. Carl Vinson congratulates Sam Nunn as Nunn announces his candidacy for the US Senate, March 15, 1972.

Photo courtesy: Roland McElroy

Announcement Day

For years, Sam Nunn had been thinking about what he might say on such an occasion, but he still needed a full three weeks to draft and polish his announcement remarks. He welcomed content suggestions from others, but the end product was written by Sam Nunn himself. Make no mistake, this speech was his. Nunn carefully considered every word, every phrase. "What does that word mean? Will it be clear? What if we put this paragraph before that one?" He was developing a habit that followed him the rest of his career. He planned to discuss the major problems facing the nation as well as the "common sense" solutions he would offer to address those problems if elected to the Senate. He used no code words for individual segments of the electorate, no platitudes to leave a "feel good" impression. Only straight talk would suffice, tough talk about the difficulties the nation faces. He would close by reminding the crowd that they must always keep in mind "the heritage of our fathers, the future of our children, and our obligation to solve present problems." He wanted the announcement speech to set the tone for the entire campaign.

Judging by the applause, I'd say his words were well received. He was still shaking hands with guests on the decorated bed of that flatbed truck when I scrambled up to position myself on one end to get a good photo for the Associated Press to consider when I got back to Atlanta. I snapped the image I wanted and got behind Nunn and Mr. Vinson as they walked down the steps to the crowd below. And just as we reached the bottom step, Mr. Vinson grabbed Nunn's coattail and gave it a good yank. "Now, Sam, give 'em unshirted hell."

I remember his words exactly because I'd never heard him use such language. Was he talking about Nunn's opponents, whomever they might turn out to be, or was it a reference to a stubborn bureaucracy waiting in Washington? Or both?

Best Speech No One Heard

As the barbecue crowd dispersed that spring afternoon, Nunn came over to me, and in a near whisper said, "There's a funeral this afternoon for one of my father's longtime farm employees. I know we have work to do, but I want to be there."

Work to do? We had been so focused on the announcement and all associated details that we had not considered anything beyond that critically important day. We were like a baseball team that focused so much on making opening day a success that it hadn't made time to schedule any games thereafter. Yes, we definitely had work to do.

When Nunn saw my questioning expression, he said, with his patented unblinking stare, "His name is Jack Norwood; he was a loyal family friend."

With that, I knew we were going to the funeral. "I'll drive," I said, "you navigate."

We turned off the main highway and drove down a long, unpaved road of loose gravel and soft sand for shoulders. Finally, we came to a little white frame church with cars packed, bumper-to-bumper, around the entire churchyard. From the open windows, I could hear a piano playing a spiritual that sounded familiar, although I couldn't recall its title. The congregation softly hummed.

"They've started," Nunn said, jumping out before we fully stopped. I walked briskly to catch up.

As we entered the crowded church, one glance around the room confirmed my fear that we would be the only white faces present, and, for a moment, I worried that we might be seen as unwanted interlopers disturbing this personal time of family grieving. But a second later, we were greeted warmly by an usher and escorted to a couple of seats in the front row. The pastor delivered his homily, and, as I listened, I worried that Nunn might be asked to participate in some way.

I've not heard Nunn mention the name Jack Norwood until today. He's had no time to focus on what he might say at a time like this. I know how carefully he selects his words, and he hasn't had a moment to prepare—

"We are honored to have Sam Nunn with us this afternoon," the pastor said, as he finished his homily. "Most of us have known Sam since the day he was born. That was certainly true for Jack Norwood." One of the ladies in the choir began to hum again. The pastor nodded in Nunn's direction. "We are most grateful for your presence here, Mr. Nunn, and I wonder if you would like to say something about our brother, Jack Norwood?"

Before the pastor finished asking, Nunn popped out of his seat and quickly stepped behind the modest podium.

What's going to happen now? He usually sweats every word when he has a speech to deliver.

In the next few minutes, Nunn delivered a moving and most revealing speech. I had never heard him speak so eloquently under any other circumstances. To a chorus of "Amens" and an occasional "Yes!" Nunn spoke of his loyal friend, a man who enjoyed a stellar reputation throughout Houston County. "But," Nunn said, "I didn't come to talk about Jack's reputation; I came to talk about his character...because character is the true measure of every individual."

Nunn devoted the next ten minutes to Norwood's impact on the Nunn family. "Jack was a role model for me, my sister, and our entire family. He taught us the importance of self-sacrifice. And he certainly made sure to reserve enough energy in every day to make a meaningful contribution to the lives of others—his family, his church, and his community. His was an incredible spirit of giving to others." Just when I thought Nunn was about to sit down, he began sharing the many sacrifices Jack Norwood had made to assist those less fortunate in the community, those who needed a friend, or simply a helping hand. "Jack embodied all the personal qualities that are most important in life, and the best way for each of us to express our gratitude for Jack's life is to try to emulate his life of service in some way, every day—even if it seems small." And then, Nunn sat down.

I felt I was being introduced to one of Houston County's finest citizens. And I was. I learned a great deal about Jack Norwood that day, but even more about Sam Nunn. As Nunn walked back to his seat, I realized that he had offered insight into his own character as well.

As the congregation of that little country church rose to sing a final hymn in celebration of Jack Norwood's life, I thought, *This is the speech those 3,000 people should have heard earlier today.* My eyes were opened as I realized the campaign was about to offer the people of Georgia someone of extraordinary mettle, someone who could make a difference in the lives of all of us. Now we needed enough time to help the people of gia discern in this young man the same qualities of leadership and character already known to those closest to him. Four months and three weeks remained until the August 8 primary, and Nunn was not well enough known to register above 2 percent in a statewide name-recognition poll.

Plan of Attack

In the beginning, there was plenty of debate among members of the small campaign staff about positions Nunn should take on important issues of the day such as amnesty, veterans, drugs, and, of course, taxes. Amnesty, in those days, was sought by draftees who fled to Canada to avoid military draft; it had nothing to do with illegal immigration. Veterans were not concerned so much about the quality of care at VA hospitals as they were about the release of prisoners of war in Vietnam and an accounting of all those missing in action. Drug-abuse discussions centered on costs inflicted on society by those addicted to illegal narcotics, not abuse of prescription painkillers. Keeping the elderly from living in poverty was the major point of welfare reform. Any discussion about taxes always came back to finding a way to provide a tax break for working people, a category wide enough to include anyone not already making millions.

Nunn insisted that the words used in all advertising be the same words he used every day when talking with voters. As a result, he personally wrote nearly every ad that appeared in print or heard over the air. Or, to be more precise, he rewrote them. Consistency was critical. Today, it would be described as "staying on message," and he was a strong manager of message.

At one point in the early days of the campaign, Nunn felt it necessary to write a memo to the handful of people who made up the entire staff explaining the approach he would be taking on major issues, and pointing out, in a not-so-subtle way, that anyone who disagreed should get onboard or choose another interest to pursue.

Two closing paragraphs made his campaign strategy clear:

> We have no gimmick in this campaign. Our gimmick—if it must be called that—is to display leadership, guts and sincerity by not only

> identifying the problem and shaking our fists at the Federal Government but also conveying the impression that we are thinking of solutions, we are capable of proposing solutions, and we do not mind making people mad. Only by displaying this leadership will we have the full impact of my own characteristics and my own personality. To those who disagree with this approach, I suggest that you speak your piece now so that we can iron it out and all travel in one direction.
>
> I am not absolutely wedded to this approach but this is Sam Nunn. This is the way Sam Nunn thinks, this is the way Sam Nunn always has thought, and this is the kind of campaign that not only would I be comfortable with, but also that I think this country needs. I am sick and tired, and the general public is sick and tired, of politicians who do nothing but shout at the Federal Government and yet have no solutions and who simply play on the emotions of our people. I intend to get tough. I intend to take a stand. I intend to propose solutions, and I am willing to let the chips fall where they may.[5]

After Nunn's memo circulated, all debate stopped. There was no doubt about who was in charge. Win or lose, the campaign would be a reflection of the candidate. He was an independent, common-sense conservative. He would not be wearing the mantle of any other person or party. I believe it was the wisest decision he made during the entire campaign. One thing was certain: his opposition would find it difficult, if not impossible, to tag him as a liberal in this race, and that would help him avoid the McGovern noose the Republicans wanted to hang around his neck every day.

"Get Tough in Washington, Put _____ in the Senate"

The campaign slogan was created to tap into a strong anti-Washington sentiment growing across the South. Complaints about Washington's ability to function as a government seemed to cover a list of issues that only grew longer with each passing day. The Nunn slogan allowed voters to interpret its meaning from the perspective of individual concerns. The campaign churned out bumper stickers as fast as the presses could roll, and the slogan soon appeared on cars and trucks across the state.

---

[5] "Plan of Attack" memo to staff, 20 March 1972; copy in author's personal files.

Get tough in Washington.
Put Sam Nunn in the Senate.

Early bumper stickers had one major fault:
the sun quickly bleached out Sam Nunn's name.

Photo courtesy: Roland McElroy

But there was a problem.

The slogan was printed in black ink on a white background. Only the candidate's name, "Sam Nunn," appeared in red ink. The red really stood out, a perfect contrast and easily readable. Two weeks after we began distribution, I got a call from a supporter in Cairo. "The sun has bleached out the red in Sam Nunn's name," he said. "We've got stickers down here with a blank space where Sam's name used to be."

"Used to be? You mean—really blank?" I asked.

"Blank as my cupboard the day before payday," he said. "I'm thinking about writing my own name in the space."

The sun had already begun to bleach out Nunn's name on my own bumper sticker, and I hoped it was not a widespread problem—but it was.

The ad agency found a new printer before sunset. New bumper stickers were distributed, and this time with a red ink that would not fade.

A few days later, when Nunn entered the campaign office, his first words were, "How much did it cost to reprint?" When I told him, his response was a dry, "Guess this campaign is going to cost us more than $50,000 after all." I shrugged. It was not a good time to tell him we were already over $50,000.

Those early bumper stickers were not our only costly mistake. There was the matter of a billboard design that hid the candidate's face. Not many people remember those first billboards because they weren't posted along roadways for more than three weeks. They featured a photo of Nunn's face on a black background with the campaign slogan printed in a reverse white font beneath the photo. In an attempt to create an artistic photo of Nunn, they had created a photo with half of his face totally hidden by a dark shadow. We were trying to help people get to know him, but the first billboard hid half of his face! That billboard might have won an artistic design contest, but it could have been displayed for a decade and most people still wouldn't be able to recognize Sam Nunn. That's when I became aware that many ad men knew even less about campaigns than I did.

An Empty Gas Station

Colleen Nunn organized the first team of volunteers in Perry and put them to work in an empty gas station in the middle of town. Their task: write letters of introduction and endorsement to their friends in every county around the state. In the beginning, the letters were written on an IBM Selectric typewriter. "Every letter had to be typed individually," Colleen said. "When we weren't typing, we were going around town gathering mailing lists from judges, court clerks, farm implement dealers, veterinarians, realtors, teachers, and even funeral home directors."[6] When an IBM mag-card machine[7] was installed, volunteer production increased significantly. Colleen couldn't say exactly how many letters went out but thought the total was probably around 5,000. At one point, eighty-one volunteers spent their days folding, stuffing, and mailing letters. She had another group of "callers" who came to the office to use the one and only WATS line the campaign installed. "No one wanted to spend their own money calling long distance," Colleen said. "In those days it was expensive."[8]

The grassroots effort that Colleen started and built upon throughout the campaign became a committed network that paid dividends in virtually every county that year and in every subsequent campaign. Twenty or more years later, while Charlie Harman was chief of staff, he received a phone call from someone asking to speak with Senator Nunn. The caller was sure Senator Nunn would want to speak with him. "Tell him it's his cousin from Toccoa."

Harman laughed. "You can't be. He doesn't have a cousin in Toccoa."

---

[6] Colleen Nunn, Sam Nunn Oral History, Washington, DC (30 September 1996).

[7] 1971 IBM sales brochure: "The secretary simply inserts a magnetic card into a small console placed alongside her desk and then types on the familiar keyboard of a specially engineered IBM 'Selectric' Typewriter. If she makes a mistake while typing, all she needs to do is backspace and type over the error with the correct letter or word and continue typing. The recording on the card is automatically corrected."

[8] Colleen Nunn, Sam Nunn Oral History.

"I may be the only one here, but I am definitely his cousin from Toccoa." Sensing he was about to be cut off, the caller decided to go for broke. "Look, I got a letter from Sam in 1972 and he wrote, 'Dear Cousin.'"

"Hold on." Harman stepped into Nunn's office and relayed the caller's message.

Nunn chuckled. "Charlie, we sent out thousands of 'Dear Cousin' letters in '72, and I think every one of them has called me—except this one. I'll take it."

In spite of the success of "Dear Cousin" letters, we entered a long slog of a campaign in the spring of 1972. Every new day came with a set of unforeseen challenges, any one of which held the potential to derail Sam Nunn's ambition before he gained any political traction at all. The first such incident occurred two days after the March 15 launch of his campaign in Houston County.

Chapter 6

St. Patrick's Day in the Waffle House

For decades, Savannah has been the site of the second-largest St. Patrick's Day celebration in the nation. It's a big deal in Chatham County, featuring all the Irish traditions, including a green-dyed river running through town. Tens of thousands of people from both sides of the Savannah River descend upon the town, drinking green beer and celebrating as long as energy and beer hold out. Participation in the parade is a "must" for every politician seeking office.

Two days after Sam Nunn announced his intention to run for the US Senate, the two of us were in Savannah to participate in the St. Patrick's Day festivities. We were sitting in a Waffle House, having breakfast, and waiting for the call to move to the parade site, where he would join Colleen in the backseat of a convertible before it rolled out to join the parade and face thousands of potential voters.

As expected, every seat in the Waffle House was taken that morning. The two of us sat in a booth, surveying the scene. We didn't recognize a face. Not one—just a sea of perfect strangers. I knew about Nunn's paralyzing fear of public speaking, but I knew nothing of his aversion to greeting strangers. His fear of standing before strangers to speak or to ask for their vote was real—painfully real, as I was about to discover.

Nunn looks nervous. Could it be the parade? No...then why?

We sat there so long that strangers at the tables were replaced by still more strangers.

He's more nervous than just a few minutes ago.

I wished that someone we knew would walk in and sit down. Nunn and I talked about every subject under the sun: the announcement speech two days before, the number of supporters we needed in every one of 159 counties, the campaign budget—everything.

What am I gonna do about this. He doesn't look ready to meet anyone.

People at the next table were laughing loudly, having a good time, and that didn't help. We ate the pancakes, all the biscuits, and all the bacon. The waitress kept bringing fresh coffee. I like coffee, but after several cups, even I am ready to move on. That's when she brought us a couple of glasses of orange juice. It may have been the longest breakfast in the history of Waffle House breakfasts. I looked out the window, wondering about the sign I hoped our sole supporter in Savannah was taping to the side of the convertible. "The letters better be large enough," I said.

"Why?" Nunn asked. "You think nobody knows me down here?" He attempted a slight chuckle.

"Well, we'll find out."

He's shaking like a leaf. Should I get up and shake hands? No, that won't work. Finally, I said, "Maybe you ought to shake a few hands right here...sort of a warm up for the parade."

"You're right; no better time than right now, is there?" With that he got up and went to the first table, and slowly, reluctantly, he offered his hand to the first stranger. "I'm Sam Nunn, and I'm running for the US Senate. Hope you'll vote for me."

It was hard. It was agony. There was no energy in him. His arm seemed reluctant to extend his hand. Some people didn't seem to have even heard his voice.

Will he make it around the entire room? I don't know. What can I do about this?

Complete strangers stared blankly at him. You could almost see them thinking, "Who is this guy who just stopped by our table; did he say he was running for the US Senate? What state—South Carolina? He doesn't look familiar." A short drive over the Talmadge Bridge will put you in South Carolina. I'm sure some of them, indeed, were wondering why someone from South Carolina was asking for their vote in Georgia.

How steep a hill have I ever climbed? This one may be higher.

But Nunn made it all the way around the room, stopping at every table and booth, even reaching out to the cook across the counter. He shook every hand.

"Okay," he said, as he got back to our table. He pulled out a ten-dollar bill, placed it on the table to take care of our breakfasts, and announced, "Let's go. I'm ready."

Well, that's the first smile I've seen all morning, and he does have some color back in his face.

"Are you sure?" I asked.

"Come on," he said, ignoring my question and almost dashing for the door.

In a few minutes, we were standing near the start of the parade, where officials quickly escorted him to the Grabber Blue Mustang convertible that was his parade transportation. Colleen, already perched atop the back seat, waved him over to join her. His sole key supporter in Savannah took him by the arm as we approached and said, "Sam, I hope you like this sign. I just finished it. Nobody knows you down here, but they'll love the reference to Colleen." He pointed to the sign, already taped to the side of the car, and there, in little green letters, it read:

Colleen O'Brien Nunn
and
her husband, Sam

"Colleen O'Brien Nunn" was easy to read, but you had to walk closer than three feet from the car to make out the name of our candidate.

A valuable lesson was learned that day. In every campaign, there are wrinkles to overcome every hour of every day. Somehow, you have to push through all of them—and keep smiling. In the end, the little sign worked perfectly. The crowd didn't know Sam Nunn and could not care less, but today they met his Irish wife, and that's what mattered to them.

It was a great first day of campaigning in the unknown world beyond Houston County. Only 157 counties remained, where no one knew Nunn—or his Irish wife.

The following week, we went through a series of meetings with potential supporters in small towns across the eastern portion of the state. At each stop, I could see that Nunn was having trouble remembering the names of those we met. I suggested he follow me as we departed each event. The plan was for me to say each person's name as I shook hands, and Nunn would follow me repeating the name. It worked fairly well the first time we tried it, but at the second stop, he tapped me on the shoulder and said, "I've got this." He paused. "I *have* to have this."

And he did.

He didn't need my help with names from that day forward. In high school, it was his speech teacher, Florence Harrison, who pushed him; now he was pushing himself. I'm sure he must have heard the voice of Ms. Harrison many times in those early days of the campaign, including that first full day of campaigning that started at the Waffle House in Savannah.

Campaign Management

Atlanta PR executive Joe Sheehan managed the campaign initially, and, later, sports marketer Ed Sieb. Sheehan, a gregarious individual and former head of the Georgia Jaycees, proved a bit too flashy for the Nunn campaign; he lasted only two weeks. His reckless spending of limited campaign funds proved to be his undoing. Not long after the campaign started, I was traveling with the candidate when we checked into a Brunswick motel and discovered Sheehan had booked a large two-room suite, complete with bar and entertainment center. The décor I can only describe as "early bordello." You are free to use your imagination. Despite its lavish, though entirely faux opulence, we could not find a shower or bathtub. We looked everywhere. Nunn continued to search while I got on the phone with the front desk from the adjacent room. Suddenly, I heard Nunn call out, "Found it!"

I hung up. *That's all I need to hear; I'll get back to the rest of my calls.*

Immediately, I heard water running and was glad that particular emergency was over.

After a while, I returned to the bedroom and found the candidate sitting in the middle of a giant marble tub located *under* the king-size bed. It was the biggest Murphy bed I'd ever seen, and somehow he'd been able to lift and fold the giant bed against the wall. The bottom of the bed was a mirror. The tub was the same size as the bed, as I recall, and appeared as if it might have been on loan from the Roman Baths.

Water spewed upward from the mouth of a gold lion before falling into the tub that was more than half full when I walked in.

Nunn looked up at me, with arms outstretched in an imperial fashion. "Senator? No! I'm running for emperor." For a moment, we laughed at the absurdity of the whole situation, but the laughter quickly subsided. He wanted to know how much the room had cost the campaign for the one night. I talked to the manager and was told the going rate was $200 a night. I persuaded him to give us the rate for a standard room, which was $40 a night, including tax.

If that wasn't enough excitement, a fire alarm went off at three o'clock in the morning, sending everyone out into the parking lot. Before breakfast, Nunn called Bill Thompson, who had volunteered to help with administrative details. "Bill, I think it's time for Joe Sheehan to return to his public relations firm."

Joe Sheehan had a Cadillac vision of the way a campaign ought to run and refused to recognize that Nunn's campaign was more like a stripped-down Chevy looking for a shade-tree mechanic to keep it running until Election Day. I never saw Joe Sheehan again. Instead, a true shade-tree mechanic showed up: Ed Sieb. I don't recall who brought Sieb into the campaign, but he was a more than an able manager. The Iowa native had one major handicap: he did not speak with a Georgia accent. In fact, his speech was closer to that of someone who hailed from New Jersey or New York—and I told him so. "You sound more like the carpetbagger from *Gone With the Wind*." I worried that his accent might adversely impact the campaign, but there was no need for concern. His amiable personality won instant friends wherever he traveled. As for campaign duties, he was unflappable in the face of impending disaster, and our campaign seemed to have a lot of those.

Richard Ray, former mayor of Perry, was intimately involved in the campaign from that first Christmas Eve meeting in 1971 to the end. His presidency of the Georgia Municipal Association gave him political connections in every city and town across the state. Nunn frequently said, "Next to my wife, Colleen, Richard was my first and strongest supporter." At the time of the 1972 election, Ray held a full-time job traveling the state as Southeastern regional manager for Getz Services. When the campaign ended, he moved to Washington to become Nunn's administrative assistant, a title later changed to chief of staff. Nine years after he arrived in Washington, Ray returned to Georgia and was elected to Congress from the Third Congressional District.

Connell Stafford was teaching history to middle school students when Nunn recruited him to be the campaign's "youth coordinator." Stafford had just finished his first year at Florence Bernd School in Bibb County when he brought several teachers to a meeting with a group of Middle Georgia legislators to discuss educational funding. During that meeting, he impressed Nunn with his grasp of education issues, and by the end of the meeting, Nunn asked him to join the campaign. Stafford came on board in late May and immediately demonstrated his skill as an organizer of youth volunteers. Although new to politics, his political instincts were rock solid.

I continued to handle scheduling, coordinate with county chairs, serve as principal contact for statewide media, and troubleshoot campaign problems as they arose.

By the time we had been in operation two-and-a-half months, our campaign management team was finally in place. Only nine weeks remained until the primary election.

The Godfather and "Great Balls of Fire"

As we struggled to get the campaign off the ground, we listened to the advice of just about anyone willing to stand still long enough to offer it. One Atlanta friend suggested Nunn should go down to Lowe's Grand Theatre and shake hands with all the people waiting in line to see the newly released movie *The Godfather*. "Let's do it," Nunn said. "I want to see that movie anyway."

At the theater, we were greeted by a ticket line that ran down the street and around the block. Suddenly, Nunn didn't seem excited to be there.

Uh-oh, I hope this is not the old butterflies thing again.

"Let's shake hands *after* the movie," he said. These people don't look like they want to greet someone running for office—not now."

I nodded. *Okay, that'll delay the pain a little while.*

That was before we saw the blood-spattered scenes in living color. Just about every version of mob assassination known to man unfolded before us. But we stuck it out right down to the last "I'm gonna make him an offer he can't refuse." When we walked out, exhausted from the violence, he felt even less inclined to shake hands with the crowd waiting for the next show. "Gotta be a better way," Nunn said, as he pulled his jacket lapel up to hide his metal "Sam Nunn for US Senate" name tag. He hoped no one would recognize him. But he needn't have worried. Everyone in line outside was focused on seeing the mayhem inside.

A few days later, another friend invited us to stop by his nightclub in downtown Atlanta, where the room would be full to overflowing with potential supporters. "Jerry Lee Lewis is performing," he told us, "and it'll be standing room only. I'll make sure Sam gets introduced before Lewis goes on." He did. Nunn waved to the puzzled crowd, and then we retreated to the back of the room, where we tried to strike up conversations with patrons who were far more interested in dancing to Lewis's music. Near the end of the performance, we were invited to come up to the stage and be recognized again before Lewis performed a final song. A minute later, Nunn was standing next to the piano, acknowledging the crowd. The owner waved me up, too, and just as I reached the stage, Lewis jumped up, kicked the piano stool backward, and slammed his fingers on the keyboard, staccato fashion. I thought he was going to destroy that unfortunate instrument. The band picked up his pounding rhythm, and they were off. The crowd roared as he ripped into "Great Balls of Fire." I'll never forget that wild look in his eye. He whipped his yellow cowlick back with a sideways jerk of his head and immediately left us for another world. Nunn and I stood there mesmerized, unable to move. From time to time, Lewis gave a little leer toward a group of girls jumping near the piano. Some in the crowd danced, and those who could find no room stomped in place until the music came to an explosive end with Lewis running his thumb up and down the keyboard several times. As the crowd yelled for more, Nunn and I skulked away into the night. "Gotta be a better way," Nunn said as we turned the corner to round the block.

The "Bird Roast"

I wanted to omit the telling of this next one, but I can't. Not if the reader is to gain a true sense of what a statewide campaign in Georgia was like in 1972. The unexpected is part of every day. Sometimes the unexpected is welcome, sometimes not.

Not long after the Jerry Lee Lewis evening, Nunn was invited to participate in a "bird roast" in deep southwest Georgia. The exact location was undetermined when the invitation was extended over the phone. We were promised that we would meet a group of local businessmen who were crucial to getting elected in the southwest region of the state. At the appointed hour, well after dark, we met a "friend of Sam's friend" at a small crossroads town, deep in Decatur County. He shook hands quickly, climbed in his truck, and called out, "Follow me." His '55 Chevy pickup pulled away slowly as if hoping to avoid unnecessary attention. At least, that's how it felt. We drove a couple of blocks from the town's only intersection, turned left, and soon left all semblance of civilization behind. Every once in a while I could see the road ahead for more than a mile, and as I searched for headlights, I realized we were the only vehicles on the road. I didn't like it; I didn't like it at all...but I wasn't sure why. I didn't say anything because I didn't want Nunn to know I had any misgivings about this "bird roast."

It had rained recently, and black swamp water was nearly up to the road on both sides of us. "Is that a log or an alligator?" I asked, pointing Nunn to an object on the passenger side ahead.

"Settle down," he said, "it's a log."

As we passed the "log," it slithered into the swamp without so much as a ripple. "That's the fastest 'log' I've ever seen." I kept a firm grip on the steering wheel. "Do you think we're still in Georgia?" Before Nunn could answer, we passed a sign that pointed the way to Quincy, Florida. We were, indeed, in the Sunshine State.

When we finally turned off the main road, we came to a stop in front of a locked gate. The pickup driver jumped out with key in hand to let us pass. As soon as both vehicles were through the gate, he locked it, and took the lead again. We followed him for what seemed like a mile, navigating around recently plowed fields and across several open pastures. On this moonless night, light was visible in only one direction—up. I'd forgotten how clearly one could see the Milky Way on such nights.

The glow of a large fire in the middle of a field just ahead pulled us closer, and the closer we got, the more unease I felt. At first I saw the shadows of those standing around the fire, then the faces of at least a couple of dozen white guys. Everyone was drinking, mostly whiskey, I think, but it was hard to tell. Some of the bottles didn't have labels. A couple of vehicles had shotguns leaning against the driver's door, and just about all the vehicles displayed a fully equipped gun rack. Someone had dug a small pit in the ground for a fire. Hot coals sizzled under the birds, which I guessed were mostly quail. Flakes of burning ash drifted into the sky. All the birds were skewered on a metal spit and turned by hand from time to time by random folk who happened by. There might have been a pheasant or two at one end because some seemed a bit larger than the rest.

Have we slipped through a time warp? Is this 1930? 1950? What's expected of us? How does this end?

We didn't have to wait long. Nunn's friend was there and greeted us warmly. He opened the tailgate on the little pickup and jumped into the bed of the truck while slapping his hand on the bare metal for attention. When all were relatively quiet, he began.

"I knew Sam's daddy long 'afore Sam was born, and to tell ya the truth, that's all ya need to know. His daddy understood Georgia politics, and ya gonna see in a minute that 'Little Sam' is jes' like 'Mr. Sam.' He's the one we all gonna support in this year's race for the U-Nited States Senate. Sam, come on up-cheer. Far 'em up!"

He reached out, grabbed Nunn's hand, and with one swift pull, had Nunn standing beside him on the tailgate of that truck. Again, a feeling of unease came over me. The light from the fire lit their faces, but when I turned to look behind me, there was only darkness.

Nunn spoke for less than ten minutes. Applause was enthusiastic from some, polite from others. There were definitely a few skeptics in this crowd. Most kept drinking whatever was at hand.

Afterwards, Nunn shook a few hands and didn't seem in a hurry to leave.

How do we know when to leave?

A door slammed. When I turned toward the sound, I caught a glimpse of a driver jumping out of the cab of his pickup. "Hey, boy," the driver called out in my direction. "Ya ever seen one of these?"

"Of course," I said. "Looks like a 16-guage shotgun."

I think he was surprised that I had any idea what he was holding. "That's right, city boy. Double barrel, for twice the fun." With one hand, and a flick of his wrist, the twin barrels snapped open.

He wants me to see them loaded—and they are.

"What-cha got at home?" he asked. The barrels snapped shut.

"Well," I said, thinking fast, "I use a 12-guage with a full choke when I go hunting. I like a full choke, don't you? Assures a clean kill."

I think he's shocked. Good. If he only knew, I just told him all I know about shotgun nomenclature.

His jaw dropped a moment, then he smiled and whacked me on the back, nearly knocking me down. "Ya know somethin' boy, you all right."

I was glad I had a gun-collecting brother. *Thanks, Frank.*

He handed me a paper cup with a clear liquid in it, and it wasn't ice water. I nodded and pretended to take a sip. Nearby, I caught a glimpse of Nunn.

"We gotta go." *If he wasn't ready, he should be. I know I am.*

A few minutes later, we followed that little '55 Chevy pickup back to the main road.

After my experience with the Klan back in 1964, I didn't know what to expect, but as it turned out, there was nothing to fear. These were just a bunch of good ole boys, law-abiding citizens in their community, continuing a tradition of celebrating the camaraderie of loyal friends. At least, that's what I kept telling myself as we followed that pickup back to the highway.

It took me a couple of days to shed the unease I felt that night.

Two Pecans in Every Envelope

Perhaps the most disheartening day in the campaign came when a retired pecan farmer from Dougherty County came by the Atlanta campaign office with what he described as "a great idea to woo black voters."

"Let's hear it," I said, not sure what to expect.

He reached over my desk and picked up an empty envelope. "Take a number ten envelope, put a campaign brochure in it, and include two pecans before you mail it to every black voter in the state."

"What?" I couldn't believe my ears. "What'd you say?"

"Well, everyone knows how much they like pecans." He started to hand the pecans to me. "These are not common Stuart variety or even Paper Shells; they're—"

"You're kidding me, aren't you?" I certainly hoped he was kidding.

"No, it'll work. I'll even provide the pecans at no cost to the campaign." He put two pecans in my hand. "You're holding the best variety I grow: Desirable. You've heard of them, haven't you?"

"Jim, you do realize this is 1972, don't you? We can't do that. In fact, you can't even make such a suggestion; it's patently racist." I put the pecans in his hand and pushed them toward him.

"No, it's not." He laughed. "Now you're kidding me."

I wasn't smiling.

He didn't see the problem at all. "You're just too sensitive. Look, I'm communicating with them in a way that I know will motivate them to the polls." He tried to give the two pecans back to me but I refused to hold them again.

"That's the worst thing anyone has suggested to me. Take those pecans with you when you leave." He started to turn for the door when I said, "Wait. Give them to me. I'll have them with my lunch, and if they're any good, *I'll* vote the 'right' way on Election Day." I was smiling, but Jim was not. He tried to slam the door on the way out, but it was spring-loaded and wouldn't slam.

Such was the mindset of many in those days.

"Half of them were against me"

There were many times in the 1972 campaign when the outcome seemed problematic, to say the least. Nunn told many audiences that his campaign took an early poll and discovered that only 2 percent of Georgians had ever heard his name. He would add, chuckling, "And half of *them* were against me."

That wasn't far from the truth. A little more than one month after Nunn's announcement on the farm, none of the nine Democratic candidates were catching on with the electorate. Duane Riner, political editor for *The Atlanta Constitution,* declared the entire campaign was "moving with the vigor of an elephant lumbering through a field of epoxy."[1] And the polls, though few, reflected Riner's view. The campaign staff was told to ignore the polls and concentrate on getting Nunn elected. In short order, he found his "campaign legs" and stepped out on an aggressive path to every corner of the state. If he expected to be successful in the Democratic primary, he'd have to run nothing short of an Ironman race.

As the campaign got underway in earnest, Nunn sent a memo to four key staffers outlining what he expected to have prepared for him every day. Of several tasks assigned to me, he wanted to be briefed daily on the people he and I knew in each town or campaign stop along the way. His memo instructed the campaign secretary to prepare cards for his review with names of all legislators, VIPs, and other persons he should contact while in a specific area. As for scheduling, he wanted no idle time. Every day should be tightly scheduled from morning to night. He wanted to be on time for all events. Finally, he also asked the staff to make sure he arrived at each event "rested and fresh-minded." He never told us how he could arrive "rested and fresh-minded" when every waking moment was spent racing from one event to the next. His instructions were clear but contradictory.

This was going to be one of those marathons where all members of the runner's crew would be required to run alongside him. In the earliest days, I helped with speeches, wrote press releases, set up his daily sched-

---

[1] Duane Riner, "Georgians Saying Ho-Hum to Senate Race," *The Atlanta Constitution* (27 April 1972): 23A.

ule of events, arranged media coverage, and recruited key supporters since almost no county came with a ready and willing base of supporters.

The breakneck schedule Sam demanded would have killed an ordinary man. One night, as we were reviewing the next day's schedule, he stopped on the first event. "Who's going to introduce me at this Columbus breakfast tomorrow?" There was a tinge of irritation in his voice that a name was not already associated with his introduction.

"I don't know," I said, which is never a good answer for Nunn, especially when you are supposed to know. "John says he'll have someone appropriate do it." John Simpkins was our Muscogee County coordinator.

"Get John on the phone."

"But, it's 11:30...at night," I said. "I think he might be asleep."

Nunn looked at me with raised eyebrows. "Look, I only have from this moment to November 7th to win this thing. John can sleep after that. Get him on the phone."

I placed the call and listened as the phone range eight or ten times in Simpkins's Columbus home. Simpkins finally picked up the phone and promptly dropped it on the floor, nearly bursting my eardrum. I heard nothing else for a moment. "John isn't speaking," I said, "but I think he's there; why don't you say something first?" I handed the phone to Nunn. "I'm sure he was asleep."

Shaking his head, Nunn grabbed the phone. "John? Sam. Who's introducing me tomorrow?"

There was no "Sorry to wake you at this late hour," none of that. It was as if the candidate assumed all of his key people were always awake and working for his victory. There's no telling how many people in Columbus heard about the "candidate who doesn't sleep" before the next day was done.

Many years later, long after I left Nunn's Senate staff, the phone rang at my house around midnight. My immediate thought was "Somebody's in trouble or somebody has died." I jerked the phone off the hook.

"'Lo," I said, clearing my throat several times.

"Roland? Sam. I didn't wake you, did I?"

"No." I was awake enough to give him the answer he expected but struggling to get my voice to work like someone who was always awake in the middle of the night.

"Do you remember that broadcast bill we voted on back in '75?"

"Vaguely," I murmured into the phone. I searched my brain's foggy cells for any trace of that bill. *Nothing.*

"Well, I'm speaking to the Georgia Broadcasters at breakfast in the morning and I'd like to mention it. What was the issue?"

We had a saying around the office, "Once an employee of Sam Nunn, always an employee of Sam Nunn." No one who has ever worked for him leaves with immunity from calls in the middle of the night. You may draw a paycheck from someone else, but you will always work for Sam Nunn.

"1975? Well, it could have been something clarifying the public interest standard in the Communications Act."

"No, that's not right," he said. "I'd remember that."

"Wait. It wasn't a bill at all," I said, the mental fog beginning to lift. "It was a ruling by the FCC on cross-ownership. Let's see, uh, cross-ownership: take away the limitations and pretty soon, you've got all media concentrated in a few hands, but—"

"That's all I need. Thanks.

(Click)

Silence.

"Or maybe it was the bill banning...hello?" *I was talking into a dead phone.*

"He's gone," I said to Ginny, now fully awake. She didn't ask who had called at such an hour. She knew.

"In it to the end"

Despite all the effort expended on his behalf by 1972 volunteers at the gas station, Sam Nunn's campaign made little progress in the first weeks, and by late May appeared hopelessly bogged down in the lower tier of candidates running for the Democratic nomination.[2] The primary

---

[2] Fifteen Democratic candidates: former governor Ernest Vandiver, incumbent US Senator David Gambrell, state treasurer Bill Burson, civil rights activist Hosea Williams, white supremacist J. B. Stoner, Jack Dorsey, Lloyd Russell, Wyman C. Lowe, Bill Aynes, former congressman W. M. "Don"

was a little more than two months away. Nunn was at home, trying to get a little rest, when the call came in. For our candidate, rest meant sitting down to go over next week's travel schedule, sign letters, call key supporters, read background papers, and, if there was time, discuss press opportunities. "Hello, this is Sam," he said to the caller, and continued to scan the correspondence in front of him.

The caller got right to the point. "Sam, I've known you a long time and have always been one of your strongest supporters, but I want to talk with you not like a cousin, but a brother."

Nunn switched the phone to the other ear and began using his ballpoint pen to scratch out whole paragraphs in the letter before him. I think he had a sense of the advice about to be offered. There was never a shortage of people ready to throw cold water on the entire enterprise. Finally, he put down his correspondence and patiently listened.

"Look, I've seen the polls; they're not moving," the caller said. "I advise you to get out of the race. There'll be no shame in getting out now, and if you get out now, your reputation will still be intact, and you can run again another day, perhaps for lieutenant governor."

I was sitting on the sofa across the room and couldn't catch every word, but I got the gist of it. Nunn let the caller have his say. When the caller finally stopped talking, Nunn spoke calmly, with words carefully considered. "If I were in this race to satisfy some personal political ambition, your advice might be appropriate, but I'm not in it to position myself for some future political office. I'm in it because I believe I can make a real contribution to solving problems that impact Georgia and the nation. If I didn't believe that, I wouldn't have run in the first place, but I do…and I'm in it to the end, no matter the result." When he hung up, he looked at me, and his only words were, "We've got work to do."

Nunn had been grinding out eighteen-hour campaign days for nearly three exhausting months, and now a well-meaning cousin had just urged him to get out of the race. Such counsel would have crushed most people, especially when coming from a family member.

Wheeler, T. J. Irwin, Austin D. Graham, Darrel W. Runyon, Gerry Dokka, and state Rep. Sam Nunn

The cousin, perhaps, was unaware that Nunn had won the grueling two-mile Freshman Cake Race before the Homecoming game at Georgia Tech in 1956[3] with absolutely zero experience in long-distance running. The race was sometimes referred to as the Freshman Rat Race because all freshmen—"rats" to upperclassmen—were required to run the race. Nunn never competed in high school track, but he had just finished his senior year of varsity basketball and, at 18 years of age, was in great physical condition. Organizers put one experienced member of the Georgia Tech cross-country team in the race to establish the pace for the runners. Nunn got behind him even though he was unaware he was behind the official "pacer."

"Gasping across the finish line, Phi Delt Nunn was rewarded with a giant cake and a kiss from Anita Wall, 'Miss Homecoming of 1956.' Martha Evans, Mr. Nunn's sweetheart from his hometown of Perry, watched the ceremonial buss with a wary eye."[4]

The natural competitive streak in him, once lit, burned white hot until the outcome was known. That same flame was not likely to allow his political ardor to cool in the middle of this race for the United States Senate. Sam Nunn, still in his early thirties, was convinced that he was uniquely qualified to make a difference in Washington. The defeatist advice of a close family member was not likely to discourage him.

Old Gray Pontiac

Jimmy Hammock, a Dublin auto dealer, provided an old gray Pontiac from his dealership for use by the campaign. Regrettably, it didn't come with a driver. If there were one thing any of us would change about that first campaign, it would be to insist on hiring a full-time driver from the beginning—even if the money had to be borrowed to pay him.

I drove Nunn for two weeks before Ginny caught up with us and complained that I was not spending enough time at home helping her raise our two boys, ages 1 and 2. Nunn suggested we make a change. "No campaign is worth making wives upset," he said. "Go home. Take care of

---

[3] Homer Meaders, "10,000 Grads Crowd Campus for Tech Homecoming Game," *The Atlanta Journal and Constitution* (28 October 1956): 16-B.

[4] Ibid.

this. We'll talk later." I rehearsed my apology all the way home, but I never got a chance to use it. Ginny actually apologized to me for being upset on the phone. "I know how important this campaign is to Georgia—and to you," she said. "Besides, I couldn't stop you if I wanted to." The next week Nunn pulled me into the campaign office to take charge of his schedule and to help Bill Pope, campaign spokesman, with broadcast media. Richard Ray, close friend and former mayor of Perry, took over the driving duties I relinquished. Ray lasted a full week before exhaustion and flu took him out of action.

I offered to go back on the road again because I knew there was no money to hire a full-time driver, but Nunn wouldn't hear of it. "I can drive myself," he said. "Besides, I need you in the headquarters." That was the worst decision he made in the campaign. Indeed, it nearly proved fatal. Nunn drove himself for at least four weeks before it began to take a toll. Previously, when he had a driver, he was getting only four or five hours of sleep a night. Driving himself, he was getting even less.

"I'd been up since about four o'clock that morning, meeting factory shifts before going to speaking engagements," Nunn said. "The day was capped with a barbecue in Canton. I finished up around eleven o'clock that night before heading back to Atlanta."[5]

There should have been someone else behind the wheel that night. Maybe it was the barbecue, but more than likely, it was simply the lack of sleep. The narrow two-lane highway twisted and turned along back roads that led to the interstate highway. It was probably a good thing that his was the only car on that road that night because he felt the car drift across the yellow centerline several times. Soon, his eyelids, heavy with fatigue, closed ever so slightly, and his grip on the wheel relaxed.

"My foot slipped off the accelerator, and the car slowed to about 20 miles an hour when the gravel shoulder woke me up. My eyes opened just in time to avoid a bridge abutment straight ahead—just barely."[6]

The next day, the campaign hired its first full-time driver, a young college student named Gil Hargett. The rigors of the campaign trail took their toll on Hargett, too, and he was replaced for a while with a mix of

[5] Nunn, Sam Nunn Oral History, Washington, DC (30 September 1996).
[6] Ibid.

drivers. Finally, in early August, the campaign found Joe Brannen, a recent graduate of Georgia Southern College. He didn't play the radio while driving, didn't talk too much, and didn't drink alcoholic beverages at all. Joe was the perfect "wheel man" for Nunn.

"I made a commitment to drive Nunn through the August 29 runoff—just three weeks," Brannen told me later. "I never realized it would turn into eight years."

Brannen always complained that I did not give the candidate enough time to travel from one town to the next, and thus, he and the candidate were frequently tardy for campaign events.

"Joe, you should've been here in the beginning when our candidate made it clear he did not want any idle time in his schedule. Better to be a few minutes late than arrive with time to kill," I advised him. "You don't want to give Sam Nunn time that can't be used productively."

The Flying Nunn

The only person who campaigned across the state in 1972 as hard as Nunn was his wife, Colleen. She was commander of a Winnebago that she christened "The Flying Nunn." Nunn's mother, Elizabeth, and sister, Betty, traveled the state with Colleen to extend the family's reach. Family friend Jim Hathaway volunteered to be their driver. Jane Beckham, a Perry friend, joined them in the summer along with a squad of Perry college girls, home on vacation. The girls bounced off the Winnebago at every stop, their old-fashioned boater-style campaign hats tilted back on their heads. With a fistful of brochures at the ready, their near evangelistic fervor was downright contagious. In every small town, the group took a photo for the weekly newspaper and accepted invitations to be interviewed on the local radio station. "If the newspaper didn't show up," Colleen said, "we used our Polaroid camera, took a picture of our team next to a local landmark, and delivered the photo to the newspaper."[7] Wherever they traveled, they generated an immense amount of free publicity for the candidate.

---

[7] Colleen Nunn, Sam Nunn Oral History, Washington, DC (30 September 1996).

Snake in the Grass

Throughout the campaign, a source of great frustration for the candidate was the difficulty he experienced obtaining free media coverage for substantive speeches he made on major issues. He didn't understand why the media weren't interested in the solutions he offered.

"They need something newsworthy," I always reminded him. "Not that everything you say isn't newsworthy, of course, but you need to be able to say it in less than 60 seconds."

"I can't possibly outline my solutions in 60 seconds," he said. "The world is not that simple."

"Well, get used to not getting much coverage," I counseled. He didn't understand the "sound-bite" mentality of the media. When I explained how it worked, he was offended and thought voters should reject any attempt to condense complex subjects into oversimplified sound-bites. "How can we have a serious discussion in sound-bites," he asked. "The people have a longer attention span than that, surely."

I have not talked with Senator Nunn about the many ways candidates are employing Twitter's 140-character limit to reach a new generation of voters who possess an even shorter attention span. I imagine his reaction would be one of disbelief—and despair.

Nunn was surprised when, two weeks before the general election, he heard his name on the car radio. He'd been dozing in the passenger seat and quickly turned up the volume in time to hear: "Sam Nunn's wife killed a snake on his front porch today. A four-foot copperhead snake was cornered on the porch by their three-year-old son, Brian, and their pet cocker spaniel, Charlie. Mrs. Nunn got down her 20-gauge shotgun and blasted away."

The Atlanta Journal ran the complete story the next day. Colleen told the *Journal* reporter that she kills about two snakes a year on the family farm. Of course, Nunn was asked about the incident at every stop after that. He smiled each time, relishing the opportunity to say, "She's the best shot in the whole family."[8] And while he enjoyed the story, he

---

[8] "Mrs. Nunn Kills Snake at Home," *The Atlanta Journal* (6 October 1972) and "Mrs. Nunn and Shotgun Take Care of Copperhead," *Atlanta Constitution* (6 October 1972).

was dismayed that it got more attention than any of his substantive speeches discussing the major issues facing the nation.

In truth, Nunn got more good press than he was willing to admit. I've often told him that somebody must have been listening to his substantive speeches. After all, he won. Of course, his victory was never a sure thing, and at least one editor went on record as wondering whether any of the candidates in the race would catch on with the voters.

"The Race Nobody Can Possibly Win"

When state newspaper editors gathered for their annual convention on Jekyll Island on June 24, 1972, Reg Murphy, *Atlanta Constitution* editor, concluded, after talking with several colleagues, that "none of the candidates can win the current Senate race."[9] Another editor at the Jekyll Island event told Murphy that the appointed senator, David Gambrell, "hurts himself every day he runs...[and] just isn't believable on the issues he has chosen."[10] Still another speculated that 47-year-old Republican Fletcher Thompson, Fifth District congressman, "will look strong by the November general election...[but] is not well known at the moment."[11] A lone Middle Georgia editor ventured, "Sam Nunn of Perry is looking a mite stronger."[12]

With six weeks remaining until the primary on August 8, not one of the candidates had caught fire. "I don't know a soul...who thinks there is any spark in this group,"[13] wrote Murphy. His conclusion: "[This race] sits there waiting for somebody strong enough to win it."[14]

When Nunn's staff read Murphy's piece, they had a right to feel a little nervous. This campaign was beginning to feel like the fourth quarter of a scoreless football game. In spite of Nunn's clear and early public separation from Jimmy Carter, the statewide ad buy in May, and the en-

---

[9] Reg Murphy, "The Race Nobody Can Possibly Win," *The Atlanta Constitution* (24 June 1972): 4a.

[10] Ibid.

[11] Ibid.

[12] Ibid.

[13] Ibid.

[14] Ibid.

dorsements of former governors Griffin and Maddox in mid-June, the campaign hadn't been able to find a way to score. If Nunn had any doubts about the eventual outcome, he never said a word. But he didn't let up. In those last six weeks before the primary, his single-minded determination served as an inspiration to keep the entire staff moving forward at full tilt.

Although of little consolation, none of the other candidates—including those with campaign experience—were doing any better. Bill Burson, state treasurer, vowed to walk the entire length of Georgia—from Brasstown Bald to Tybee Light—to meet voters where they lived and worked. Burson attempted to copy the success of Lawton Chiles, who won his Senate seat in Florida in 1970 by walking from Key West to Pensacola. Unfortunately, Burson took the pledge literally and spent many valuable campaign days walking alone along highways lined with longleaf pines.

After former governor Ernest Vandiver declared his candidacy, he stepped onto an RV and pledged to pay a personal visit to all of Georgia's 159 counties. His brand of retail politics worked well during the days of the county-unit system but had no chance in 1972, when people in urban areas were learning about Senate candidates from their television sets.

"Is there anyone still watching?"

Ten days before the August 8, 1972, Democratic primary, Nunn participated in a televised debate in the studios of WSB-TV featuring fifteen candidates for the Democratic nomination and three candidates for the Republican nomination. With so many candidates participating in a 60-minute debate, hardly anyone had a chance to do more than introduce themselves and state one or two reasons why they should be the nominee. In the course of the hour, debate moderator Dick Horner asked Hosea Williams, the lone African American on the panel, if he thought a black man ought to be selected to visit the moon. Before he could answer, J. B. Stoner, avowed segregationist, raised his hand to gain the attention of the moderator. "I'll gladly pay for a one-way ticket for Hosea." Stoner waved high the Confederate flag he always displayed in his jacket's breast pocket.

It was that kind of debate.

Near the end of the hour, the moderator asked each candidate to tell the audience the most important question remaining that, in their view, had not been asked. Sam Nunn, shocked by the circus atmosphere of the event, looked into the camera, and with a straight face, said, "The major question remaining: is there anyone still watching this program?" Viewers throughout the state howled, and the remark became the single most remembered comment of the evening.

Chapter 7

All the Difference

In the years following the 1972 Senate campaign, former campaign staffers reached a general consensus about a number of decisions, events, and fateful encounters that ultimately made the difference in the outcome of the election. This chapter can be read as "the campaign in miniature" because it recounts the most significant steps that actually moved the "doesn't have a chance" campaign forward and ultimately made the difference between winning and losing. Some may argue over which action on this list was the most important, but that is a waste of energy; all were critical to Sam Nunn's success.

Support of Home Folks: December 1971

When the home folks got behind Nunn, as they did early, their influence reached into the farthest regions of the state. The loyalty of his Perry neighbors led them to write letters to friends and family across the state urging a close look at their native son. Most followed up several times with personal phone calls. As Nunn campaigned, he was often approached by strangers who began conversations with, "My friend (or relative) called me (or wrote me) about you and I came out to see if you were as great as he (or she) said you were. His (or her) word carries a lot of weight with me." The effort by Houston County friends and family to introduce Sam Nunn through phone calls and correspondence gave him instant credibility in communities where residents had never heard his name.

Separation from Governor Carter: May 10, 1972

In early May 1972, the campaign continued to encounter voters who thought Nunn was running for the US Senate not to win but to become better known across the state, perhaps to run later for lieutenant governor. Some said Governor Carter himself was spreading that word. It was certainly believable. After all, Nunn was very young, and, many reasoned, too close to Carter to mount a serious challenge to Carter's appointee. In spite of the fact that Jimmy Carter had pulled the rug out from under him when Nunn tried to carve out a new Middle Georgia congressional district in the fall of 1971, their relationship remained cordial, if not particularly close.

Nunn strongly resisted any suggestion from advisers that he find a public way to separate himself from Carter, especially if the campaign must launch a personal attack. Some of the staff wondered if he had the courage to "go for the jugular" in order to separate himself from Governor Carter and Carter's appointed senator. That's when Gambrell stepped in to create an unintentional path to a separation from Carter that was unmistakable. During a press conference, a reporter asked Senator Gambrell how much he had contributed to Carter's gubernatorial campaign, and Gambrell responded, "I only gave $100." That was too much for Nunn, who was aware of substantial contributions from Gambrell's wife and his father to the Carter campaign. Nunn recorded a radio ad in which he suggested the wrong questions were being asked of the appointed senator: "The question is not how much Gambrell gave to Carter. The question is: How much of the Gambrell family fortune did his wife and father give in 1966 and 1970? How many bank notes did they sign? Were any paid back? If the aim of this campaign is to restore confidence of the people in their government, he needs to tell the whole story, not just part of it."[1]

Gambrell did not respond, but Governor Carter did. He was not amused. Carter wrote to his friend Sam Nunn: "I've never been so surprised and disappointed in anyone before. I just don't understand you. If you really believe that I sold the US Senate appointment, then you're absolutely mistaken but honest. We are asking the TV and radio stations to monitor this abusive advertisement by you against me."[2] The scab had

---

[1] Transcript, radio commercial (10 May 1972).

[2] Governor Jimmy Carter, handwritten personal letter, 16 May 1972.

been completely pulled off their "cordial" relationship. The slight laceration was now a deep cut—and everybody knew it.

In response to a media question the next day, Nunn said, "I have no quarrel with Governor Carter but if he wants to speak for Senator Gambrell, it makes my questions more pertinent."[3]

This little public spat seems rather quaint in comparison to the hard-knuckle negative ad campaigns that typify modern campaigns, but the exchange between Nunn and Carter was considered pretty brutal in those days.

Carter's objection was mild compared to that of Nunn's mother. Elizabeth Nunn detested anything in politics that smacked of a personal attack, and she implored her son to pull the ad. "I took it off the air, not because Carter didn't like it but because my mother wanted it stopped," Nunn said.

I recall the ad ran only one or two times, but that's all that was needed. The desired effect had been accomplished. No one suggested again that Nunn was running for any office but United States Senate.

But Governor Carter wouldn't let it go.

Carter continued to interject himself into the campaign even though Senator Gambrell took every opportunity to say he did not want Carter involved in his race. Three months later, when the Democratic runoff between Gambrell and Nunn was heating up, Governor Carter came out swinging yet again. He warned that if Nunn "persists" in alleging that Carter "sold" the Senate seat to David Gambrell, Nunn could lose the support of the governor's office in the fall if Nunn should become the nominee.[4] Carter was not very popular in Georgia at that time, so his words carried little threat. Throughout his first year in office, anti-Carter sentiment had grown. Most voters thought he had sold himself as a conservative in the gubernatorial race but was turning out to be "one of those liberals." Regardless, every time Governor Carter put himself in the race, he sent a message that Sam Nunn was definitely not a "Carter Demo-

---

[3] Tom Linthicum, "Carter Hits Nunn on Ad," *The Atlanta Constitution* (20 May 1972).

[4] Bob Fort, "Carter Warns Nunn on Charges," *The Atlanta Constitution* (11 August 1972): 9-A.

crat." That helped Nunn's campaign immensely. One newspaper editor even asked me if we had Carter on the payroll.

Republican Fletcher Thompson, who represented the Fifth District in Congress, unintentionally opened a couple of doors for Nunn as well. It started with an exposé in the Atlanta newspapers alleging Thompson was abusing his congressional franking privilege by sending mail statewide, far beyond the boundaries of his district, and all at taxpayer expense. It became an attack line for Nunn and made it harder for Fletcher to position himself as a fiscal conservative. Separating himself from Jimmy Carter's politics in the summer and painting Thompson as fiscally irresponsible in the fall demonstrated Nunn's independence from national party influence and facilitated his creation of a broad coalition of support at the precise political moment when such a coalition was needed most.

Thompson admitted months later that he had trouble outside of his home base in the suburbs of Atlanta because Georgia voters were not ready to accept a Republican candidate in a statewide race. He described a time when he was campaigning in Waycross with his brother, Spencer. "Spencer handed this lady this one thing [a brochure]. She looked at it and said, 'He's a Republican, isn't he?'

'Yes, ma'am,' Spencer said.

'Well, he's a Yankee, and I'm not going to vote for any Republican.'"[5]

Fletcher always thought he would have done better under the old county-unit system, but the story he told about the Waycross voter indicates that he was probably wrong about that. The time had not yet come for a new Georgia Republican to win statewide.

Early Statewide Ad Buy: May 15, 1972

In mid-May, Sam Nunn made the decision to take nearly all remaining campaign funds and make a statewide advertising buy on television and radio. It was radical and risky and defied all conventional political wisdom. There was no record of anyone having spent campaign funds

[5] Fletcher S. Thompson, 10 July 1996, Sam Nunn oral history collection, 1996–1997, Manuscript, Archives and Rare Book Library, Emory University.

on a statewide buy so early in a campaign. In those days, most campaigns reserved funds for a saturation of the airwaves during the last few weeks of a race. But Nunn felt he had to crack the top tier of candidates early or there would be no reason to spend reserves later. He needed a way to alter campaign dynamics—and soon—so he instructed the ad agency to make the buy.

Fancy production techniques were out; the campaign couldn't afford them. On the day of the "shoot," Tom Little of McDonald & Little advertising agency walked into the studio, picked up a large black curtain, and draped it over a couple of stage pipes left from a recording session the day before. Next, he selected a plain, unfinished stool, about thirty inches tall, on which Nunn would sit to deliver his message. Nunn had rewritten the script for the ads by the time he arrived, and it took a few minutes to load his edited words into a teleprompter. The words he uttered came straight from a set of deeply held convictions.

As the videotape rolled, Nunn talked directly into the camera about his "common-sense, conservative solutions" to the problems facing America. The camera slowly zoomed in from about waist high to a tight head and shoulders. Tom Little shot six or seven commercials that day, and all had an immediate impact on Nunn's race. This dramatic roll-of-the-dice recording session took less than two hours. I credit the words to Sam Nunn and the advertising genius of Tom Little for creating the remarkable impact of those ads. Voters on the other end of that electronic connection certainly understood each message, and thousands decided to give this guy a good hard look. He spoke their language, he made sense, and, importantly, Nunn connected with each viewer.

As I watched the finished ads play, I thought of a letter we discussed in graduate school that Marshall McLuhan had written to Canada's prime minister Elliott Trudeau in 1968. McLuhan had watched the television image of Trudeau speaking to students gathered in a large auditorium, and he wrote to advise Trudeau to avoid such venues in the future. "Television demands close, casual, intimate discussions," McLuhan wrote. "Also, no notes, no script, no debating."[6] I've watched thou-

[6] Letter, Marshall McLuhan to Pierre Elliott Trudeau (13 November 1968).

sands of political ads since 1972, but have never seen any that connected with the viewer in such a personal and intimate way as the ones Nunn recorded that morning in May 1972. The ads came across, as "close, casual, and intimate" in their connection. McLuhan would have approved. Nunn's instincts in such moments were a result of the retail politics he experienced daily. In a very real sense, he was conducting his own polls when he shook hands with voters and looked them in the eye. That daily experience qualified him to write effective 30-second messages that listeners and viewers accepted. He was his own focus group. I don't know of a candidate anywhere today who is qualified by personal voter connectedness to write his or her own ads.

Frequently, Nunn would return at the end of a day of campaigning and tell us that he wanted to record a radio ad about economic development (or some other local issue) for the town he'd just visited. My job was to call our best local contact and ask, "If we record an ad on (x subject), will you raise the money locally and put it on the air for us?" If our local contact agreed to those conditions, Nunn would record his message that night and the staff would put it on the first bus out of Atlanta the next day.

Maddox and Sanders Choose Not to Run: June 14, 1972

Carl Sanders and Lester Maddox enjoyed strong support across the state in 1972, although their political leanings were the opposite on just about everything. Sam Nunn didn't expect to win 50 percent or more of the vote in the primary; he expected a runoff all along. He also knew that if candidates with more than nominal strength diluted the pool of contenders, the task of making a runoff would be difficult— perhaps impossible. We'll never know what effect the presence of Maddox and/or Sanders would have made on the outcome. Both decided to forego the Senate race. Sanders was the last to bow out of the race, and he did so on the morning of the last qualifying day.

Endorsement of Griffin, Kind Words from Maddox: June 21, 1972

On June 21, one week after the filing deadline, former governor Marvin Griffin held a press conference in the capitol and endorsed Sam

Nunn. His words were delivered in classic Griffin style. "I waited 'til all the can-di-dates had jumped in the wagon, and the tailgate was shet good 'n tight. Then, I peeked thru' the cracks, an' peeked out the man I thought would make the best sen-a-TOR. Well, sir, Sam Nunn stood out by himself."

As I listened, it was easy to imagine Griffin traveling the state in the 1940s and 1950s, entertaining crowds as he campaigned for state representative, lieutenant governor, and, later, governor. He enjoyed being Marvin Griffin. His personality was such that I'm confident he woke up smiling every day. Griffin retired from politics after his loss to Atlanta attorney Carl Sanders in the 1962 gubernatorial race and became full-time editor of the *The Post-Searchlight*, a weekly newspaper owned by his family in Bainbridge since 1907.

Very early in the Nunn campaign, Griffin invited him to visit Bainbridge, located in the deep southwest corner of the state—about forty miles from the Florida line and fifty miles from Alabama. He offered to escort Nunn around town and introduce him to his friends. Nunn and I arrived in Bainbridge on a beautiful April morning about a month after his official announcement. As we entered his office, Griffin stood up and gave us one of his trademark smiles, ever expanding, it seemed to me, as it stretched from ear to ear. "I don't know much 'bout-cha, Sam," Griffin said, "but I knew ya daddy, and that's enough for me. Les' go."

As we walked around town shaking hands, Nunn would say to those he met, "Great to meet you; I hope you'll help me out."

On the third "I hope you'll help me out," Griffin tapped him on the shoulder. "Sam, ef-thyse[7] you, I'd stop sayin' 'hep me out.' I knew an ol' boy who kep sayin' that, and they hepped him out aw-right, they hepped him right outta office."

Griffin's endorsement at the June press conference was welcome but not likely to be a game changer, so we looked for a way to enhance the impact of his endorsement. The most logical was to have Lester Maddox join Marvin Griffin at his press conference. After all, they were longstanding friends. By inviting Lieutenant Governor Maddox to drop

[7] A horrible mash-up that occurs in the Southern idiom when several words are spoken as one. In this example, "If I were you."

by the press conference, we hoped he would find some way to interject a few kind words about Nunn's candidacy. But Maddox demurred. Indeed, he gave no assurance that he would show up at all. As the press conference neared its conclusion, I looked around the room. Every member of the Nunn team wore an expression of abject disappointment. Maddox was a no-show.

Unnoticed, Maddox had slipped into the room and was standing behind the cameras in the back of the room. An instant later, he stepped into the light, grabbed Griffin's hand in the presence of the media, and shook it vigorously. Print cameras flashed and television cameras rolled. "You made a wise choice, governor." Maddox shook Griffin's hand as long as he heard shutters continuing to click. Then he turned to Nunn and shook his hand just as vigorously. "There's nothing wrong with you, and there's a lot wrong with those other fellows." Those words led media coverage that night on television and appeared in nearly every daily newspaper in the state the next day. Suddenly, the conservative Maddox base had received its marching orders. As a result, Nunn's gasping campaign began to pick up discernable momentum.

And Nunn never said "Help me out" during the rest of the campaign.

The Atlanta Constitution *Endorsement Hours before Primary: August 7, 1972*

One day before the August 8 primary, *The Atlanta Constitution* endorsed Nunn as the best candidate in the field: "By background and experience, he is qualified to serve in the United States Senate. As for endurance, he has run this race with courage and precision. We commend him to those who have found this campaign uninspiring."[8] For the next twenty-four hours, I made sure the message got on every radio station in the state, and though it was too late for the dailies to make a difference in the Tuesday primary, I wanted to make sure all editors of major newspapers around the state had taken note. *The Atlanta Constitution*'s endorsement helped undercut Gambrell's support in the densely populated Atlanta area, and that was important, particularly since Nunn carried

[8] "U.S. Senate," Editorial, *The Atlanta Constitution* (7 August 1972): 4a.

only thirteen of 159 counties when the August 8 vote was counted. Most of the thirteen were in Middle Georgia, where, in spite of the *Macon Telegraph*'s endorsement of Gambrell, Nunn enjoyed a solid majority. Hall County was the only county outside of Middle Georgia that he carried in the primary, and there were two reasons for this: Dr. Henry Jennings and his brother, Dr. Robert Jennings, a dentist. Both were cousins from the Cannon side of the family. These two highly respected members of the Hall County medical profession made sure the most populous county in northeast Georgia would be counted in the Nunn column. Without Hall County, Sam Nunn could not have made the runoff with David Gambrell. It pays to have willing and influential cousins in every political campaign.

"Sam Nunn is tough, Sam Nunn is young...": August 10, 1972

At some point in campaign history, jingles were considered an important tool to help a candidate establish name identity in a memorable way. By 1972, however, most campaign veterans thought musical jingles were a waste of money. For a jingle to work, it should be clever, memorable, and reinforce the candidate's key message. If a jingle could do all that, we needed one—desperately—in the waning days of that summer.

One late July night, after a full day of campaigning, Nunn returned to his Atlanta apartment totally frustrated with the current status of his campaign. He'd already asked a small group of key staff members to meet him there. The group included Tom Little of McDonald & Little ad agency and two or three more staffers. To say Nunn was frustrated would be an understatement. "Nobody knows what I'm running for." He was exhausted but directed most of his ire toward Tom Little. "We've got to get something out so people know my name." He collapsed on the nearest bed. "They don't know my name, and they don't know what I'm running for." Frustration, born of six months of intensive, morning-to-night grind on the campaign trail, was erupting just days before the primary. Would Nunn be the choice to face David Gambrell in a runoff or would he be returning to Perry to practice law? The answer was far from certain—and we knew it.

That night, in his Landmark apartment, no one had an answer for him. And still didn't have an answer when voters cast their ballots on August 8, 1972.

Fortunately, a number of factors worked together in those closing days to put Nunn in second place and ahead of Vandiver when the primary votes were counted. He would meet Gambrell on August 29 to decide the Democratic nominee for the US Senate. But we had two problems: we were running out of money, and Nunn was still unhappy that he wasn't well enough known around the state. Just twenty days remained before the runoff to raise his name recognition and connect it to the office he sought.

About mid-morning of the day after the primary, Tom Little stepped into Bill Thompson's office and asked to be paid for the work his agency had done to get Nunn into the runoff. I had been in conversation with Thompson about the debates now scheduled when Little interrupted.

Thompson exploded. "Paid? You wanna be paid?" Thompson stood up and leaned over his desk. "Paid?" His elbow hit the bottle of Milk of Magnesia he kept on his desk to calm his stomach ulcer and nearly knocked it over. He saved it just in time. "Let me tell you something," Thompson said, with a rigid finger in Little's face. "We've been at this for months now, and there are still people in this state who've never heard Sam Nunn's name. It's a miracle we're still in it." He took a long, slow swallow from the blue bottle before putting it down gingerly. Most people would make a face or give some sort of reaction to drinking such a large dose of antacid, but Bill consumed so much regularly that his system probably thought it was Coca-Cola.

"But we *need* to be paid." Little was not going to back down. He was more than a little agitated and didn't want to engage in any further discussion unless he had a check in hand. "We're not doing any more work until we get paid."

"Listen," Thompson said. His stomach acid must have been running at full throttle. "If you don't deliver a jingle to me by tomorrow morning, you're fired. And I don't care what it says, but it better say Sam Nunn's name over and over." For emphasis, he added, "Sam Nunn! Sam Nunn!

Sam Nunn!" Everyone in the campaign headquarters could hear the conversation now.

Little didn't say anything more. He simply turned and walked out. Neither of us had any idea if we would ever see him again.

I knew Thompson wanted a jingle and guessed this might be the occasion he would demand it. Thompson already knew my view but asked me again if I thought a jingle was a waste of money.

"Probably," I said. "I doubt a jingle can be created on such short notice that would make a difference in the outcome of this election."

"We have to do something," Thompson said, and took another swig from the blue bottle. "This thing is far from over."

The next morning, Little stormed into Thompson's office and threw a three-inch reel of magnetic tape on his desk. "There's your jingle, you SOB." He turned straight for the door. "Now pay me." He slammed the door and headed for the elevator.

"I think he just resigned," I said.

"Good," was Thompson's only comment.

But Thompson loved the jingle when he listened to it later that day, and so did Nunn the first time he had a moment to hear it. The jingle started running on radio stations around the state immediately and continued through Election Day.

Several weeks after Little's abrupt departure from the campaign, I got the rest of the story on the jingle's creation from Little himself while attending a party at his home. (My relationship with Little was never as strained as Thompson's.) I asked him how the jingle was created so quickly when he had opposed it so adamantly.

"That night, after Thompson's ultimatum," Little said, "we were in a recording session with a group of singers, finishing a jingle for another client—a bank, as I recall, and a paying client, by the way. We were wrapping up when I remembered I was supposed to produce a jingle for the Nunn campaign. Your guys hadn't paid me so I really didn't care whether we did it or not."

"I asked the singers to wait." He began to chuckle as he recalled the night in more detail. "I had nothing in mind. Nothing. First, I rummaged through our library of production music searching for something that had not been assigned to another client. I found one unused track, threw it on the tape deck and listened. It played one time, and I scribbled the words of the campaign slogan on the empty page. I wrote one verse and repeated it over and over." He began to shake his head. "The jingle was awful, but if Thompson wanted a jingle, he was going to get one."

"But it wasn't awful," I said. "It was great."

"No, the jingle *was* awful. I was sure we would be fired, and, by the way, that was fine with me."

What made the jingle a success? The music had a pounding energetic beat. The lyrics? I offer the lyrics here for the reader to evaluate: "Sam Nunn. Sam Nunn. Sam Nunn is tough, Sam Nunn is young. Put Sam Nunn in Washington, Sam Nunn in Washington! Sam Nunn!" That one line mentions the name of the candidate *seven* times. And that single line repeated for 30 seconds. That's what Thompson wanted and that's exactly what he got.

The jingle might have been corny and unsophisticated by ad-agency standards, but it worked. Soon, disk jockeys across the state were taking requests to "play the Sam Nunn jingle."

A few days later, Thompson replaced Little's firm with Dot Wood of Wood/Bowes Advertising. Dot had already begun to tape ads for us before the official switch to her firm. She was not only less expensive than McDonald & Little, but was willing to devote something Nunn sorely needed: 100 percent of her time and energy through Election Day.

Television Debates between Primary and Runoff: August 14–28, 1972

David Gambrell garnered the most votes in the primary, 31.4 percent. Sam Nunn was second with 23.17 percent, and former governor Ernest Vandiver was third with 20.5 percent. The twelve remaining candidates were in single digits.

When the primary vote was counted, Bill Pope announced, "It's over."

"What do you mean—'over'?" I asked. "How can you make such a final declaration when we still face a runoff?"

"Gambrell got 31 percent of the vote; that's all he's got. He needed to be in the 40-percent range to have a chance. In the runoff, he'll get a few more, but Sam is going to have more than 50 percent, considerably more, because he's going to pick up most of what went to the other candidates in the primary."

Pope may be right, I thought, *but this race seems far from over to me.*

While primary night results were still being announced on Atlanta television stations, a reporter asked Nunn, in the middle of a live interview, if he would be willing to participate in a debate with Senator Gambrell before the runoff. Nunn had come in a strong second in the voting and sensed momentum beginning to build in his campaign, but campaign funds remained as scarce as they had been from the beginning. He needed the exposure that free media would grant him, so he jumped at the chance to use the interviewer's question to challenge Gambrell to a series of debates. He would even be glad, he said, to participate in as many debates as could be arranged between that night and the day of the runoff.

"I think it will be interesting to see if a Georgia-educated boy can handle all that Harvard wisdom," Nunn told reporters, as the final returns on primary night confirmed early reports. He anticipated there might be two or possibly three debates. Gambrell quickly agreed to the debates, but by granting Nunn an almost unlimited number of debates, Gambrell was making a gift of free media exposure worth tens of thousands of dollars to a campaign that was out of money and already operating with a significant financial deficit.

It was a short night for those of us who worked in the state headquarters of the Nunn campaign. I'm sure I got no more than three hours of sleep that night. I think I was afraid to go to sleep out of fear I would wake up to find the final count was not quite in, that one county was still out and leaning toward our opponent. But sleep did come, and so did the dawn, and the result was the same: Sam Nunn had come in second and would be facing the appointed US senator David Gambrell on another ballot in three weeks. Every member of the staff was higher than a kite.

At 7:00 A.M., I began fielding calls from producers at television stations around the state, and by 8:00 A.M., I had scheduled debates in each of the major television markets. We didn't have cell phones in those days, so there was no way to consult with the candidate, who was out greeting workers during a 7:00 A.M. shift change at the Ford assembly plant.

When Nunn arrived at the campaign office a few minutes after 8:00 A.M. and heard what I had done, he was not happy.

"You did what?!" He paced back and forth, shaking his head, and must have said "Jeepers!" a dozen times. It was not that he didn't like the schedule so much as he was uncomfortable about a decision to schedule so many so quickly. His basic sense of caution had been violated. He hadn't had time to consider all the possible implications of such a sudden development, but it was too late for that now. In the end, the decision to quickly schedule as many debates as possible made him look decisive and in control of the race. Gambrell, we learned later, was even more upset than Nunn that so many debates had been scheduled.

The question we had to answer quickly was who would be responsible for briefing Nunn before each debate. The question was never satisfactorily answered. In the car, driving from Perry to the first debate in Albany, Nunn was accompanied by five or six people who gave him conflicting and sometimes confusing advice. Little wonder that he didn't have his "A game" in the first debate.

Nunn could have used Norman Underwood at that time, with his skill as a tactician and his command of the issues. Underwood was an Atlanta attorney with the Troutman Sanders law firm, and Nunn knew of him from the 1970 gubernatorial race when Underwood worked as a speechwriter for Carl Sanders. Although they were on opposite sides in that campaign, Nunn became familiar with his work and knew him to be an excellent writer. Sanders lost that race when Jimmy Carter successfully painted him as too liberal for Georgia. In bringing Underwood into the campaign, Nunn hoped to pick his mind for lessons learned in the 1970 race. Unfortunately, Underwood was not available until after the August 29 runoff. Nunn would be on his own in debate preparation.

With the experience of a single debate behind him, Nunn began analyzing Gambrell's strengths and weaknesses, mentally preparing to respond to the issues Gambrell was most likely to raise. Most puzzling to the staff were those weird barbs Gambrell threw in from time to time in the first debate. Gambrell called Nunn "a shined up Charlie McCarthy" in the Albany debate. Was he suggesting that Nunn was someone's puppet? Or that Nunn's views were scripted for him? It made no sense to me, but if that was the best Gambrell could do, Nunn would be just fine.

Nunn did what a team of consultants would do today: conduct a "murder board" with the candidate. The difference? Nunn would sit on both sides of the table. He would ask himself the most anticipated questions and attempt to respond in the clearest, most direct terms with his answers. And he would keep his questions for Gambrell focused on the issues, asking, for example, "Why did you vote against the compromise anti-busing bill in the Senate? Why have you built an attendance record that reflects the highest rate of absenteeism in the Senate?" Nunn planned to take command of the remaining debates. And he did.

In the twenty days between primary and runoff, Nunn participated in a total of eleven debates—seven on TV and four on radio. The free exposure gave voters a chance to see the two men alone, up close, answering questions and asking each other questions. The debates were a valuable opportunity to make a final impression on voters before the runoff. It was not without risk, of course. One major gaffe could have been disastrous. But there wasn't one unintentional slip or forced error. With each debate, the groundswell of support for Sam Nunn grew.

On August 30, 1972, "Nunn had 301,933 votes, or 53.8 percent, to Gambrell's 259,373 votes, or 46.2 percent."[9] Nunn had won 120 of 159 counties. The voters had seen what I saw a year earlier at the Goals for Georgia conference when the two men appeared together for the first time: Nunn can beat this guy—and did.

Senator Talmadge was now free to throw his support openly to Sam Nunn. "Gambrell was a fine man—integrity, good judgement—but he came across just like a statue. If he'd had the personality his wife had, Nunn would never have defeated him."[10] Not many would disagree. Thankfully, Luck Gambrell was not on the ballot.

A Labor Day Call: September 4, 1972

By Labor Day of 1972, most of the staff were exhausted, not to mention the candidate, but he wasn't about to admit it. Qualifying for a

---

[9] Bob Fort, "Nunn Rolls Over Gambrell," *The Atlanta Constitution* (30 August 1972).

[10] Herman E. Talmadge, 17 July 1996, Sam Nunn oral history collection, 1996–1997, Manuscript, Archives and Rare Book Library, Emory University.

runoff had been problematic at best. Coming from behind to win a three-week runoff campaign to become the nominee had been far from certain. We didn't know on Labor Day, but Thompson's staff was preparing to release a poll showing him 8.5 percentage points ahead of Nunn.[11] The poll also showed President Nixon getting more than 70 percent of the vote against Democrat George McGovern. Nixon actually received 75 percent of the Georgia vote, so the poll may have been entirely legitimate. Fall was, indeed, going to be even tougher than the summer.

I was in Athens on Labor Day, enjoying burgers on the grill with my family and thinking about the tough dash our team was about to make to the November finish line. Suddenly, my musing was interrupted by the sound of a ringing phone.

"Hello."

"Roland. This is Sam."

Uh-oh.

"I hate to ask you to do this," he said, "but I need to ask you and Connell to move into the Atlanta campaign office and live there until the campaign is over."

How am I going to explain this to Ginny? How?

"Go ahead." I didn't mean to, but I'm sure I sounded a bit hesitant.

"We have too much left to do, and not enough time to do it."

I understood what he was asking and tried to inject some enthusiasm into my voice. "We'll do it!" I took it upon myself to speak for Stafford. Of course, Stafford was single and had no problem moving. Nunn also called Norman Underwood that day and asked Underwood, who already lived in Atlanta, to be in the office all day, if possible, every day, until the election.

As I put the phone back on its cradle, I remembered Bill Pope's advice for surviving the demands of a marathon and difficult campaign: "There are three things to remember," Bill said. "Eat when you can, sleep when you can, and never pass a restroom without going inside. You never

---

[11] United Press International, "Thompson says he's leading," *The Augusta Chronicle* (21 September 1972): 4b.

know when, or if, any of those opportunities will come again." All three rules were about to be adopted by the members of Nunn's A-team.

We were entering the tough final weeks, and the campaign was almost broke. On some days, the campaign was broke. A paucity of funds would be our albatross all the way to the general election on November 7.

Bill Pope had told us not to worry, that eventual winners were frequently left with significant campaign debt, but the debt would be wiped out by grateful supporters. His words carried little comfort, because none of his predictions about financial support had come true in the past. For the fall campaign, breaking even became our day-to-day objective.

Nunn's mother, Elizabeth, was keenly aware of campaign expenses and kept a sharp eye on every expense. On one occasion, she was campaigning in Gwinnett County, handing out brochures to everyone she met on the street. One man took her brochure and began walking away. At a safe distance, he turned and said, "Lady, I don't like your son, and I'm not about to vote for him."

She called after him, "That is your right, sir, and I admire your independence." She stepped quickly toward him. "You can vote for anybody you like, but give me back that brochure." She snatched the brochure out of his hand. "It costs a penny and a half." Elizabeth Nunn was a real Scrooge when it came to protecting precious campaign resources.

In the early days of September, raising the required funds was not the campaign's only challenge. With victory within our reach, Nunn was asking us to redouble efforts to earn unpaid media exposure, and that meant maximizing the time of all volunteers at all public venues, from county fairs to local shopping malls. We needed to redouble the efforts of surrogate speakers and keep them moving from one civic club to another. If they were doing one speech a day, we needed to schedule them to make two or three speeches. We needed to record sound-bites daily from every Sam Nunn appearance and feed those audio slices to statewide media via telephone hook-up. Our phone bank in the campaign headquarters included two phones dedicated to feeding sound-bites to radio stations. We borrowed secretaries from law firms to help make those "feeds" happen.

Stafford and I moved into the campaign headquarters the day after Labor Day, and, going forward, when we weren't sleeping, we were working in the campaign office. Management of the Travel Lodge, headquarters for the campaign, agreed to rent us two rooms adjoining the campaign office for the duration of the campaign. We slept when exhaustion dictated a break. The two of us went home on weekends just long enough to pick up enough fresh clothes to last the next seven days. For the final nine weeks, Stafford and I worked a minimum of eighteen hours per day. The speed and complexity of campaign activity increased, and so did my daily intake of caffeine. But our presence in the campaign office sent a clear message to supporters and volunteers that Nunn intended to win this race, and thus no effort expended by them personally would be wasted.

Although Norman Underwood was not with us from the beginning, his presence in the campaign headquarters was a boost for the fall campaign and a very real asset to the candidate across a breadth of issues.

"Maybe it was unstated," Underwood told me later, "but my perception of the campaign from afar was that Sam Nunn was working hard not to let Fletcher Thompson get to his right on any issue. All the elements were there in the political environment of 1972 to create a backlash against all Democratic candidates, but Sam Nunn was not going to let Fletcher get to his right or tie McGovern around his neck."

"What about the race question?" I asked Underwood. "That's been a part of every Georgia campaign for as long as I can remember."

"You're right," he said. "I think Sam saw what Jimmy Carter did to Carl Sanders in the 1970 gubernatorial race."

"Are you referring to the photo that Carter's team circulated in South Georgia barbershops, the one showing Sanders standing in a locker room while members of the Hawks basketball team poured champagne over his head?"

"That, and other things." Underwood said. "Carter was always positioning himself to the right of Sanders, and, in the end, voters elected someone who was far more liberal than Sanders. I think Sam was determined not to let that same thing happen to him."

Meeting with the Godfather: September 20, 1972

Most personal endorsements aren't worth the time it takes to arrange them. They usually have very little influence on the outcome of a race. However, if a candidate didn't have any, or didn't have the "right" ones, he might be subject to the question, "What's wrong with you that no one will endorse you?" Not the kind of question you want to have thrown at you near the end of a campaign.

For the record, former governor Carl Sanders endorsed the night of the runoff. Senator David Gambrell conceded the election at 10:45 P.M. on August 29 and simultaneously endorsed Nunn along with Governor Jimmy Carter.

Governor Carter, who had supported Gambrell vigorously, said, "Sam and I will be meeting tomorrow to discuss the potential issues and the part of other Democratic officials in the fall campaign. I should think Sam will want to continue to run an independent campaign, but I will help him if he asks me to."[12]

Speaker of the Georgia House, George L. Smith, endorsed on October 9.

Lester Maddox based his early endorsement on Nunn's support of George Wallace in the presidential race. Relying on Nunn's public position, Maddox gave his support to him and disappointed many Georgia Republicans. Maddox, however, turned a cold shoulder on the Nunn campaign after the runoff when he saw the voting ticket that state senator Leroy Johnson had prepared and distributed the weekend before the August 29 runoff. The ticket indicated that Julian Bond, Coretta Scott King, and Reverend J. E. Lowery of the Southern Christian Leadership Conference were joining Johnson in endorsing Nunn. Julian Bond was not happy with Johnson because he had never given permission for his name to be on the ticket; he wanted to stay neutral in the race. "I was incensed as hell that they used my name without my permission," Bond told a reporter. "They put me in a pretty embarrassing position."[13] The

---

[12] Ibid.; Fort, "Nunn Rolls Over Gambrell."

[13] Jeff Nesmith, "Endorsement Put Bond on the Spot," *The Atlanta Constitution* (1 September 1972): 22A.

ticket, which Johnson distributed to black voters through the mail, became the subject of several critical news stories in Atlanta newspapers following the runoff.

Nunn's opponent was ecstatic. "I'll be damned"[14] was Thompson's reaction when he saw the ticket. That's the way Republicans expressed their excitement in those days.

Bud Barron of Dublin, self-declared chairman of the Democrats for Thompson Committee, collected the news stories and prepared a collage of them for an ad that ran once in rural weeklies and a few dailies under the headline "How Julian Bond and Sam Nunn Teamed Up to Deceive Georgia Voters."[15] Thompson at first denied having anything to do with the ad, but later admitted he had actually suggested language for it. Nunn labeled the ad "scandal-sheet advertising."

Lester Maddox began putting out the word that he was switching from Sam Nunn to Fletcher Thompson. Therefore, a Nunn meeting with Wallace was critically important. At first, the campaign considered inviting Wallace to Georgia to appear with Nunn at a campaign event, but Wallace was too severely injured in the May shooting to consider such a trip. Overtures were then made to permit Nunn to visit Governor Wallace in his Montgomery office. That meeting was finally scheduled for September 20, 1972.

Just about every Democrat in the South was seeking Wallace's blessing that year as McGovern's chances for a November win continued to plummet. Nunn's Muscogee County chairman, John Simpkins, worked out meeting details with Billy Joe Camp, Wallace's press secretary. Accompanying Nunn on the flight from Atlanta's Peachtree DeKalb Airport were Norman Underwood and Bill Gray from the campaign. John Simpkins drove to Montgomery and was waiting at the airport with Billy Joe Camp when Nunn's charter flight arrived.

---

[14] David Nordan, "Fletcher Thompson Denies Using Racist Digs," *The Atlanta Constitution* (10 September 1972): 6A.

[15] Bob Fort, "Thompson Admits He Knew about Controversial Ads," *The Atlanta Constitution* (27 September 1972): 19a.

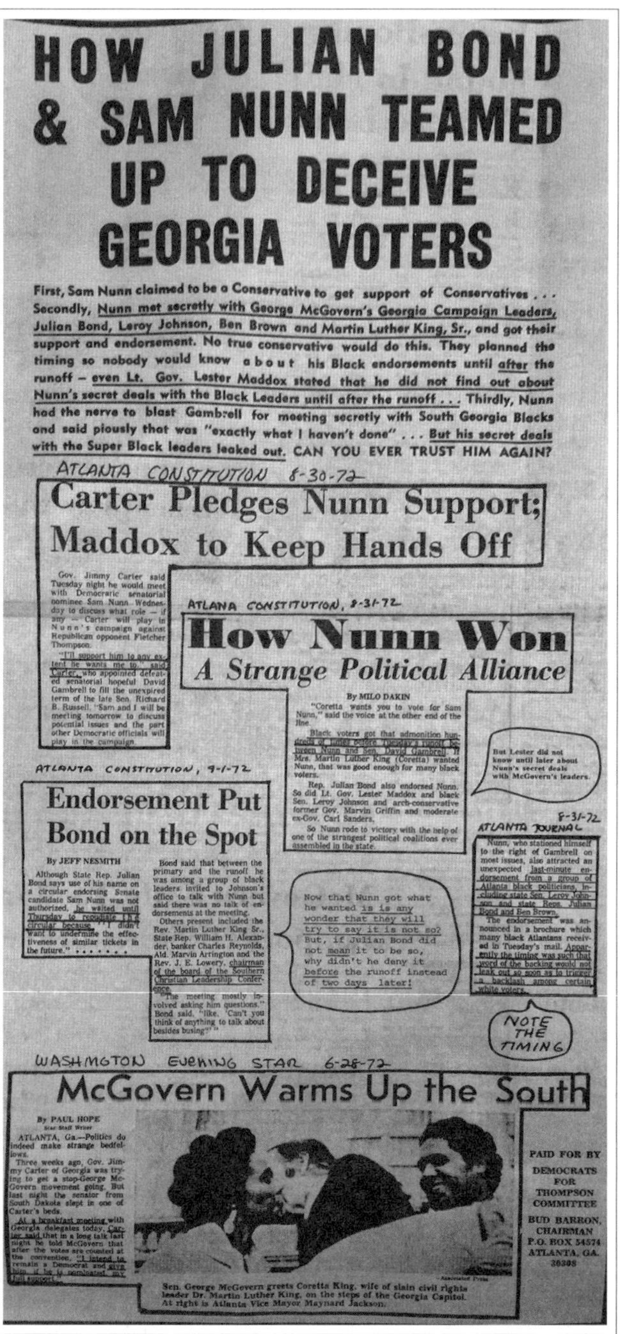

HOW JULIAN BOND & SAM NUNN TEAMED UP TO DECEIVE GEORGIA VOTERS

First, Sam Nunn claimed to be a Conservative to get support of Conservatives . . . Secondly, Nunn met secretly with George McGovern's Georgia Campaign Leaders, Julian Bond, Leroy Johnson, Ben Brown and Martin Luther King, Sr., and got their support and endorsement. No true conservative would do this. They planned the timing so nobody would know about his Black endorsements until after the runoff – even Lt. Gov. Lester Maddox stated that he did not find out about Nunn's secret deals with the Black Leaders until after the runoff . . . Thirdly, Nunn had the nerve to blast Gambrell for meeting secretly with South Georgia Blacks and said piously that was "exactly what I haven't done" . . . But his secret deals with the Super Black leaders leaked out. CAN YOU EVER TRUST HIM AGAIN?

ATLANTA CONSTITUTION 8-30-72

Carter Pledges Nunn Support; Maddox to Keep Hands Off

Gov. Jimmy Carter said Tuesday night he would meet with Democratic senatorial nominee Sam Nunn Wednesday to discuss what role — if any — Carter will play in Nunn's campaign against Republican opponent Fletcher Thompson.

"I'll support him to any extent he wants me to," said Carter, who appointed defeated senatorial hopeful David Gambrell to fill the unexpired term of the late Sen. Richard B. Russell. "Sam and I will be meeting tomorrow to discuss potential issues and the part other Democratic officials will play in the campaign.

ATLANA CONSTITUTION, 8-31-72

How Nunn Won
A Strange Political Alliance

By MILO DAKIN

"Coretta wants you to vote for Sam Nunn," said the voice at the other end of the line.

Black voters got that admonition hundreds of times before Tuesday's runoff between Nunn and Sen. David Gambrell. If Mrs. Martin Luther King (Coretta) wanted Nunn, that was good enough for many black voters.

Rep. Julian Bond also endorsed Nunn. So did Lt. Gov. Lester Maddox and black Sen. Leroy Johnson and arch-conservative former Gov. Marvin Griffin and moderate ex-Gov. Carl Sanders.

So Nunn rode to victory with the help of one of the strangest political coalitions ever assembled in the state.

ATLANTA CONSTITUTION, 9-1-72

Endorsement Put Bond on the Spot

By JEFF NESMITH

Although State Rep. Julian Bond says use of his name on a circular endorsing Senate candidate Sam Nunn was not authorized, he waited until Thursday to repudiate the circular because, "I didn't want to undermine the effectiveness of similar tickets in the future." . . . .

Bond said that between the primary and the runoff he was among a group of black leaders invited to Johnson's office to talk with Nunn but said there was no talk of endorsements at the meeting.

Others present included the Rev. Martin Luther King Sr., State Rep. William H. Alexander, banker Charles Reynolds, Ald. Marvin Arrington and the Rev. J. E. Lowery, chairman of the board of the Southern Christian Leadership Conference.

"The meeting mostly involved asking him questions," Bond said, "like, 'Can't you think of anything to talk about besides busing?'"

ATLANTA JOURNAL 8-31-72

Nunn, who stationed himself to the right of Gambrell on most issues, also attracted an unexpected last-minute endorsement from a group of Atlanta black politicians, including state Sen. Leroy Johnson and state Reps. Julian Bond and Ben Brown.

The endorsement was announced in a brochure which many black Atlantans received in Tuesday's mail. Apparently the timing was such that word of the backing would not leak out so soon as to trigger a backlash among certain white voters.

WASHINGTON EVENING STAR 6-28-72

McGovern Warms Up the South

By PAUL HOPE
Star Staff Writer

ATLANTA, Ga.—Politics do indeed make strange bedfellows.

Three weeks ago, Gov. Jimmy Carter of Georgia was trying to get a stop-George McGovern movement going. But last night the senator from South Dakota slept in one of Carter's beds.

At a breakfast meeting with Georgia delegates today, Carter said that in a long talk last night he told McGovern that after the votes are counted at the convention, "I intend to remain a Democrat and give him, if he is nominated, my full support."

—Associated Press

Sen. George McGovern greets Coretta King, wife of slain civil rights leader Dr. Martin Luther King, on the steps of the Georgia Capitol. At right is Atlanta Vice Mayor Maynard Jackson.

PAID FOR BY DEMOCRATS FOR THOMPSON COMMITTEE
BUD BARRON, CHAIRMAN
P.O. BOX 54574
ATLANTA, GA. 30308

Anti-Nunn ad created by Fletcher Thompson supporter as general election got underway, 1972.

Image courtesy: *The Dublin Courier Herald*

Originally, the meeting was to take place in the governor's office in the capital, but Wallace was not feeling well that day so the meeting was moved to the governor's mansion. In the short ride to the mansion, Camp informed the group that Wallace remained in great physical distress from wounds suffered in the shooting five months earlier. As Underwood related,

> *The Godfather* was the big movie that year, and on the flight to Montgomery—trying to lighten things up—I told Sam he was going over to kiss the ring of the Godfather. But when we got to the mansion, we were taken into this dimly lit room to wait for Wallace. It really did look like a scene from *The Godfather*. Dark, foreboding, no air moving at all. A few minutes passed before an aide pushed Wallace in, slumped in a wheelchair. I knew he was small of stature, but he looked nothing like the formidable political fighter depicted on the nightly news. Wallace's voice was weak and raspy, a sound that made the scene all the more eerie. "Sam Nunn." Wallace's voice was barely audible. "Sam Nunn." He even sounded like Marlon Brando, and he repeated the name as he looked Sam over. "Now here's what we'll say if the press asks." Wallace had clearly thought about it and wanted to be clear. "We'll just say that you came over to pay your respects; that's all." Cornelia, his wife, came in about that time. "This is Sam Nunn." He sort of nodded in Sam's direction. Cornelia shook Sam's hand, and said in a rather perfunctory manner, "How do you do?" Wallace looked at her with an amazed expression. "Cornelia, don't act like you don't know who he is. This is Sam Nunn from Georgia. He just won that primary for the United States Senate over there." And with his thumb, he pointed in the direction of the Georgia line.[16]

Underwood interpreted Wallace's comment as reflecting genuine respect for the young man who had come to see him. Nunn had won the primary, and, in Wallace's eyes, was likely to be the winner in November.

I asked Underwood if Wallace gave any campaign advice to Nunn before he left.

"Yes. Here's what stuck with me. Wallace told him, 'Sam, you go to Washington, and the first thing you know, somebody will whisper in your ear that you could be the next *VEEP*! All those monuments, all that

[16] Norman Underwood, telephone interview with author, 17 June 2015.

power; it can go to your head, but don't go for that.'" Underwood chuckled, as he recalled the scene. "Wallace really emphasized 'VEEP'!"

I'm sure Nunn found the advice interesting, but the danger of being overwhelmed by the Washington experience was far from his mind that day. He was hoping Wallace would say something positive, something that could be interpreted as an endorsement, but he came home able to say nothing more than, "I went to Montgomery to pay my respects to Governor Wallace." It wasn't much to report, but it was more than other candidates who were never granted an appointment with Wallace. Fortunately, there was more to come from Wallace before the November 7 election.

Someone from the Thompson camp told him that the visit did not take place. Thompson took the opportunity at the next joint appearance with Nunn to charge that Sam Nunn had "deliberately planted false reports of a visit with George Wallace."[17] Nunn, in the same appearance, labeled Thompson's source as "a complete liar." Thompson later apologized.

Seven days before the general election, Governor Wallace sent a letter wishing Nunn "every success," and he closed with, "I expect to see you in Washington soon."[18] His letter, published the next day in Georgia newspapers, had arrived at precisely the right moment for maximum effect.

"I admired Wallace," Nunn said, "not for his racial views, but because of his willingness to stand up and shake a fist at Washington occasionally. There's something therapeutic about that in the South."[19]

---

[17] Bob Fort, "Nunn-Wallace Visit Fake, Says Thompson in Debate," *The Atlanta Constitution* (30 September 1972): 2A.

[18] Nunn visited Governor Wallace in his Alabama home, Wednesday, 20 September 1972. News of the visit weakened claims by Nunn's opponent, Rep. Fletcher Thompson, that Nunn was tied to the unpopular Democratic nominee for president, George McGovern. On 1 November 1972, Wallace wrote to Nunn: "I feel confident that your talents as well as the strong stands you have taken for those things in which we all believe will be recognized and rewarded by the voters on November 7th."

[19] Phil Gailey, "Sam Nunn's Rising Star," *The New York Times* (4 January 1987): 29.

That's how I interpreted the slogan "Get Tough in Washington." Others have told me they read it as a coded message pertaining to segregation. I suppose there was a small portion of the electorate who saw it that way, but nothing was farther from the truth. It was truly an expression of the willingness to "stand up and shake a fist at Washington occasionally."

As the campaign progressed, only twice did I have a moment of doubt about achieving success. Both moments involved matters completely out of the control of the campaign. The first instance was when it appeared *The Atlanta Constitution* might endorse former governor Ernest Vandiver a few days before the primary, and the second occurred after the primary, when Vandiver, third-place finisher, refused to endorse either candidate in the runoff. Instead, Vandiver announced he would remain neutral. Vandiver was shocked and deeply hurt by his defeat. For some time, a rumor was passed around political circles that Jimmy Carter had promised to appoint Vandiver to the US Senate if there should be a vacancy. Vandiver felt betrayed when the appointment did not occur. No proof of such a commitment was ever found. Vandiver, nevertheless, claimed a number of people close to Carter reported to him that "he [Carter] was going to appoint me."[20] Carter, for his part, has always asserted there was never such a promise. "I never promised anyone that I would appoint them to any position,"[21] Carter said.

Later, Herman Talmadge characterized the promised appointment as "common gossip."[22]

Nevertheless, Vandiver's defeat in the Democratic primary was a bitter pill for him and effectively ended his political career.

The Atlanta Constitution endorsed Nunn for the primary, and Vandiver, perhaps inadvertently, through one of his supporters, let it be known that he would be voting for Sam Nunn in the runoff. It was not a technical endorsement, but it had the desired effect of reducing Gam-

---

[20] Ernest Vandiver, 29 May 1996, Sam Nunn oral history collection, 1996–1997, Manuscript, Archives and Rare Book Library, Emory University.

[21] Jimmy Carter, 16 July 1997, Sam Nunn oral history collection, 1996–1997, Manuscript, Archives and Rare Book Library, Emory University.

[22] Ibid.; Talmadge, 17 July 1996, Sam Nunn oral history collection.

brell's strength in the Atlanta suburbs. We never learned if Vandiver gave his blessing for his voting preference to be released, but it was welcome news in the Nunn camp.

Another month passed before Vandiver agreed to send a letter to 22,000 of his key supporters, urging them to vote for Sam Nunn in the November election. He called Nunn "qualified and worthy to represent Georgia in Washington"[23] and said he believed Nunn's election "will strengthen the Southern position in the Senate."[24]

Vandiver toured northeast Georgia with Nunn in late October, and Sen. Herman Talmadge traveled two days with Nunn in the last week of the campaign.

Ninth District Congressman Phil Landrum, dean of the Georgia delegation, endorsed Nunn on November 2.

The affirming actions of all these men helped mitigate the impact of the unpopular Democrat, George McGovern, who was at the top of the ballot in 1972.

Another potentially damaging event took place when Nunn's general election opponent, Congressman Fletcher Thompson, invited Sen. Barry Goldwater to campaign on Thompson's behalf. Thompson's campaign unwisely selected Warner Robins (near Nunn's hometown) as the venue for the endorsement, specifically, the Houston County Fair.

A dozen years later, I had a chance to talk with Senator Goldwater about that experience while I was traveling to Taipei with him and six Capitol Hill ham-radio operators. All of us were making a good-will visit that included setting up the first ham station to be licensed to Americans by the Taiwanese government. The agreement permitted us to operate the station for ten days. On the first night of our visit, our delegation gathered in Senator Goldwater's suite in Taipei's Grand Hotel, a suite that turned out to be the entire top floor of the hotel. At one point during the evening, Goldwater asked each of us to tell him how we came to our Capitol Hill jobs. When I told him of my association with Sam Nunn, he laughed aloud.

---

[23] S. Ernest Vandiver, personal letter, Sam Nunn Archives, Emory University (September 1972).

[24] Ibid.

"Did you know I went down to Georgia to campaign for Sam's opponent in 1972?"

"Oh yes," I told him, "we were very much aware of your visit."

"Craziest damn thing I ever did," he said. "They took me right into the heart of Nunn country. Just damn stupid. They [the Nunn campaign] had these young people all along the side of the road on the way to the fairgrounds. When I got up to speak, all I could see was Sam Nunn signs. What was his opponent's name?"

"Fletcher Thompson."

"That's right. Thompson. I remember him."

Goldwater's expression conveyed no sense of having remembered, but it didn't matter.

"I got down there and talked more about Carl Vinson and his nephew than Thompson. Why'd they put me in Warner Robins?"

"I have no idea." *Maybe that was a rhetorical question.*

"The air force base, of course, but hell, we weren't far from Milledgeville where Carl Vinson lived. I wanted to visit him but...." He poured himself another glass of Scotch. "Damn Republicans wouldn't let me, said it would confuse people if I stopped in Milledgeville to pay my respects to the chairman."

"You did manage to endorse Thompson," I said. "The R's should have been glad about that."

"Yes, but I caught hell for saying nice things about Sam and Chairman Vinson. Sam knows that; I've told him. One thing I remember damn well, and I told Sam 'bout this, too. We were pulling out of the fairgrounds when I saw this great big sign, must have been held up by two-dozen screaming kids. '*Welcome, Barry. In Your Heart You Know Nunn's Right.*' Funniest damn thing I ever saw."

In late October, even President Richard Nixon showed up to help Thompson. Just as President Roosevelt was unsuccessful in influencing the Georgia US Senate race of 1938 (in favor of District Attorney Lawrence Camp over Senator Walter George), so, too, was Richard Nixon unsuccessful in persuading voters to elect Fletcher Thompson over Sam Nunn for the seat of Richard Russell. President Nixon had nice things to say about Thompson, but he stopped short of an outright endorsement. That hurt Thompson and astonished the Nunn campaign.

Thompson never succeeded in connecting Sam Nunn to the candidacy of George McGovern. Perhaps if Thompson had been more politically adept, the outcome might have been different.

Of course, Sam Nunn took every opportunity to remind voters, "He [McGovern] has his race to run. I have mine." Such comments helped define Nunn as a candidate who was running as a Democrat but would be an independent voice in the Senate. Someone once asked Nunn if he would be campaigning with George McGovern if he came to Georgia. "Not if I see him first" was his oft-repeated response.

Nunn was taking questions at a Marietta civitan club when a strong Republican in the room stood up to lecture him on problems created by a "liberal takeover of the Democratic Party." The speaker pointed a finger into the air and concluded with, "The South must turn to the Republican Party for leadership."

Nunn replied in a dry monotone, "Let's don't start this year." The crowd roared. Apparently, there were still a few Democrats in Cobb County.

"Every Republican in Georgia owns an umbrella": November 7, 1972

Early on the morning of November 7, 1972, Sam and Colleen Nunn cast their votes at the courthouse in Perry. Their two children, Brian and Michelle, full of energy on that special day, scampered about them. While Nunn voted, Brian peeked around the voting booth curtain, and that set off a rattle of camera shutters capturing his antics. Michelle took her dad's hand as they emerged from the booth, held up two fingers, in the style of Churchill, to signal an anticipated victory. The media loved it.

"Did you vote twice?" Nunn asked Colleen as they walked away.

"I did, but I almost missed it," Colleen said. "Aren't you worried that others might not know they are supposed to vote twice—once for the two-month period remaining on Russell's term, and second for a full six-year term for yourself?"

"Do you think Fletcher might win the short interim election?" Nunn asked.

I'm sure they were both wondering if the campaign had overlooked reminding people to vote twice.

Nunn wasn't smiling anymore. Colleen just kept walking.

"Get Roland on the phone," Nunn said to Joe Brannen, who was waiting to drive the family to Atlanta. Nunn knew I talked with the county coordinators nearly every day and kept a list of names and phone numbers beside my phone and in my briefcase that never left my side. A few minutes later, Nunn was on the phone with me from the county clerk's office.

"You've got to put everybody in the headquarters on the phone right now to every county coordinator in the state," Nunn said. "Remind them to tell everyone to vote twice."

"We'll get on it," I said. "It was pretty obvious on my ballot in Clarke County," I said, trying to diminish his anxiety. "See you in a couple of hours."

As I hung up, I wondered if Thompson would actually want to serve two months if somehow he did win the short eight-week period left in Russell's term. I mentioned this possibility to Bill Pope, who thought it not worthy of a comment. He waved me off. Pope always thought I worried too much. But I told him, "Sam is worried, so all of us are worried. That's what we do."

Connell Stafford overheard the end of our conversation as he stepped into the room. "Let's hope we don't have to contend with *that,* but, just the same, I think we ought to get someone to check the election law."

"It'd be like Thompson to want to serve if he won that eight-week period," I said, "you know, so he could say, 'I was once a United States Senator.'" I turned to Stafford. "Here's a list of our county coordinators."

"Hell, Congress isn't even in session," Stafford said, as he picked up his phone.

"I know, but it'd be embarrassing just the same," I said, pulling up a chair. "Start dialing."

"There is one county we don't need to call," Stafford said.

"Okay, which one?" *Why does this always happen in Georgia?* "Not—"

"Yep, Taliaferro. Sam told me he went there about two weeks ago to talk with his old friend Emerson Chew, who moved there from Perry years ago. Emerson had some good news for Sam."

"I think you better tell me what happened."

"Sam thought Emerson had pulled together a group of local supporters. Instead, the two of them went to the home of the ordinary. It's called the county judge in most counties. He was dressed way down, according to Sam. Might've been in his briefs, that's my guess. They were there about thirty minutes, and the whole time, the ordinary spoke in the past tense. Emerson asked him, 'How's Sam doing over here?' And the answer was, 'Well, he's done well. He's done well.' Then Sam asked, 'Will we carry the county?' And the ordinary said, 'You done great, young man, you done great.' As they got in the car to head back to town, Emerson kept repeating, 'That's it. That's all we need to do.'"

"Old habits are hard to break," I said. "You don't think Sam will get 100 percent of the vote down there, do you?"[25]

Stafford didn't answer. He was already into conversation with the first county coordinator on the list.

In Perry, Sam Nunn and family piled into the campaign car with Joe Brannen at the wheel. Rain fell in sheets and whipped across Interstate 75 as they started for Atlanta. A few minutes into the drive, Nunn turned to Joe and, with a straight face, said, "Every Republican in Georgia owns an umbrella." Joe smiled, but he smiled alone. Not one of his passengers said another word until they reached Atlanta's perimeter highway.

When dawn arrived the next morning, Sam Nunn had defeated his Republican opponent by an 8-point margin. Apparently, Democrats had found enough umbrellas to make a difference. And Emerson Chew had, indeed, delivered 100 percent of the vote in his county. That's what he reported to me personally the night before.

However, it wasn't clear that Nunn had won the short-term election for the remaining two months in Senator Russell's term, the period from November 8, 1972, to January 3, 1973. Not clear at all, because some

[25] The official vote tally in Taliaferro County was Nunn, 721 votes; Thompson, 0.

voters had forgotten to vote twice—once for the full six-year term that started January 3, 1973, and a second time for the remaining eight weeks in Russell's term. To be sure that every citizen we spoke with understood the impact of the final tally, the campaign staff quickly abandoned the informal "Sam" when addressing the new senator the next day and formed a fast habit of referring to him as "Senator Nunn."

At first, Thompson thought he had won the short eight-week period and let it be known that he would take the seat if the outcome revealed he had won it. By end of the second day, however, it was clear that Nunn had been elected *twice* on November 7.

The number of notable Democrats from around the nation who called election night to extend personal congratulations surprised everyone. Lyndon Johnson was the first. At that time, he was fully retired, living in Texas, but not in good health. I was impressed that he was paying such close attention to the Georgia race. Some years later, when I told this story to President Johnson's daughter, Lynda Bird Robb, she smiled and nodded. She'd heard a similar story many times from Democrats across the nation. "Daddy kept a keen eye on all the races around the country and always made sure to call the Democrats," she said. "He was sick when he called Sam—I know that—but he was never too sick to take care of business." Two months later, President Johnson died at the LBJ Ranch.

Democrats from Georgia now held both Senate seats, nine of the ten Congressional posts, and the Republicans recorded no increases in membership to the Georgia General Assembly. It appeared the state Democratic Party had been strengthened by the results of November 1972.

Unfortunately, there was no time to take a winner's victory lap around the state.

The most immediate need was to pull together a staff in Washington, and get to work. Already, the new senator was receiving 200 to 300 letters per day in his Washington office. The workload was significant before we had a chance to recoup the physical energy expended during the campaign. Richard Ray, the former mayor of Perry, and Senator Nunn made a trip to Washington almost immediately after the election. Their goal was to ask Senator Gambrell's staff to remain in place until Senator Nunn could assemble his own team. While in Washington, Nunn announced that Richard Ray would be his administrative assistant, a position equivalent to today's chief of staff. I joined as press secretary a few days later. Avon Buice, Nunn's attorney friend from Perry, agreed to serve temporarily as legislative assistant. Buice remained in Washington three or four months before Atlanta attorney Joel Feldman took over legislative duties. We were off and running—literally.

As Nunn added one new face after another to his staff, a reporter from *The Atlanta Constitution* asked Nunn if he, as a 34-year-old senator, wouldn't be better off with more experienced hands on his staff. "There is some merit in staffing up with experienced minds," Nunn said, "but given a choice between young, energetic staff and experienced staff, I'll take the former every day. They will gain experience, but experienced staff will never be young and energetic." It made sense to this 28-year-old.

Before I left Georgia in the fall of 1972, I visited a few friends in my hometown to give them the news that they would not be seeing me as often as they used to. One of those was Henry Taylor, the father of a close friend who owned a dry-goods store in Quitman. Instead of offering his congratulations as many others had done, Henry's only comment was, "Roland, just don't become cynical."

Not a smile on his face. I was surprised. How could I become cynical when I was going to Washington to assist Sam Nunn in serving the best interests of Georgians and, possibly, the nation? Cynical? Not possible. But his words have come back to me many times over the years. I have had more than a few opportunities to stare cynicism in the face. Not pretty. And I have thanked Henry for his good advice silently many times through the years.

A republic is hard to keep. Ben Franklin expressed that sentiment the day our Republic was created. He knew our nation was fragile and that its continued health depended on an informed and involved electorate. Attempts to hold it together and move it forward with some degree of moral authority have always been difficult. The degree of difficulty is often made worse by participants who contribute to the public's distrust by their self-serving actions or statements. I left Georgia naively expecting those who had earned the public trust through fair elections to honor that trust through the honorable exercise of their official duties. Was that too much to expect?

(l-r) US Senator Sam Nunn, Roland McElroy, and Richard Ray.

Photo by Steve Deal for the *Atlanta Journal and Constitution Magazine*, January 21, 1973

Chapter 8

On Capitol Hill

Christine Till, press secretary to Senator David Gambrell, met me at Washington's National Airport and began my orientation to life on the staff of a United States senator. We weren't out of the parking lot before she glanced my way and said, "I want to prepare you for rooms that are much smaller than you might have expected."

Her words startled me but I didn't want to show it. "It'll be fine, I'm sure."

It's a Senate office, I thought, *in the United States. On Capitol Hill.*

She parked her car on Northeast Drive, a slight curl of a driveway almost directly in front of the Capitol itself. Diagonally across the street was the Dirksen Senate Office Building. We nodded to security guards as we entered, and they waved us toward the main elevator. No need to check credentials in those days.

"We're halfway home," Till said. "Suite 3327, at the back of the building—the very last office up there. Senator Gambrell didn't have much seniority, you know. Neither will Senator Nunn."

"Maybe that'll change when 'Number 87' is sworn in on January 3rd."

"Eighty-seven?"

"Yes," I said. "Nunn is first in his class of thirteen new senators, and by virtue of his being elected to fill the unexpired term of Senator Russell, Sam Nunn will rank eighty-seventh in seniority when the swearing-in takes place."

Till didn't smile.

Maybe I should have kept that one to myself.

As we walked into Senator Nunn's new office, Till informed me that suite 3327 consisted of five rooms, the same number of rooms as

Senator Talmadge's suite. I nodded, not really paying attention to what she just said, and began absorbing everything in sight: two rooms to the left of the entrance, two rooms to the right, and a very small reception area in the middle. Two assistants were answering phones constantly.

"But," she said, "Nunn's five rooms are not as big as Talmadge's five." Her voice trailed off and I almost didn't catch her last words. "Press is on the right." She stepped briskly into the last room on the right, which was by far the largest room in the suite. Nine staffers were crammed into the space and sat at desks placed back to back. Not one staff member had a private office, and, worse, everyone seemed to be on the phone. The noise level was perhaps the greatest surprise to me. I've heard the noise a thousand looms make when they're weaving cloth in a textile mill, and this reminded me of that mill.

"How do they think?" I asked Christine Till, half shouting. She didn't answer; she just stared blankly straight ahead. *Maybe she didn't hear me.*

No Chandelier for You

"Where's *my* office?" I asked, louder. I was beginning to worry about the whole thing.

"There," she said, pointing to a small desk in a corner with a view down the passageway that had been our entrance. I sat in her chair and realized that if I turned my head to the right, I could see all the way to the senator's office at the opposite end of the suite. I could also hear much of the noise from the other rooms in the suite.

"You *are* kidding," I said. "You must be."

I had given my blood, sweat, and tears for the last eleven months to a cause that has brought me to a small desk jammed into a corner. I had more room in the tiny campaign boiler room at the Travel Lodge headquarters. How can this possibly work? Everybody is on the phone or yelling at each other.

"No, I'm afraid not," Till said. "No one has time to kid around here. I bet you were expecting a room with a crystal chandelier, weren't you?"

"No, but...." *Actually, that would have been nice.*

"Even the senator doesn't get that without seniority."

"Nunn is first in his class of thirteen," I said. "Doesn't that count for something?"

"Not much, but you'll have a chance to move up when the 93rd Congress is sworn in and the office shuffle takes place," she said.

"Shuffle? What's that?" *I don't like the sound of any of this.*

"When defeated or retiring senators leave," she said, "everyone beneath them gets a chance to move up to larger quarters. You'll always have five rooms; that's determined by the population of your state, but the *size* of those five rooms will be determined by your seniority; at least, it's supposed to be."

"How does any taxpayer get the nerve to complain about Washington when the people elected to represent them—and their staffs—are crammed into quarters that even a sardine wouldn't tolerate? Does OSHA know about this?"

"Congress has exempted itself from OSHA rules," she said. "The member can stuff you and a few sardines in here if he wants to and not have to worry about government regs."

"You're kidding me. This won't do."

"I'm sure the taxpayers would be delighted to pay for larger quarters for Senator Nunn's staff," Till said, in what was probably her most sarcastic voice. "And stop saying, 'You're kidding me.'" She turned and walked away.

I don't think she's happy here.

A day later, I called the sergeant at arms' office to talk with the person responsible for room assignments. The first assistant who answered passed me along to another assistant and then another. Each had the same cheery, "Welcome to Washington. What can I do for you?"

My call must have been transferred many times in order for everyone there to have a good laugh. "We have to have more space," I said to the last assistant, who must have drawn the short straw in the office and was actually talking to me.

There was more laughing in the background before the assistant finally said, "Tell you what, we'll send someone to see you right away." He cautioned, "But don't hold your breath about more space."

In about an hour, the Dirksen building superintendent arrived. As soon as he walked into the office, I shook his hand and repeated, "This won't do." I held up my arms to indicate the entire office. "There's not enough room here for the present staff, much less the number we will need when Senator Nunn moves in."

The superintendent rolled his eyes. "That's what they all say."

"What can we do about it?" I asked. "I'm serious; we WILL need more space."

He looked around the room a moment, as if trying to assess the possibilities. "Oh, you've got Robert Kennedy's old office."

"Really?" *Is he pulling my leg?* "I don't believe it."

"Well, believe it, and he had a lot more staff in here." The superintendent looked around the room as if looking for something that should be there but wasn't. "In fact, in this room alone, he had space for eighteen people."

"Not possible," I said. "Absolutely, not possible." *He IS pulling my leg.*

"Yes, he did." He walked to the back of the room and began looking behind some of the file cabinets pushed against the wall. "Nine worked from 7 A.M. to 3 P.M., and nine more worked from 3 P.M. to 11 P.M." He pulled two of the file cabinets away from the wall. "Ah, here they are." He motioned me over. "Take a look."

I hadn't moved since he told me the office once belonged to Robert Kennedy. "Are you saying his employees shared these desks?"

"Well, not all of them." He pointed to a series of large bolts protruding slightly and evenly spaced across the back wall. "We built a platform back here for three desks. The ceilings are fourteen feet high, as you can see. When we put the platform in, the staff on the upper level had private desks. The downside: everyone up there had to be less than six feet tall."

"Now, I know you're pulling my leg, because there's not enough money in the clerk-hire fund [official funds set aside to hire all staff] to accommodate that many staff members."

"That's right," he said, as he began walking toward the door. "Senator Kennedy paid for the second shift out of his own pocket. Some of the people he hired were being paid more than the Senate cap on salaries allowed, and, of course, that had to come from his pocket, too." He was now standing halfway into the hall, next to the open door, more than ready, it seemed to me, to escape this conversation. "Just let me know what you want to do. We can put that platform back, if you like."

Taxpayers have no idea what they are getting for their money. No idea at all.

New Year's Eve at the Lincoln Memorial

I expected the fall to be busy as we worked through the process of setting up a new office in the Dirksen building—and, indeed, it was non-stop and frenetic. With the holidays fast approaching, most of us were praying for a brief respite from the pace, but it was not to be. Someone forgot to send out the invitations for the January 3rd swearing-in ceremony to Nunn's key supporters. When the mistake was discovered, Senator Nunn calmly asked Joe Brannen and me to take care of it. Once again, the "go-to" guys stepped in. With our wives, Joe and I spent Christmas Day in the office finishing the job of stuffing envelopes and getting them to the regional post office as fast as possible. The post office did its best, but with holidays on both sides of our mailing, there was little chance the invitations would arrive in time for recipients to make plans to attend the swearing-in eight days hence.

Maybe New Year's Eve will be less eventful.

In Georgia, Ginny and I always spent New Year's Eve with friends in Athens enjoying a dinner of traditional Southern food. Now we were in a new home in Virginia with very few friends and no plans for a New Year's celebration. At the last minute, a couple from Senator Gambrell's staff invited the two of us to join a small staff party in the District. We accepted, but as we drove across Memorial Bridge, I had a sudden urge to stop in front of the Lincoln Memorial. "The ways things are going, this may be the last opportunity we have to visit Mr. Lincoln."

There were plenty of parking spaces in the circle surrounding the memorial. "Not many people visit Mr. Lincoln on New Year's Eve," Ginny said, as we began the long walk up the steps. In a few minutes we stood directly in front of President Lincoln's statue.

A feeling of peace came over me as I stood in the quietness of the place, and I hadn't expected that; it surprised me. A moment later, I felt a surge of energy. *This president gave it all to preserve the Union. He left nothing on the field. Those who follow him—all of us—owe a debt that is only partially paid when we do our duty wherever we find it and pass the obligation to the next generation. And no one, from any generation, has the freedom to shirk that obligation.*

Somewhere in the distance fireworks exploded and echoed across the National Mall. And then it was quiet again. As we walked slowly to the car, I said, "I think this already qualifies as the best New Year's Eve we've ever had."

And, no, the invitations Joe and I—and our wives—worked so hard to mail on Christmas Day did not arrive at their intended Georgia mailboxes until well after January 3rd. Every time another call came in to report the sad news that the invitation didn't arrive until mid- to late January, Joe and I had to endure that special kryptonite stare of Senator Nunn because we had been the last to touch them.

January 3, 1973

It was nearly noon. The man who sat on the curb next to me at Dublin High School fifteen months earlier and discussed his political future was now standing at the rear of the Senate chamber, waiting to be escorted down the center aisle to be sworn in as Georgia's newest United States senator. For the swearing in, each new senator had been given only one ticket for the staff gallery. When the ticket arrived, Richard Ray looked at me and without hesitation put the ticket in my hand. "You've been with him longer than anyone on staff," he said. "You deserve to be there."

"Are you sure?" I asked. "Because you were there, too."

"Not on the darkest days," he said, smiling, "and not on the shortest nights. Take it. You earned it."

As I sat in the gallery that day, I felt a genuine sense of pride in what Sam Nunn had accomplished with the assistance of a small staff of inexperienced neophytes. I was especially proud of the voters. In the final analysis, they were responsible for putting Sam Nunn in the Senate. They showed the whole country they could take the time from their lives to carefully discern which of the eighteen candidates was best equipped by intellect, integrity, and understanding of their concerns to represent them successfully in the United States Senate. They made their choice without blindly following the lead of the president or any of the other partisans who campaigned in Georgia on behalf of Representative Thompson.

Senator Nunn, waiting at the back of the chamber, was surrounded by 100 mahogany desks, arranged on four cascading tiers in a semicircle around the well (the spot where senators often stand to cast a vote). Among those waiting to be called was the youngest member ever to be sworn in, Joseph Biden of Delaware.[1] Nunn, at 34, was an old man compared to Biden. Joe Biden was elected at 29 but turned 30 in December, more than enough time to be declared constitutionally eligible to take the oath on January 3, 1973.

Vice President Spiro T. Agnew waited at the dais for the names of the newly elected senators to be called. The group included thirteen freshman senators who would be escorted by their home-state colleague down the aisle to the well of the chamber, where the presiding officer of the Senate would administer the oath of office.[2] Fully one-third of the Senate would be sworn in before the ceremony was completed.

As the Senate clock struck noon, Vice President Agnew picked up the gavel, a solid ivory pestle, and rapped the desk several times.[3] "If the senators to be sworn will now present themselves at the desk in groups of four, and as their names are called in alphabetical order, the Chair will administer the oath of office." The clerk, sitting at Agnew's left on the lower tier, nodded to the presiding officer to indicate he was ready. Agnew gave the gavel a sharp rap. "The clerk will read the names of the first group."

---

[1] Henry Clay of Kentucky was only 29 when he began his service in 1806, but Senate records indicate he was allowed to begin his service before reaching the required age of 30, which he did in the same month as his swearing in.

[2] Senator Nunn's class included: Floyd Haskell (D-CO), Joseph R. Biden Jr. (D-DE), James McClure (R-ID), Dick Clark (D-IA), Walter D. Huddleston (D-KY), J. Bennett Johnston (D-LA), William D. Hathaway (D-ME), Pete V. Domenici (R-NM), Jesse Helms (R-NC), Dewey F. Bartlett (R-OK), James Abourezk (D-SD), and William L. Scott (R-VA).

[3] The ivory pestle was a gift to the United States from India in 1954. It replaced the original ivory gavel first used by Vice President John Adams in 1789.

Back Row, Third Desk from the End

The Senate in the 93rd Congress was controlled by Democrats, who enjoyed a fourteen-seat majority. Standing in his traditional spot at the first desk nearest the dais on the center aisle was Sen. Mike Mansfield (D-MT), whose sixteen years as majority leader was a new record. Across the aisle from him stood Minority Leader Hugh D. Scott (R-PA). Both Senators Mansfield and Scott were respected by the entire Senate as partisans who understood that governing requires bipartisan cooperation. Ideology was one thing; governing was another. They were committed to the latter.

The chamber was surprisingly dark. The only light came from a single chandelier in the center of the room and a series of wall sconces placed at regular intervals along the outside walls.

"Mr. Biden, Mr. Haskell, Mr. McClure, Mr. Nunn," boomed the voice of the legislative clerk. Nunn, accompanied by Georgia's senior senator, Herman E. Talmadge, walked to the dais, where he repeated the oath read by the vice president:

> I do solemnly swear (or affirm) that I will support and defend the Constitution of the United States against all enemies, foreign and domestic; that I will bear true faith and allegiance to the same; that I take this obligation freely, without any mental reservation or purpose of evasion; and that I will well and faithfully discharge the duties of the office on which I am about to enter: So help me God.

"Congratulations." The presiding officer shook each hand. The four men signed the official oath book as other senators rose at their desks to applaud.

In the family gallery, Nunn's mother, Elizabeth, wife, Colleen, and two children, Michelle and Brian, applauded loudest of all. As I watched the family beaming, I thought of the instructions I received from Senator Nunn when we arrived in Washington not two months earlier. "Put all family activities on my monthly calendar first and work everything else around those events." It was a discipline he followed throughout his Senate career. But that didn't mean that business was excluded from those events. Through the years, as the children matured and became more involved in sports, members of Nunn's staff often tagged along to discuss upcoming legislation or hearings.

"Part of the discipline in being a senator," he told a reporter in early 1973, "is to strike a proper balance between your senatorial duties and your family. In the long run, I don't think you can do an adequate job as a United States Senator unless you also do an adequate job of being a father."[4] His words came back to me two years later when tragedy struck the family of Herman Talmadge. Senator Nunn and I had just left his office and were on our way to the Capitol for a media interview. I was about to ask Nunn a question when we noticed someone approaching slowly from the far end of the hall. Only a few lights burned in the hallway and that made it difficult to make out the face. Whomever it was walked very close to the wall as if to avoid making eye contact with passersby. A moment later, we realized it was Nunn's colleague, Herman Talmadge. Senator Talmadge had just returned to work after the funeral for his youngest son, Robert, who, at age 29, drowned while on a Memorial Day outing with friends on Lake Lanier. Nunn greeted the clearly distraught Talmadge with a handshake and placed the other on his shoulder. Talmadge, his shoulders slumped, seemed older to me. Words exchanged were few, but near the end, Talmadge took a deep breath and slowly let it out, shaking his head all the while. "Sam, Bobby was a grown man before I got to know him." With that, a large tear trickled down his cheek. "I *never* got to know him." Talmadge turned and walked away, his footsteps sounding slower than before.

Neither Senator Nunn nor I said a word as we resumed our walk, but a minute later, Nunn said in a quiet voice, "I'll quit and return to Perry to practice law before I let that happen to me." He meant it.

Colleen was an equal partner in keeping the family anchored at home. She was committed to having at least one meal each day when the whole family could be present, and typically it was a 7:30 P.M. dinner. Of course, it didn't work perfectly every night. Nunn missed a few dinners altogether, but he was committed to attending as many of his children's extracurricular activities as possible. Brian Nunn remembered one partic-

---

[4] Maurice Fliess, "A Day in Life of Freshman Sen. Nunn," *The Atlanta Journal and Constitution* (25 March 1973): 1A.

ular night vividly. "My basketball team made it to the state finals in Maryland. Dad had a speech to make that evening, which he cut short and raced out for the game in Cole Field House [University of Maryland campus]. It was already second quarter by the time he got there, but I spotted him in the crowd—in full tuxedo. Even though my friends teased me unmercifully, I was proud to see him."[5]

"Dad spent a lot of time videotaping us at basketball games," daughter Michelle Nunn recalled. "We have video footage that is shaky and crooked—almost makes you seasick to watch it—and that's usually the footage he took. He helped us in so many ways but took care not to project onto us what he thought we should be as much as he let us realize what we wanted to be."[6]

"The majority leader is recognized," said the vice president, and with that pronouncement, the 93rd Congress was underway. The four senators moved to their assigned desks. Senator Nunn's desk was third from the end in the back row. Seating assignments are made strictly on seniority, and even though he was the most senior of the freshmen sworn in that day, Nunn was relegated to the back row with the rest.

His desk seemed only slightly larger than the old-fashioned kind that one might have found in an early nineteenth-century schoolhouse. But this was no ordinary schoolboy's desk; it was one of the forty-eight desks constructed in 1819 to replace those the British had burned in 1814. Senator Nunn raised the hinged mahogany top and scanned the names inside. He knew about the Senate's tradition of asking each senator to write or carve his name in the desk he was using when he retired from the Senate. He had been told that he would not have Richard Russell's desk, the desk of the president pro tempore of the Senate, at least not right away. Allen Ellender of Louisiana claimed it when Russell died in January 1971. And when Ellender died in July 1972, the desk fell to the next president pro tempore, James Eastland of Mississippi. Eastland sat at the Russell desk until his resignation in December 1978. That's when Herman Talmadge asked for it, but Talmadge sat at the Russell

[5] Brian Nunn, videotaped interview with author, 18 July 1996.

[6] Michelle Nunn, videotaped interview with Joe Fab, 18 July 1996.

desk for only two years before his defeat in the fall of 1980. Finally, in January 1981, Sam Nunn was able to claim the desk of the legendary Richard Russell, and it remained with him until the end of his fourth term, January 1997.

Sun? What sun?

A few days after the November 1972 election, Bill Pope, our campaign media spokesman, invited me to join him for an after-work drink at Manuel's Tavern in Decatur. We hadn't been there long when he told me he didn't envy those who signed on to work for Senator Nunn in Washington. "That first year is going to be a bear," he said. "No one will be able to do enough to keep up with Nunn or meet his expectations." He tipped his warm beer to me and gave a little "good luck" smile. "Never enough."

"Maybe so," I said, "but we owe it to him and to the people who gave him the job to make sure he succeeds."

Pope laughed. "Were you a Boy Scout, too? You sound just like him."

"No, but—"

"Let's drink the rest of our beer outside; this may be the last time you see old *sol* for a very long while."

Pope was right about the long days ahead for Nunn's staff. That first year in Washington was rough. I don't remember seeing the sunshine at all that year. Most of us arrived around dawn and left well after dark. The days were extended to some degree because we were handicapped by the lack of modern technology. There were no computers, just typewriters and telephones connected to the wall. Fax machines had not been invented. Correspondence to constituents required typing and filing of multiple copies by hand. We made four carbon copies of every letter: yellow, pink, green, and white, a different color for their internal destination.

Learning the players as well as the protocol for playing politics in Washington offered its own set of challenges. Just ten days into January 1973, as I was working at my desk, I noticed a well-dressed gentleman sitting alone in the reception room. Fifteen minutes later, he was still there. Thirty minutes later, I decided to take a closer look.

Oh no, I think that's Elliot Richardson!

Fortunately, when I set up my office on the second day of January, the first thing I posted on the bulletin board above my desk was a page from the Federal Directory displaying the names and photos of all the members of President Nixon's cabinet *Ah, there he is.* My finger stopped at the image of Elliot L. Richardson, secretary of Health, Education, and Welfare. He had just been tapped by Nixon to be the next secretary of Defense.

Holy smokes, he's here to see Senator Nunn. He doesn't have an aide with him, and nobody from our staff is talking to him.

I jumped to my feet and took off for the reception room. "Mr. Secretary," I said, introducing myself and shaking his hand. "Wait here; I'll be right back." I don't think I even stopped walking toward the senator's office while I was shaking his hand. Martha Tate, Senator Nunn's secretary, was sitting at her desk typing a letter as if nothing else was going on. "Where's Senator Nunn?" I said. "Secretary Richardson is here to see him. How did we miss this appointment? Never mind; we need Senator Nunn—now!"

Martha, who had worked in Senator Russell's office, understood the urgency. "I'll find him," she said. "The Secretary must be here for a courtesy call."

Every Cabinet-level appointment must be approved by the Senate, and it is standard protocol for nominees to visit each member of the Senate committee that will consider his nomination and vote on whether or not to make a recommendation to the full Senate. Richardson was expecting a face-to-face meeting with Senator Nunn.

Several minutes passed before Martha tracked down Senator Nunn in the Capitol. He asked her to apologize to Richardson and try to persuade him to wait a few minutes more.

Martha had an animated way of talking under normal circumstances. Often, she spoke so fast her words didn't have time to connect in a coherent manner. On this occasion, her words spilled out much faster than usual, and her hands gestured freely in all directions, as if she were trying to arrange her words in a way that would convince Secretary Richardson to wait a little longer. "Senator Nunn is on his way...two minutes, Mr. Secretary. That's all. I saw you on the news last night. You were great. What channel was it? Senator Nunn...two more minutes...Walter Cronkite, I think."

Five minutes went by and Richardson waited. He shuffled and rearranged the papers he had been reading. He was in no mood for idle conversation. Suddenly, he stood and said, "I think I have waited long enough." If he'd been close to a window, the window would have been covered in frost. A second later, Richardson was out the door and headed for the elevators.

I walked with him to the end of the hall, apologizing profusely for the misunderstanding. I explained that Senator Nunn's Washington scheduler was new and did not understand that a request from a cabinet nominee for a courtesy visit is not a Georgia-style "drop-by." Such appointments are a fixed time for a senator and nominee to meet prior to a hearing on the nomination. Richardson stared straight ahead and didn't seem to hear any of it.

Is it necessary to assume such a patrician air? The scheduler made a mistake, for crying out loud.

At that precise moment, the elevator doors opened and Senator Nunn stepped off. Secretary Richardson never looked up as he stepped into the same elevator, now going down. "I am very sorry to keep you waiting, Mr. Secretary," Senator Nunn said, as he tried to shake Richardson's hand. "My staff is green and misunderstood your request for an appointment."

By that time, the doors were closing. Secretary Richardson had just enough time to give us an icy, "How unfortunate."

The doors closed and he was gone.

Such are the lessons learned daily by a new and inexperienced staff.

Richardson made a return visit a couple of days later. All seemed forgiven and forgotten. After all, he was the one who needed something only Senator Nunn could provide: a vote in favor of his confirmation. In May of 1973, Richardson became President Nixon's new secretary of Defense. As it turned out, Watergate soon gave Secretary Richardson more headaches than any lapse in protocol might.

"If his lips are movin'..."

In the belief that experience is a safe light to travel by, I asked Gordon Roberts, longtime press secretary to Senator Talmadge, if he had any advice to offer this newcomer or any pitfalls to avoid. Roberts agreed to see me right away, and when I arrived, I found a wizened and wiry individual, leaning back in his chair as far as it would go. He looked me over carefully as I approached. I don't know what he was thinking about the very young press secretary before him. Whatever his thoughts, he kept them to himself. He didn't get up to shake hands or offer a chair. He simply lit his pipe, took a couple of puffs, and said, "Shoot."

He's probably tired of sharing his knowledge with the parade of novices who must come through his door.

"Shoot," Roberts repeated, with a tone of impatience. A couple of weak smoke signals rose from the pipe's bowl before it went out completely. He reached for his tobacco pouch, less than an arm's length away, and with a couple of quick scoops, the pipe was reloaded and back in service.

In the course of our conversation, I asked him how I should interpret the overly polite remarks often made in the chamber when senators are addressing each other. "Their language seems to be a bit florid," I said. "Why are they so effusive in their praise of each other?"

Roberts smiled, but I could tell by the crooked way he smiled that I should be on guard. "Well, there is a lot to learn 'bout that, and I'm not sure I can tell it all in one sittin'," he said. He pulled air rather vigorously through the pipe and was silent while the resulting smoke rose to envelope his entire face.

The scene reminded me of Marvin Griffin, about to spin one of his great yarns. Or maybe he's going for Eatonton's Joel Chandler Harris, of Br'er Rabbit fame.

"The one thing to take away from what I'm sayin' is this: senators nearly always mean the opposite of what they say 'bout each other."

"Excuse me?"

"You heard right. If a senator, in the middle of debate, addresses a colleague 'cross the aisle, he might say, 'My distinguished friend from the great state of X is the recognized expert in this area.' That means he thinks his colleague actually knows nothin' 'bout the subject of the debate and wishes he would just sit down. If his colleague says to him, 'Let me make one thing perfectly clear,' that means 'I'm 'bout to obfuscate as much as possible and you'll be lucky to follow anythin' I say.' If another colleague starts his comments with, 'The fact of the matter is,' you can be sure that you will hear no facts at all, 'cause it's a setup line that all politicians use when they're desperate to find somethin' persuasive to say. That new fellow from Wyoming says it all the time. What's his name—Cheney, I think. He picked it up from Nixon when he worked at the White House. Nixon says it a lot."

He stopped for a moment. I couldn't tell if he was looking for a reaction from me or just catching his breath. Irony is better than sarcasm, I thought, so, I decided to play along. "Surely, there are times when comments about each other are genuine and sincere."

Gordon stood up, tucked in his shirttail, and pulled his trousers up. With his wiry physique, I could tell he had trouble keeping his trousers near his waist.

"Genuine and sincere? Hmmm. You want one that is genuine and sincere? Well, Russell Long [Democratic senator from Louisiana] told one the other day about a colleague he felt was genuine and sincere."

"Good," I said, leaning forward. "Let's hear it."

"He was talkin' about a senator from—I can't recall. Long asked the question: 'How do you know whether senator so-'n-so is tellin' the truth or not? Easy, if his lips are movin', he's lyin.'"

"So, his colleague was known for always telling the truth? The opposite, right?"

Roberts howled, then with a straight face, said, "No, no. That one is utterly and completely true—genuine, sincere—and true. You asked for it; there it is."

For the rest of my time in Washington, whenever I heard a senator address another in the Senate chamber as "my distinguished colleague" or "recognized expert in this area" or begin an explanation with "let me make one thing perfectly clear," I thought of Roberts and smiled. Maybe that's what he hoped for—a smile and a sense of humor for all the craziness I would encounter over the years.

Roberts wasn't the only press secretary to give me advice that could not be followed. Jim Brady, press secretary to Sen. Bill Roth (R-DE) before he joined President Reagan, taught me a "guaranteed way" to get media coverage on substantive issues. Brady asked me to join him one day at a press conference where his boss, Senator Roth, would outline the ways he would propose cutting the federal budget. Intrigued, I tagged along to see how Brady could possibly guarantee media coverage on such a dull subject. As the news conference began, Senator Roth put on a green eyeshade, picked up a giant pair of scissors, put a copy of the federal budget between its two large blades, and pretended to cut a massive book that represented the federal budget. Network film cameras rolled and shutters of print-media cameras chattered. The event made all three networks that night. I understood, but I could not imagine any way to persuade Sam Nunn to put on a green eyeshade and pretend to cut the budget with giant scissors. Nunn would have none of it, before or after becoming senator. His aversion to public-relations gimmicks, as he called such antics, meant statewide exposure for any otherwise newsworthy event or speech would always be hard to come by.

A Disciplined Constant

While the staff struggled in many ways that first year, Sam Nunn was a quick study of his environment—Senate rules, procedures and schedule, committee and subcommittee areas of jurisdiction, staff organization, and management of constituent service functions. He couldn't read enough or learn enough to satisfy his voracious appetite for knowledge. Along the way, he earned a reputation as one who always wanted to become better informed than most of his colleagues on issues to come before the Senate. When debates started, that intellectual strength earned him enormous respect from both sides of the aisle.

A member of the Capitol police force took notice of Senator Nunn's seemingly unlimited energy one day and stopped me on the steps of the Capitol. "Has Senator Nunn always been as intense as he seems to be every day?"

"Oh, yes," I said. "Oh.... YES."

He shook his head, "Well, he'll get over it; they all do."

"No," I said, "he won't. He is what he is—a disciplined constant—loaded with energy and plenty of stamina. He is not about to change."

The policeman just smiled. He'd heard it all before. But he hadn't met this Georgian.

Sam Nunn was a disciplined student of his early mentors: John Stennis (D-MS), Mike Mansfield (D-MT), Russell Long (D-LA), and Henry "Scoop" Jackson (D-WA). Nunn and Jackson became so close that Nunn withheld his endorsement of fellow Georgian Jimmy Carter until Jackson dropped out of the presidential race in 1976.

In time, those first mentors were replaced by colleagues closer to his own age, many of whom became close friends: Lawton Chiles (D-FL), Bennett Johnston (D-LA), Pete Domenici (R-NM), Dewey Bartlett (R-OK), David Boren (R-OK), Bill Cohen (R-ME), John Warner (R-VA), and Dick Lugar (R-IN).

In time, Nunn rose in seniority on the Armed Services Committee to become the ranking member and, ultimately, chairman. He went from a student of nuclear-arms negotiations to the senator sought out by presidents for advice and counsel on all issues surrounding nuclear proliferation. His broad command of issues was reflected in all his committee assignments: Government Affairs, Permanent Subcommittee on Investigations, Intelligence, Small Business, and Armed Services.

Some Republicans in Georgia have dismissed such laudatory assessments as nothing more than Nunn loyalists attempting to "deify Sam Nunn."[7] To that I have always said, "He is mortal, I can assure you, but few who serve in the Congress today are his equal in ethical behavior, dedication to the public good, and in the enormous intellectual capital he brings to the table on every issue."

Give It to an Intern

Our first summer in Washington, Nunn's office hosted a large group of political interns—sons and daughters of key supporters who wanted their offspring to have a Washington experience to add to their resumes. There was nothing wrong with that, but it didn't meet Senator

[7] R. Robin McDonald, "Explain It Sam," *Atlanta Magazine* (July, 1992): 42.

Nunn's standards for excellence in all phases of his office operation. "We should create an intern program that offers a benefit to both parties—interns and staff," Nunn said.

In a short time, we arranged for the Institute of Government at the University of Georgia to sort through all intern applications and select three to send to Washington each quarter of the academic year. Participants from all schools in the university system were free to apply. All participating institutions agreed to grant one academic credit to each intern for their time in Washington. The result was a continuous flow of talented and gifted interns through our office every three months. Other Senate offices were soon establishing similar programs in conjunction with colleges and universities in their states. Among the intern "graduates" of our press operation were Jim Galloway, political editor of the *Atlanta Journal and Constitution*, and Deborah Blum, who won a Pulitzer Prize for a newspaper series exploring ethical issues in primate research. Intern Gordon Giffin came to Nunn's office while a senior at Emory Law School. He was hired as Nunn's legislative director and years later served as US Ambassador to Canada during the Clinton Administration. Intern Dubose Porter of Dublin was elected to the General Assembly and for a time was minority leader in the Georgia House. Today he serves as chairman of the Democratic Party of Georgia. Another intern, David Ralston, also followed a political path and became Speaker of the Georgia House of Representatives. Arnold Punaro of Macon came as an intern and never left. For a while, Punaro handled military affairs on Senator Nunn's personal staff. Later, he was named staff director for the minority on the Senate Armed Services Committee. When Democrats regained majority status in the Senate in 1987, Punaro became staff director for the entire committee. Today, Punaro, a retired Marine Corps major general, is sought out for his expertise on military-reform issues.

I have taken the time to include these outstanding interns in the story because they typify the extraordinary men and women who passed through Nunn's intern program and used their Washington experience to make a significant contribution to the civic affairs of our nation.

Roe v. Wade: First Out of the Gate

In the first month of Senator Nunn's first term, I got more than a taste for the challenges a Senate press secretary faces every day.

On January 22, 1973, the Supreme Court issued its landmark *Roe v. Wade* decision, and ten minutes later, Atlanta media wanted to know Senator Nunn's reaction. As his newly minted press secretary, I grabbed the Associated Press wire story and walked briskly across the street toward the Senate. Walking to the Senate chamber with a breaking news story was the fastest way to get reaction to satisfy media requests in those days. As I crossed Constitution Avenue, I tried to think of how many times Nunn was asked about his position on abortion during the campaign. Answer: not many. Abortion was not a hot-button issue. Georgians were more concerned about school busing, inflation, Vietnam, drug addicts, and welfare cheats. Nunn was opposed to abortion except in the case of rape, incest, or the health of the mother, but I had also heard him say it ought to be a decision between the woman and her doctor.

In the Senate reception room, I showed him the story and asked if he had a reaction for the media. He looked at me as if I were from another planet. "But I haven't read the decision; how can I give a reaction?"

I was astounded. "It cuts away most state restrictions on abortion and gives a woman the right to make her own decision on the question. You've answered this question before; it should be easy. You can say you still have questions about the constitutionality of—"

"Do you have a copy of the Court's decision?"

"No, but the AP story has a detailed summary—right here—near the bottom." I pointed to the last paragraph.

"Has Joel read it?" Nunn asked without taking the document. Joel Feldman was Nunn's legislative director, and, more important, a lawyer. He needed a legal eye on the decision before he would comment. No layman should attempt to offer a legal opinion on such matters. In fact, even some lawyers are suspect.

"Yes, he's read it," I assured him, "and he agrees you don't need to read the decision itself. He says the debate will continue and—"

"I will not be stampeded into making a statement without the benefit of reading the decision myself. The press can wait." He turned and started to walk toward the chamber.

"But you'll miss their deadline, and your reaction won't be in the news story about the decision." Even as I uttered those words, I knew I wasn't helping my case. He hated being rushed into anything. Anytime. Anywhere.

"There'll be no knee-jerk reaction to the news from me—ever." And he disappeared through the door leading to the chamber.

I walked slowly back to the office and informed the reporter that Senator Nunn's reaction would come later, *after* he had read the decision. "But he'll miss my deadline." The reporter was incredulous. "It doesn't work that way; don't you know that?"

"You'll have it tomorrow," I said.

"Nobody will be interested tomorrow," the reporter said, clearly exasperated.

"I know that. Get used to it," I said. Again, I walked across Constitution Avenue toward the Supreme Court, less than a block away. By the time I got back to the office, the sun was going down. I put the decision on Nunn's desk, and he read it that night.

Thus was born his reputation as "Cautious Sam." But his reticence was more than simple caution. He was always uncomfortable when he knew his words might become a sound-bite. Nunn preferred to demonstrate to the listener his understanding of all sides of an issue before speaking. That takes time. I understood his reasons for a cautious review of an issue before speaking, but his approach was at odds with the speed demanded for effective news dissemination in 1973.

By the time I got home that cold January night, my sons, ages 2 and 1, had already enjoyed my birthday cake. German chocolate cake was all over their faces. I didn't know it at the time, but I was home much earlier than I was going to be on other birthdays. Eventually, I taught the boys to save a piece of cake for dad.

Every member of Nunn's Senate staff learned to accept his considered deliberation when preparing to respond to media inquiries. We tried to anticipate news stories that required a response, hoping to prepare in advance the necessary background documents to put in front of him when a story broke. Reporters, however, never understood. In responding to one reporter who insisted he was too cautious, Nunn said, "I plead guilty to charges that I take a long time to make decisions on crucial matters. I try to balance the matter. I try to look at both sides of it. And I don't decide those matters until I'm confident of them or until I have to. There are a lot of things you have to fire from the hip on, but I'm never comfortable shooting from the hip." He paused to check the reporter's reaction, then added, "It must be very comfortable for those people in Washington who are so philosophically bent in one direction or the other that they have an automatic position and answer on everything. They don't have to look at the facts. They basically have a position and hunt for the facts to justify that position. I plead guilty to being swayed by facts. I start with the facts and then arrive at a position rather than the other way around. It's not the easiest way."[8]

And that's why he refused to give a knee-jerk reaction to the *Roe v. Wade* decision on January 22, 1973.

While the media may have been unhappy with his careful analytical approach to issues, it was precisely that care that engendered respect for his views and support from across the political spectrum. On more than one occasion, I have been with him when we entered a room filled with individuals who did not agree with his position on a specific issue, and watched their mood change as he explained the issue at hand thoroughly. He presented his own views first, as they expected. Then he discussed thoroughly the other point of view—theirs. In the course of examining all sides, they would begin to nod, not always in agreement, but in acknowledgement that this senator had given their issue more thought than anyone in the room. Suddenly, there would be a lot more questions from those who wanted to understand more, and he became the teacher. Often, they shook his hand as they left the meeting, saying, "I don't agree with your position on this matter, but I respect your judgment." Some would say they were persuaded by his logic and appreciated learning what they had not previously considered. Not every politician can do that. Senator Nunn could because he made it his business to know all sides of an issue before he started talking.

---

[8] Scott Shepard, "Nunn not a one-issue senator despite defense work, he says," *The Atlanta Constitution* (9 December 1986): A14.

While chief of staff, I often advised lobbyists who came by to reconsider the reason for their visit if they were only familiar with their side of an issue. Some, unfortunately, ignored my advice. Often, as they walked out after a visit with the senator, a furrowed brow and downcast expression told me which ones went in unprepared to discuss the merits of *both* sides. If you want to get on the same page with Sam Nunn, you had best do your homework.

Agnew Resigns

Senator Nunn's first two years in the Senate were full of unexpected historic events that changed America in significant ways. In addition to the landmark *Roe v. Wade* decision in the first month, January also witnessed the signing of a four-party cease-fire agreement in Paris, which effectively ended the Vietnam War, although, of course, the fighting did not end. Direct American involvement in the fighting continued until August 1973, and the war did not formally end until April 1975 when the North Vietnamese captured Saigon. I sat in my office that day watching a black-and-white television newsreel that showed the dramatic and chaotic withdrawal of American forces. People nodded to one another in the halls that day but hardly anyone spoke.

Before the month of January 1973 was out, Secretary of Defense Melvin Laird ended the military draft when he announced that henceforth the US would rely on voluntary enlistment. Thus was the All-Volunteer Force born. Senator Nunn quickly let it be known that he opposed relying on a volunteer force to defend America, believing instead that every American should be required to serve in some capacity to protect and preserve the freedoms so many before them had sacrificed to secure.

Draft resolutions were also circulated that year among the members of the Senate that contained language to clarify once and for all who in our government had the power to declare and wage war. Most people probably thought the Constitution had settled that question many years ago, but that was before the excesses of President Nixon in prosecuting the Vietnam War came to light.

Under the US Constitution, only Congress has the power to declare war, raise the troops, and provide money to support them. The same document declares the president is the commander in chief of all armed forces. There is some room for ambiguity, I suppose. In January 1973, the actions of President Nixon, including secret bombing missions in Laos, forced the Congress to debate a resolution that would clarify the obligations and responsibilities of all parties concerned. While this summary runs the risk of oversimplifying a complex issue, I mention the War Powers Resolution here as an example of the terribly difficult issues Senator Nunn and his staff faced in the early days following swearing-in. Ultimately, the war-powers question was resolved—at least temporarily—nine months into 1973 when Congress overrode the president's veto with a two-thirds vote in both chambers on the War Powers Resolution.

I was still catching my breath when the Senate set up a Select Committee on Presidential Campaign Activities in February 1973 to investigate the Watergate burglary. I don't recall anyone talking about impeaching Nixon at that point, but the story, of course, was just beginning to unfold.

Nunn's office couldn't afford a newswire machine, so I depended on the good graces of staff in a nearby Senate office to let me know when a breaking news story came across the wire. On October 10, 1973, my door opened and the press secretary from down the hall popped his head in. "Your boss won't believe this one," he said, and handed me a wire story.

I scanned it quickly. "I don't know about Sam Nunn, but I never expected to see anything like this!" I was out of my chair and headed for the door. "Gail, you've got the conn!"[9]

My assistant, Gail Bramlett, was already handling calls. As the door closed behind me, I heard her say, "Resignation? What resignation?"

I raced toward the Senate across the street. I was leap-frogging the steps toward the entrance when I spotted Senator Nunn descending them.

---

[9] "You have the bridge" or "You're in command." A well-known line from Captain Kirk of *Star Trek*.

"The vice president has resigned!" I said, and handed him the wire copy, just a couple of paragraphs in length. Senator Nunn was quiet as he read the story. Out of breath, and not a little excited, I said, "If we stay here another thirty years, we're not likely to witness anything that tops this."

Senator Nunn must have thought the comment amusing because he gave me an ever-so-slight smile before handing the wire story back to me. "It says he pleaded 'no contest' to tax evasion. Is that right?"

I nodded. "I guess it was those envelopes filled with cash from contractors while he was governor that did him in."

"Has any other vice president in our history resigned?" Nunn asked.

"Calhoun is the only one. David Brinkley was talking about that on NBC last night. Calhoun resigned to run for the Senate in 1832. But Agnew is the first to resign accused of criminal activity. Tax evasion, for heaven's sakes."

If I detected a lack of astonishment in Nunn when I delivered the news of Agnew's resignation, it was, as I learned years later, because President Nixon had told him and a small group of Democratic senators the afternoon before to expect the news.

"I have a feeling the worst is yet to come," Nunn said.

Ten days later, I was having dinner with friends at Hogate's Restaurant on DC's waterfront when the maître d' came to my table and tapped me on the shoulder. "Mr. McElroy?"

"Yes." *Nobody has this number except the babysitter.*

"I'm sorry but you have a call." I jumped up almost certain one of the children was seriously injured or ill.

At the phone, I listened to an excited reporter from *The Washington Post*. "We're trying to find Senator Nunn tonight." It was October 20, 1973, the night of the so-called "Saturday Night Massacre," when President Nixon ordered Attorney General Elliot Richardson to fire special prosecutor Archibald Cox. Richardson refused and resigned, along with his assistant, William Ruckelshaus. Nixon then asked Solicitor General Robert Bork to do the deed, and he obliged.

As I listened to the reporter's inquiry, I wondered why the Watergate story seemed to be without an ending. *Or maybe it has an ending; it's just not the one anyone is enthused to see.*

I never told the *Post* reporter that Senator Nunn was in Europe on a trip with other senators. Several of the senators with him served on the judiciary committee and rushed home as soon as they heard the news.

It occurred to me years later that while I was working for a believer in the highest ethical standards of public service, another public servant at 1600 Pennsylvania Avenue was defining his personal code of ethics in a purely self-serving manner. The reins of power could not be held thusly, so the power Nixon coveted slowly, inexorably, slipped from his grasp.

Before Nunn's first six-year term was completed, he had served with three presidents (Nixon, Ford, Carter) and four vice presidents (Agnew, Rockefeller, Ford, Mondale). It was an unsettling period of time, to be sure, filled with unexpected and historic changes in American governance.

Stennis, the "Conscience" of the Senate

We were still in the first month of Senator Nunn's first term when we received word that Sen. John Stennis, chairman of the Senate Armed Services Committee, had been shot during a mugging in front of his Cleveland Park home in the District of Columbia. He survived, but his days of traveling abroad were over. When Stennis returned to his duties, he asked Senator Nunn to chair the new manpower subcommittee he had created just before Nunn's election, and he assigned Frank Sullivan, one of the most talented members of the committee staff, to work with Nunn.

Stennis, 71 years of age when he was shot, understood that the time was rapidly approaching when the baton he held with other senators elected in the aftermath of World War II must be handed to a new generation. From his point of view, Stennis knew the process had already begun. The Mississippi senator had recently mourned the passing of his close friend Richard Russell, and he had witnessed the retirement of several contemporaries with whom he was close, including Rep. Carl Vinson of Georgia. When Sam Nunn arrived, Stennis was more than ready to take Georgia's newest senator under his wing, school him in the arcane rules of the Senate, and, in general, expedite Nunn's legislative maturity. Stennis described Nunn as "the last but not least" member of the Armed Services Committee. No one was surprised when Chairman Stennis handed the reins of the newly created manpower subcommittee to Nunn, but nearly everyone was surprised by the immediate impact of Stennis's appointment.

Nunn was 35 years old and slightly more than a year into his first term when he and Frank Sullivan visited NATO installations during the February recess and returned with a comprehensive report on US manpower requirements in Europe.[10] The Senate was facing a contentious debate over the so-called Mansfield Amendment, an annual legislative exercise by Majority Leader Mike Mansfield (D-MT) to unilaterally cut the number of US troops in Europe. In the latest iteration of Mansfield's amendment, the Leader wanted to reduce the number of American troops by 125,000. This memoir is not the place to go into detail on the subject, but in typical Nunn fashion, he shepherded the debate into an ideologically neutral field with three amendments that ultimately carried the day: the first addressed the combat support ratios of US forces in Europe, a second focused on the security of US nuclear weapons in Europe, and a third addressed the interoperability of US and Allied forces and equipment in Europe. All were adopted by the Senate and became law.

The debate is mentioned here because the second amendment Nunn offered signaled his commitment to raising the nuclear threshold for the use of nuclear weapons. He argued that reducing the number of troops, as Mansfield wanted to do, would likely lead to a decision for an earlier, not later use of nuclear weapons. His legislative eye was always searching for ways to reduce the risk of using nuclear weapons.

The debate on the Mansfield Amendment in the summer of 1974 earned Nunn a reputation as the Senate's resident expert on the North Atlanta Treaty Organization. The experience also telegraphed to his colleagues that this new senator would come to debates armed with "a good bit of background," as he often said, and they would be well advised to do likewise.

Stennis, no doubt, was proud of his protégé and pleased that he had given Nunn an early opportunity to demonstrate his own integrity, diligence, and judgment.

---

[10] Sam Nunn, "Policy, Troops and the NATO Alliance," Report of Sen. Sam Nunn to the Committee on Armed Services, United States Senate, 93rd Congress, 2nd Session (2 April 1974).

"No partisans at a round table"

For the length of his first term in office, Senator Nunn satisfied himself with the five smallish rooms in the Russell building assigned to him across the hall from Senator Talmadge. Six years later, following reelection to a second term, Nunn jumped at the chance to use his new seniority to move up to a corner office in the Dirksen building. Although it would be farther from the Senate chamber, the new suite would afford enough room in his personal office to include a certain circular table he'd seen in another senator's office just after arriving in Washington. Eyes rolled when he announced that he wanted that specific table for his office.

No one, including the sergeant at arms, had seen the table in years. Indeed, some suggested the table no longer existed in the Senate's inventory.

Senator Nunn could not be dissuaded from the search. Members of his personal staff also looked for it but had no luck. Finally, one Saturday morning, he trekked down to the basement storage facility himself and began searching through the entire inventory of tables. A couple of staff members tagged along, convinced the search was futile. An hour later, there it was—its top separated from its base and leaning against a back wall. It had a few scratches here and there but nothing objectionable. The superintendent looked at me with eyes wide open. I don't think he'd seen such a determined senator in his entire career. For the next seventeen years, that round maple table was Nunn's favorite place to meet.

"There are no partisans at a round table," Nunn said. "No place to take sides. It's perfect for my office."

When Senator Nunn retired from the Senate in early 1997, Sen. Richard Lugar asked for the table and kept it in his office for the rest of his career. And when Lugar left the Senate, he bought the table and took it with him. That simple table, eight feet in diameter and solid maple, provided a venue for discussion and mark-up of major national security legislation, including the Nunn-Lugar Program that passed as the Cooperative Threat Reduction Act in 1991. Nunn has described the Act as the most important national security legislation to become law during his twenty-four-year tenure in office.

Chapter 9

Ramrod Straight

Half way through his first six-year term, Senator Nunn was pulled back into the campaign chapter of his life by an allegation that his 1972 campaign had accepted $2,500 in cash from Gulf Oil Corporation's Washington lobbyist, Claude C. Wild Jr. The Watergate special prosecutor's office accused Wild of funneling cash to the Committee to Re-Elect the President, and still more cash to eight senators and representatives, including Nunn, whose name appeared on the list. (Contributions from corporations and labor unions were prohibited, and all contributions and expenditures had to be reported. Abuses uncovered during the Watergate investigation led to the creation of the Federal Election Commission in 1974.)

Senator Nunn said he personally received no money from Gulf Oil or Claude Wild. Nevertheless, he asked his campaign finance officials to conduct a thorough investigation to determine if there was any evidence of having received cash from Claude Wild. When the answer came back that there was no record of such a contribution, Senator Nunn was not satisfied. He retained legal counsel to conduct a detailed audit of all campaign receipts and expenditures in an effort to be absolutely, positively sure there had been nothing even slightly irregular in the handling of funds. A year later, Senator Nunn issued a statement that said, in part, "When this matter first came to my attention, I asked those responsible for handling my campaign finances to conduct a full and complete investigation to determine if any such contribution had been received by them. I have been informed by them that they received no such contribution."[1] He spent nearly $30,000 to determine that the Gulf Oil lobbyist had not made a cash contribution of any amount to the Nunn campaign.

The charge was baseless, and Sam Nunn knew it, but in the end, he felt it necessary to exhaust every possible thread that might be used far down the road to connect his good name to any charges from the special prosecutor's office.

The code of ethics he learned from his father was thoroughly ingrained in his character and never forgotten. Nothing made that clearer than an incident related to me in late 1972 by Perry attorney Avon Buice, who accompanied Senator Nunn on an orientation trip to Washington shortly after his election. Apparently, neither was properly dressed for Washington's unpredictable weather. "We didn't expect the weather to be so cold," Buice said. "It was miserable, and then it began to rain. Both of us were wearing lightweight summer suits, and we needed raincoats."

"What'd you do?" I asked. "I know Sam doesn't carry cash—ever."

"That's true, and he didn't that day," Buice said. "I offered to use the campaign money I was carrying and buy raincoats." Buice thought buying raincoats under such conditions could be easily justified as a legitimate use of campaign dollars. "But if that makes you uncomfortable," he said to Nunn, "we'll pay it back later."

Nunn shook his head and pulled his jacket up. "No, we won't do that. Even if no one else hears of it, I'll always know about it."

They were both soaking wet the rest of the day.

"Who gave this to me?"

Only once did Nunn accept cash that could not be accounted for. The incident occurred at a Georgia Bulldog football game on Saturday, November 4, 1972, just three days before the election. Nunn went down to the field prior to the kick-off to have a photo taken with UGA II, the team's bulldog mascot. Although we still couldn't afford to take a poll, crowd reaction was telling us a Democratic win was in the offing. As we attempted to sprint up the aisle from the field to the exit at the top of the stadium steps, fans shook his hand and slapped him on the back in a

[1] Public statement by US Sen. Sam Nunn (12 March 1976).

show of support. But they also did something else we didn't expect. They put cash in his pockets.

Former governor Marvin Griffin once told me of such a custom, but I'd never actually seen it practiced. "In the old days, when can-di-dates barnstormed from county to county, that cash was what kept 'em goin'," Griffin said, laughing. "Cash paid for everythin' and if ya had plenty in yo' pocket, why that was betta' than any poll. Ya knew instantly where ya stood."

When we reached the top of the stadium steps, Nunn turned to me as he turned his pockets inside out. "Look at this! Can you believe it?" Cash was literally in every pocket of his jacket, trousers, and shirt. People had been shaking his hand, and with the free hand, putting money in his pockets." We started collecting the cash, mostly $5 and $10 bills, when suddenly, he froze. He held up a $100 bill and waved it as though it was stuck to his fingers and wouldn't come unglued. "We've got to find out who gave this to me."

He held the $100 bill with his thumb and forefinger like it was something unpleasant he picked up by accident in a cow pasture. "Here" He extended his arm in my direction, and I grabbed the bill.

"Did you see who gave it to you?" I asked. *He doesn't even want to touch it.* "Can you describe the person?"

"No, of course not." He brushed himself off vigorously, as if he had discovered a stain that couldn't be removed. "Why don't we get them to put a message on the scoreboard," Nunn suggested. "We can ask whoever gave me a $100 bill to please call my office."

"You've got to be kidding," I said. *The odds of finding the person who slipped that Ben Franklin into his pocket are, let's see, how many people are there in this stadium—okay, about 65,000 to one.*

"No, I'm not kidding," he said. "I promised we would report all cash contributions of $100 or greater—and we will."

"Okay, but we don't have time to do it today. I'll call the athletic office next week and ask them to post a message on the scoreboard at the next home game." That seemed to satisfy him. We left for an event in Clayton County before the game started. Just as well, since Tennessee won 14-0.

UGA II welcomed Sam Nunn to Sanford Stadium prior to Georgia-Tennessee football game, 1972.

Photo courtesy: Roland McElroy

Later, I discovered the next home game wouldn't be until December 2 against Georgia Tech, well after the election, but I called the athletic office anyway. Their first reaction was disbelief. "You want us to do what?" When I explained why we wanted the message posted, they asked a very good question. "How do you know the person who gave the $100 will be there?"

"We don't," I said. "Okay, forget it."

I explained it all to Nunn, and eventually he agreed to simply report the cash as "$100 cash from unknown source at football game." And so, we did. To my knowledge, that was the last time a statewide candidate for office experienced that longstanding tradition of stuffing a candidate's pockets with cash—at least publically.

A Plan Is Essential

Some member of Congress is always getting into trouble for some act of personal or public indiscretion, or so it seems. Therefore, preparation for such awkward moments is essential if you are a competent press secretary. Your plan better be a good one and ready to be implemented if you hope to have a prayer of getting the story off the front page quickly.

I was thinking about such a plan one day when I walked into Senator Nunn's office. He was signing correspondence but was accustomed to interruptions. Maybe that's why he didn't look up at first.

"Consider this for a moment," I said. "What's to keep a woman you've never met from walking into your office, pointing a finger in your direction as she drops a paternity suit on your desk, and saying, 'You're the father of my baby and this news will be in the Atlanta papers tomorrow'?"

Senator Nunn still didn't look up. "Well, if you're going to be in public life, you have to live your life so far above reproach that a charge like that will fail for lack of credibility." And he never stopped signing letters.

"That's a pretty heavy burden to put on an elected official," I said. "Pretty soon, only monks, cloistered away on a mountaintop for years need apply for these jobs."

He finally looked up. "That's the price you've got to pay if you wanna avoid such a charge."

"Got it." I walked back to my office and checked that potential problem off my list.

To this day, every time I read about a politician's fall from grace, I think about Sam Nunn's words. One elected official told me he thought Nunn's standard too high. When I shared that view with Senator Nunn, his only comment was, "He'd be well advised to choose a profession other than public service for a career."

That's the reason why, for many years, his field representatives in Georgia were all male. Only late in his career did he permit himself to travel alone with a female staff member. "No reason to give anyone an opportunity to start a rumor," he said.

Only once did we have an experience that demonstrated how easy it is for an elected official to suddenly find himself in an awkward position that could have been fodder for a rumor of possible misconduct.

During his first term, Senator Nunn and I were touring the state as participants in the Georgia Chamber of Commerce sponsored prelegislative forum. The governor, a couple of key state legislators, and Senator Nunn were the principal speakers each day. The five-day tour made scheduled stops in three towns per day. Tagging along for the entire week were about a dozen state lobbyists and reporters from the major news outlets. Not every lobbyist who started the week remained for the entire week; several shared duties with colleagues from their home office who relieved them midweek. None of us were surprised when, on the third night, a vivacious young lady showed up for the reception at the end of the day at the residence of one of Nunn's key supporters. She talked with Senator Nunn as much as she could and always stood near him while he talked with other guests. If he wasn't available, she attached herself to me, asking a million questions. She never gave me a straight answer when I asked about her employer, so I decided the best thing to do was keep talking and steer her away from Senator Nunn. When all guests had departed and the time had come to retire for the evening, our host offered the young lady the spacious guest room he had reserved for Senator Nunn.

After she was comfortably in her room for the evening, he apologized to Senator Nunn for putting the two of us in a smaller bedroom with two twin beds. "Well, at least there is a connecting door between you and your staff assistant," our host said. "By the way, what's her name?"

"I don't know," Senator Nunn said. "She's not with us."

"I thought *you* knew her," our host said.

My jaw dropped as I realized a serious mistake had just been made by all of us. "She's with you, isn't she?" I asked.

"No, no, no," our red-faced host said. "I'm sorry; I can't believe this."

"Well, *we* don't know her," Nunn said. "I assure you of that."

"Damn, I was certain she was with you." Our host was scratching his head trying to think of a way out of this mess. "She seemed so close."

"Yeah, well, we just met her for the first time tonight," I said. "I don't think we caught her name."

"Well, I never would've offered her a bedroom if I'd known you didn't know her. I'll ask her to leave right now." He started for the connecting door, then stopped, and with a bewildered look in our direction, said, "But she's already in there. How do I do this?"

"Don't do anything," Senator Nunn said. "Just leave things the way they are for tonight. We'll make sure it doesn't happen again." He gave me a look with an exclamation point in it, if that is possible to imagine.

Later, when lights were out, and the house was quiet, I heard Senator Nunn chuckling in his bed, and I began to relax.

It's times like these that I'm glad he has a sense of humor.

Rules of the Road

Most people have never seen, let alone actually read, Sam Nunn's 1972 platform, but near the end of it, he wrote one line that could have been written yesterday: "The distrustful attitude of citizens toward elected officials is one of the most serious situations facing this country today." He continued by pledging to make a full disclosure annually of his financial holdings, decline any further legal fees from his law practice, and refuse any additional payments from US farm programs. In Nunn's view, such a pledge should be sufficient, but he also left no doubt that he would do whatever it took to avoid even the appearance of conflict of interest during his years of service.

When Nunn became ranking member of the Senate Armed Services Committee in 1983, he asked the minority staff director, Arnold Punaro, to create a code of ethics for the Democratic staff that went beyond the requirements set for other Congressional committees. It was more evidence of his personal commitment to avoid even the appearance of impropriety.

In 1987, when Democrats regained control of the Senate after a six-year hiatus, he became chairman of the full Armed Services Committee. He immediately asked Punaro to work with the committee's chief counsel, Jeff Smith, to "revise and update the old standards using the ethics rules of Congress as 'the basic format' for a broader code."[2] The result was something the committee staff referred to unofficially as the "rules of the road." When a procurement scandal hit the Pentagon in early 1988, Senator Nunn was proud to note that it did not touch the committee or its staff. "Some members of the staff chaffed a bit at being asked to sign the code when they were hired," Nunn said, "but in my years as chairman, we did not have even one problem."[3]

Nunn's Rules of the Road

- Prohibited any staff or their spouses from owning any stock in defense industries.
- Prohibited taking an honorarium for any defense-related speech. (At the time, Congress allowed members to accept $2,000 per speech as an honorarium.)
- Prohibited any staff from trying to influence the Pentagon in selecting one contractor over another.
- Prohibited any staff from accepting travel expenses from a defense contractor, even though Congressional rules at the time allowed such travel under some circumstances.

---

[2] Scott Shepard, "Nunn Sets the Standard With His Ethics Code," *The Atlanta Journal and Constitution* (3 July 1988): A22.

[3] Ibid.

- o And required any staff member who left to become a lobbyist for a defense contractor to wait one year before contacting the committee.

"The committee's restrictions were tame by today's standards," said Punaro, "but at the time, they were considered very restrictive."

"I can tell you I slept better at night because the rules were there," said Nunn.

A Place at the Table

Nunn's high ethical standards were not universally adopted on Capitol Hill, a discovery I made shortly after I left his office in 1986. For several years, I tried my hand at representing corporate interests in Washington—lobbying, in other words. Lobbying should be an honorable profession, but its ability to quickly infuse large sums of money into the political process has earned it an unseemly reputation. That is unfortunate, because a good lobbyist can play an important role—some would say, essential role—in the legislative process. The educational value of listening to an informed lobbyist with information that only he or she possesses is frequently lost, however, in the corrupting sound of easy money cascading from a hose that no one is willing to shut off.

Add to that a few congressmen who get elected without a moral compass at all, and you will understand why I quickly soured on wearing the lobbyist label. For me, the saddest day of my brief lobbying career began the morning I walked into a board meeting of a corporate client and found a member of Congress sitting next to the chairman of the board at the head table. I was shocked, to say the least. I couldn't take my eyes off the scene. I wanted to believe my eyes had intentionally deceived me.

This is very wrong.

Yet there he was. I felt physically sick. When it came time to hear a status report on legislation pending in Congress, the chairman turned to the member of Congress—as he might to a staff member—and asked him to report on a bill that would impact the chairman's industry. The congressman proceeded to outline all action pertaining to the bill in his committee of jurisdiction, of which he was the ranking member at that time. Before he finished, he described how and when Congress was likely to take up the bill and whether or not amendments of interest to this particular company would be passed.

Just when I was beginning to feel sick again, I recalled the words of my Quitman friend: "Roland, don't become cynical."

Is this what he meant? Well, this makes me sick.

A few days later, I recounted this incident to another lobbyist. His reaction was telling.

"Look, my friend," he said, putting a hand on my shoulder, "it's very simple: if you didn't buy it, you don't got it."

"Surely," I said, "the merits of an issue will carry—"

"You really are a Boy Scout, aren't you? It doesn't work that way, and the sooner you learn that, the sooner you'll earn a place at the table.

"I don't—"

"No, if you didn't buy it, you don't got it," he repeated. "Got it?"

Chapter 10

"You think this job is funny?"

In the years following Sam Nunn's election to the US Senate, his father's serious and sober influence was frequently on display. Many of his closest friends often thought the younger Nunn appeared too serious in television interviews, even stone-faced.

"Not only does he not smile, he doesn't even blink," said his friend Ed Beckham. "Is he reading from a teleprompter? Because when I watch, he seems to be staring at a fixed spot in front of him, never blinking, only staring."

"Why don't you tell him all of that," I suggested.

"No, I don't believe I'm the one for that," Beckham said, smiling. "*You* ought to do it."

I'd heard similar sentiments about Nunn's stoic expression from other friends and even some in the media. One reporter had the temerity to describe his demeanor as "funereally sober."

I waited and made sure I picked a good day to raise Beckham's observation. It was the close of a busy but productive legislative day when I walked into his office, where Nunn was signing correspondence. There's no reason to waste time, I thought, so I offered the following suggestion in my most "by the way" voice. "Why don't you try to smile a bit more the next time you're interviewed on television?"

"Why?" He didn't look up.

"Smiling makes you appear more approachable and will help you connect with your constituents."

He acted like he hadn't heard me. Finally, he looked up with a pained, squinting stare, somewhat like the one he might give an aide who brings him a lunchtime sandwich loaded with mayonnaise. After what felt like ten minutes of cold silence, he said, "You think this job is funny?"

"Well, no, I…uh…" *This was not a good idea.*

"Would you prefer this?" He turned as if speaking to an unseen camera. "The threat of a terrorist attack with a nuclear weapon is real." Then he gave the imagined camera an exaggerated Cheshire cat grin that went from ear to ear.

I started to laugh but thought better of it. "No, of course not, but...okay, forget it. You have to do it your way." I never suggested smiling occasionally again, even though well-intended people kept suggesting that I do so. His comment was his way of telling me, and anyone else who cared to know, that he took his job and the issues seriously, and that's all that should matter.

As I returned to my office, I thought of a comment his mother made early in the first campaign. "Sam's serious demeanor is inherited from his father," she offered one day when I asked her why Nunn's facial expression seemed so—well, expressionless. "And Sam's not about to change," she said. It was as if that was all that need be said on the subject.

"But," I tried again, "every once in a while it would be good to see a little charisma."

She laughed and walked into the next room. A few minutes later, I heard her laughing again. Apparently, she found my suggestion amusing.

Nunn's sense of humor had a way of surfacing in the most unlikely of circumstances. A week after our exchange in his office, he addressed a conference at Williamsburg for members of the Democratic Leadership Council. His speech was crafted to focus on national security issues. Our conversation must have been on his mind, because he opened his speech with words he purposely delivered in an exaggerated deadpan. "I've been asked to demonstrate some charisma..."—he paused and looked in my direction—"by talking about throw-weight, hardened silos, megatonnage, and multiple independently targetable reentry vehicles." The crowd of mostly Washington types burst into laughter.

He knew instinctively how to take a complex subject, lighten it up, and bring the audience on board for a serious discussion of the perils of nuclear proliferation. His audience understood what he was doing, and for them, he had charisma enough.

Maybe that's what a Nunn supporter had in mind the day she wrote a letter to Senator Nunn in the late 1980s, urging him to make the plunge into a race to succeed President Ronald Reagan. "Dear Senator Nunn," she wrote, "Please run for President. My husband and I will vote for you. We need a change. This nation has had all the charisma it can stand."

I wished I had written that line.

"Short, balding, and owlish looking"

For some reason, many of the nation's most seasoned reporters had trouble describing Senator Nunn's physical appearance. Gene Methvin, a Dooly County native, described him in a profile he wrote for the *Reader's Digest:* "He doesn't turn tourists' heads on Capitol Hill; he looks more like a subcommittee aide."[1] Way back in 1979, Al Hunt wrote in a *Wall Street Journal* profile: "Much attention will soon focus on a short, balding, owlish-looking senator."[2] Senator Nunn usually took such descriptions in good humor, but Hunt's choice of words was not well received. I tried to point out that Hunt also wrote, "If not especially imposing physically, he is intellectually."[3] I could tell by the look Nunn gave me that it was too late; the damage had been done.

Michael Kramer, writing in *Time* magazine, didn't even attempt a description. He simply declared, "Sam Nunn has never flirted with charisma."[4]

"What about the headline on Kramer's piece?" I said. "'*Smart, Dull and Very Powerful.*' Two out of three's not bad."

Nunn gave me a Dick Cheney kind of smile; it strayed crookedly up the side of his face and seemed a bit irritated.

---

[1] Eugene H. Methvin, "Sam Nunn: Senator for the Defense," *Reader's Digest* (October 1981): 23.

[2] Albert R. Hunt, "Little Giant: In the SALT Debate, Sen. Sam Nunn's Role Could Prove Decisive," *The Wall Street Journal* (22 March 1979): 1.

[3] Ibid.

[4] Ibid., 24.

A Thimbleful of Charisma

Sam Nunn established a fairly impressive record for one who worked without the charisma many thought essential to Washington success. In 1986, Senate press secretaries named him the "workhorse of the Senate." In 1990, a survey by the *National Journal* rated Senator Nunn one of the five "most respected members" of the Senate.

Sen. Carl Levin (D-MI) explained why Sam Nunn is held in such high regard by his colleagues. "He knows more about the subject he talks about than anybody else by the time he starts talking about it."[5]

When Nunn decided to retire, a survey of senior Senate staff, published in *Washingtonian* magazine, determined he would be the senator "missed most."[6]

Sam Nunn must have been doing something right, because syndicated columnist George Will concluded his retrospective on his career with, "the Georgia Democrat is among the best presidents this nation never had."[7]

Imagine what he might have accomplished if he'd had even a thimbleful of charisma.

About That Golf Game

Yes, golf *is* a serious subject to him, but there have been occasions when golf has revealed his particularly wry sense of humor. In October 1974, Nunn was suffering from a severe case of laryngitis and trying to save his voice from all unnecessary conversation. When three of his friends showed up for a round of golf, he handed them a memo that outlined the rules that would guide their game and stipulated the concessions, if any, they could expect from him:

---

[5] Pat Towell, "Sam Nunn: The Careful Exercise of Power," *Congressional Quarterly* (14 June 1986): 1329.

[6] "Best and Worst of Congress," Annual Survey, *Washingtonian* (September 1996).

[7] George Will, "The Best President We've Never Had," *The Washington Post* (22 June 1998).

My handicap is 6. I'm not interested in hearing that you aren't playing to your handicap, and until I've seen you play a few holes, I'm not interested in playing for more than a dollar Nassau. If at any time I'm interested in press bets, I'll let you know.

Do not embarrass me by asking that I concede any of your putts. I will volunteer to do so if in my judgment, it is deserved.

I admit it is a nice day for golf, that the weather has either been hot or cold, and the greens keeper is doing an excellent job.

Kindly refrain from telling me of your past performances on the golf course. The only round which interests me is the one we are about to play.

I would appreciate your refraining from such remarks as: "That would have been a beauty—if it hadn't caught the trap." "You got a bad bounce or it wouldn't have gone out of bounds, etc." I am capable of doing my own sympathizing.

The scorecard contains the rules. I shall expect you to apply them as scrupulously as though I were watching—because I might be.

If I happen to be up on the last tee, I do not wish to give an additional half-stroke or more and play the last hold double or nothing.

I prefer, while at golf, not to be drawn into a discussion of business or economic subjects, nor hear such discussions pursued by others in the middle of my backswing.[8]

The memo continues for another page, but surely that's enough to convince any doubters that he does, indeed, have a sense of humor—as well as a passion for golf.

---

[8] Sam Nunn, personal memo to Mell Tolleson, Ed Beckham, and Bill Jerles (6 October 1974).

Chapter 11

1978 Reelection Preparation

Starting in early 1977, every political strategist in Georgia advised Senator Nunn to prepare for a tough reelection campaign. Conventional wisdom says the most vulnerable moment in a senator's career is his first reelection campaign because that's when a senator has a full six-year record of votes to defend. "If you've been in office six years, there are at least two votes you don't remember that could be used against you in a campaign—and probably more," Nunn acknowledged. The closer we drew to the election, the more we heard that comment.

We were told the challenger might be one of those who had thought about running in 1972 but didn't. Or it might come from a self-funded conservative Democrat who possessed the requisite funds to mount a credible challenge, someone who would attack Senator Nunn from the right side of the political spectrum. A Republican challenger was not obvious, nor would it change our planning. It was still a Democrat's game in Georgia.

Every Vote, Every Issue

As 1978 approached, Senator Nunn's potential vulnerabilities were on his mind a lot. I remember well a day in the winter of 1977–1978 when he called key members of his staff into his office and said, "I want to review every vote I have cast in the Senate since I arrived." Jaws dropped as he explained how he'd seen the otherwise exemplary tenure of other senators demolished because a challenger brought up a single vote in a televised debate that the senator couldn't remember and thus couldn't defend. "Here's what I want you to do," Nunn said. "Prepare a three-ring binder that contains every vote on every issue I've cast over the past six years. Include with each vote a brief discussion of controversial aspects of the issue as well as my rationale for voting the way I did." He assured us it wouldn't take long to pull the material together. He was wrong. It took a team of staffers and interns three months to pull the basic information together and another three months to fine-tune his rationale for votes.

We soon filled not one but three binders, divided by issues, and included all votes on a specific issue. Emphasis was given to the most controversial, e.g., congressional pay raises, extension of voting rights, Panama Canal treaties, federal taxes, and federal spending. It turned out to be a long list.

"And not just votes on final passage of a bill," Nunn said, "I need to know if the votes were on procedural issues or amendments." He looked at his legislative director, Gordon Giffin. "You and your staff will need to take that one."

"I'm on it," Giffin said, with more enthusiasm than anyone else in the room had been able to muster. In fact, I think he was downright happy to have the assignment.

"You don't have to include votes on motions to adjourn, or motions to instruct the sergeant at arms to request the attendance of absent senators, or—"

"In other words, we can use some discretion?" I was hoping for some way to reduce the overwhelming number of roll-call votes to consider.

"Not much," Nunn said. "Not much. I'd rather see more than not enough."

Giffin took overall responsibility for the project, thankfully. When finished, he presented Nunn with eight, three-ring binders, each three-inches thick, containing analysis of more than 2,500 votes cast in his first six years.[1] Giffin also prepared a set of binders that analyzed each of the fourteen planks in Nunn's 1972 platform to demonstrate the amount of progress made in fulfilling his campaign promises. Has anyone ever prepared with such a comprehensive effort for a reelection to the US Senate? I doubt it.

---

[1] Number of recorded votes in the US Senate in the five-year period of 1973–1978: 3,581.

Nunn reviewed each binder, and committed to memory those votes with the potential to become part of a campaign debate. Fortunately, he never had to use any of the material—but he was prepared, nonetheless, for any question about his record.

Pecan Orchard Announcement

The 1978 reelection campaign was launched on the Nunn family farm outside of Perry, just as it was six years earlier. But this one reminded me of another political barnstorming day in Houston County exactly forty summers earlier—a 1938 event on the courthouse square at which Nunn's father endorsed Sen. Walter George for reelection, defying President Roosevelt, who had come to Georgia in the spring and endorsed Senator George's opponent.

The1978 announcement featured a flatbed truck decked out in the obligatory red, white, and blue bunting. Fortunately, the hour for convening was scheduled early enough to avoid the threat of afternoon thundershowers. Humidity was tolerable and the orchard shaded by more than enough pecan trees to keep everyone cool. Congressman Vinson wasn't able to attend the 1938 event, but he enjoyed a seat of honor in 1978 close enough to the podium to clearly hear his grand-nephew describe his own vision for America's future.

Fincher's Barbecue in Macon delivered enough of their award-winning product to satisfy all 4,000 in attendance. Several hundred bales of hay provided plenty of seating, and the Nunn campaign provided hand-held fans to ward off flying insects. Funeral-home fans, we called them in the old days. Rev. Leonard Cochran, pastor of Perry Methodist Church, was present to deliver the invocation. Others on the flatbed, in addition to Nunn's colleague, Senator Talmadge, were Georgia Secretary of State Ben Fortson, and former governors M. E. Thompson and Lester Maddox. Maddox was serving as Georgia's lieutenant governor in 1978.

Mayor James McKinley presided and introduced a local African American pastor who opened the festivities singing the patriotic anthem "The House I Live In." Most in the crowd knew it as "What America Means to Me." The pastor's deep bass held everyone in rapt attention, especially on the words "the faces that I see, all races and religions, that's

America to me." His voice filled the orchard. Cows just beyond the fencing raised their curious heads. I thought of all the times past when a black man wouldn't have been asked to perform such a song on such a stage. I wondered what Maddox and Talmadge were thinking as they heard "my neighbor white or black, the people who just came here, or from generations back." They stood with everyone else to offer a lengthy ovation when the pastor's performance was over. Of course, Lester Maddox had retired long ago the last of his ax handles, and Herman Talmadge had put away any remaining copies of his 1955 book, *You and Segregation*. As I scanned the crowd, I could find no one wearing red galluses like Talmadge's father, segregationist governor Gene Talmadge, wore to public occasions like this one.

Maybe the times have changed. Indeed, maybe.

Nunn's speech focused on the federal budget. "A balanced federal budget is the best way to fight inflation," he said. "We must make inflation public enemy number one."[2] The inflation rate was 7.41 percent in May 1978 and rising. He talked about a number of defense issues, including a needed evaluation of the security of nuclear weapons in the US arsenal. Only a few in the crowd recognized a theme they had heard before and would hear as long as Sam Nunn served in the US Senate: we must find ways to reduce the threat of nuclear annihilation.

As the speeches concluded and the people began to disperse back to their hometowns, newspaper reporters scrambled for the nearest phone to file their stories. Television film crews rushed back to stations to begin processing their 16-mm film for the evening news. Senator Nunn and his family retreated to his A-frame home on the farm to recuperate from the excitement of the day. I went along to visit a while and rehash events of the day.

The sun was setting by the time I passed the orchard again. Pecan trees, planted by Nunn's ancestors, were in full leaf, sporting a fresh green hue. The combined aroma of fresh hay and barbecue filled the air. The pastoral scene before me begged to be captured on film. As I

---

[2] "4,000 Attend Kick-Off Here Saturday," *Houston Home Journal* (1 June 1978): 1.

stepped from my car and uncapped my Rolleiflex, I was struck by the natural solitude of the place. A few stray cattle had grazed their way into the orchard again, but aside from the hay and a few of those handheld fans dropped by departing guests, there was little evidence of the historic scene that played out hours earlier. Elected officials and distinguished guests, some of whom had clashed publicly many times in their careers, were gone. Indeed, with the light of a setting sun playing among the trees, the earlier scene seemed more like a postcard from Georgia's political past than a reflection of the present political landscape. Today, the little pecan orchard had said goodbye to all the old men of yesteryear, with the noise of their collective past—Georgia's past.

I cranked the film forward to the last negative on the roll and pointed the lens toward the pasture beyond the pecan trees. I don't know why I thought of Ben Franklin, my favorite founding father, at that precise moment, but I did. Ben Franklin said it would be hard work to keep this Republic. But he didn't say it would be impossible. In quiet cow pastures under pecan trees and in the halls of Congress, it is noble work that occupies our time—all of us, especially our elected representatives—every day.

"The pecan trees look mighty healthy," I said as I returned to my car. "Going to be a good crop this year." Several cows looked at me; one even mooed. "A vote in agreement—good enough."

When the people voted in November, Senator Nunn captured 83 percent of it, defeating former US Attorney John W. Stokes. The win was a big improvement over the 54 percent he earned in 1972 when he was still a relatively unknown quantity around the state. Years later, Senator Talmadge was asked what Senator Nunn did to diminish his vulnerability in his first reelection campaign. "He was a hard worker," Talmadge responded. "He had good press. He went to Georgia. He kept his fences mended. He voted in accordance with the wishes of the people of Georgia on most occasions. So, he became very popular in short order."[3]

---

[3] Ibid.; Talmadge, Sam Nunn Oral History, Washington, DC (17 July 1996).

Senator Nunn's reelection in the fall was expected. Therefore, much of the pre-election attention of media pundits was focused on the prospects of a history professor from West Georgia College: Newt Gingrich. Gingrich had tried twice and failed (1974 and 1976) to unseat the incumbent, Rep. Jack Flynt of the Sixth District. But Flynt didn't run for reelection in 1978, and Gingrich defeated Democratic state senator Virginia Shapard by 7,500 votes. Nunn told me that the outcome might have been different if not for a motorcade that blocked traffic on Friday afternoon, three days before the Sixth District election. First Lady Rosalind Carter had come to town to campaign on behalf of the Democrat, Virginia Shapard. When the Secret Service blocked traffic on surrounding roads for more than two hours to allow the motorcade to pass, they created a hornet's nest of angry people—make that, voters—shaking their fists at the passing officials. Nunn was in that motorcade and an eyewitness to the unfolding political debacle. "If not for that motorcade," he said, years later, "with furious voters forced to sit behind their wheels for hours, the entire course of US history might have been changed."

Whether or not the blocked streets caused Shapard's defeat was never determined, but the outcome of the race was the same: an about-face for the district and a serious blow to the state's Democratic leadership.

An even bigger political upheaval took place two years later. Indeed, every Democrat in the state felt a political tremor when the Talmadge dynasty came to an end at the hands of an unknown Republican challenger by the name of Mack Mattingly. There would be no automatic blessing of a Democratic nominee by the voters from that day forward.

Chapter 12

Avoid Alcohol, Sex, and Personal Attacks

By 1981, I thought all those old fears of public speaking were behind Sam Nunn. They weren't. They all came back the day Nunn's close friend Sen. Henry "Scoop" Jackson (D-WA) called to ask Nunn if he would be willing to accept the Alfalfa Club's spoof nomination to be president of the United States.

Alfalfa Is More Than Hay

Most people have never heard of Washington's Alfalfa Club. When the National Geographic Society organized the Alfalfa Club in 1913, its leadership decided its name should be taken from the plant that agronomists say will extend its roots to any length in search of a drink. Membership applications do not exist. If you are deemed worthy by the club's unnamed leadership, you will be invited to join about 200 of the club's members on the last Saturday of January for a steak and lobster dinner and a convivial good time. Until Justice Sandra Day O'Conner was admitted in 1994, it was a male-only club. Times have changed, but the dinner remains a private affair, no working media allowed. As a result of the dearth of information about the event, media reports usually include little more than a tale or two from the nominee's remarks elicited from departing guests.

It doesn't sound like something a serious person would consider attending for one minute. Scoop Jackson had delivered the keynote speech a couple of years previously, and he thought it would be good for Nunn's political future if he accepted the opportunity too. Nunn had joined the club in 1978. From his point of view, it was a fun evening for Washington leadership and a few invited guests, a chance to relax and enjoy the fellowship and dinner. Nothing serious was scheduled for the evening.

The honoree selected as keynote speaker was expected to deliver a twenty-minute humorous speech.

"I have to be honest with you," Jackson said over the phone. "The success of this speech will determine what the nation's top corporate and political leaders think of you for the next twenty years. I just thought you ought to know. And I should tell you that you must avoid any stories that include alcohol, sex, or sexual relations."

I walked into Nunn's office in time to see the blood drain from his face as Jackson explained the importance of the speech.

"People will judge my abilities based on a speech full of jokes? Jokes?" Nunn watched me walk into the room and began shaking his head.

I could tell this speech was going to be a hard sell. *He does NOT want to do it.*

"That's right. Nothing serious, Sam, just jokes," Jackson said.

"But I don't do humor, Scoop; I do substance. Besides, I don't have anyone on my staff who can write that kind of speech."

If it had been anyone other than Scoop Jackson, the conversation would have been over. Jackson was insistent, however, and in the end, he suggested Nunn seek outside help.

"My speech was written entirely by one of Bob Hope's speech writers. I'll give you his number, and you'll be all set."

Nunn scribbled down the number. They exchanged a few more words and Nunn hung up. "We may be in real trouble," Nunn said to me.

I'd been tipped off by the society's secretary, who also emphasized how important this speech would be to Nunn's career. Nunn was ashen; I needed to find words to reassure him.

"It's just one speech," I said, "we can do it."

Both eyebrows went up. "The most important speech of my career?" Standing up, he threw his hands into the air. "There's nothing of substance in it. It's ridiculous." He frowned and began shuffling papers on his desk. "I do substance, not jokes." A paperweight landed with a thud on top of the papers. "We may be in trouble."

You've already said that.

"No, no. We *can* do it," I said, with all the confidence I could muster. I was careful to use the inclusive "we" to telegraph that he would not be alone in the preparation process. "Some of those selected have even gone on to become the actual president."

I wish I hadn't said that.

"What's wrong with this world," Nunn said, "that we turn to people who make light of serious issues and somehow that's supposed to make us feel better about electing them president." He twitched his mouth to one side and then the other and seemed lost in his own self-doubt.

A moment later, as if another switch had been turned on, he sat down again. "Scoop gave me the name of one of Bob Hope's joke writers and said I should call him." He handed me a slip of paper with a name and California phone number. "Get him on the phone, will ya? We've got five weeks."

When I handed Nunn the phone, he explained the purpose of the call to the joke writer and mentioned Scoop Jackson as a reference.

"Stop right there," the writer said, "I wrote a terrific speech for Jackson and sat in the back of the room to hear him deliver it. But his delivery was terrible; his timing was awful; he blew every line. I never want to be associated with that event again—ever."

The writer hung up.

Nunn was quiet as he placed the phone on its cradle. "We may be in trouble."

I kept searching for professional humorists to help craft the Alfalfa speech, but all of them were engaged to help others who also were scheduled to speak at the dinner on the same night.

"Well, I guess you'll have to put aside everything for the next several weeks and focus on pulling this speech together." Nunn sounded a little desperate.

I didn't bother to point out that, according to my calendar, the holidays of Christmas and New Years were usually celebrated during the time set aside for our speech preparation. Holidays are not recognized when there is urgent work to be done in Nunn's office, so bringing up the holiday schedule would have been foolish and totally lost on him. I knew I would be working during the holidays again—that didn't bother me—but I worried that assets I counted on, people whose talents I expected to call upon for stories and anecdotes, would be unavailable to me during that time.

Oh, well—full speed ahead.

I had no idea at the time how many joke writers I would be calling or visiting in person over the next few weeks. There was Washington's Bob Orben, who told me he read *The Washington Post* every morning and used the headlines to write a hundred one-liners before breakfast. Orben taught me how to write jokes based on the "rule of threes." Example: A hippie, a priest, and Henry Kissinger are on a plane when the engines quit. Only three parachutes are on the plane. The pilot came to the back where the three passengers were sitting, strapped on one of the three chutes, and jumped out, leaving two parachutes for the three passengers. Now, you know where this is going, and if you're familiar with the rule of threes, you know that the punch line will have something to do with Henry Kissinger. It's actually the easiest way to write a joke because it works every time—well, almost every time.

I also sought material from a couple of well-known Georgia humorists, Lewis Grizzard and Bob Steed. I knew Grizzard from his sportswriting days at the *Athens Banner Herald* in the early 1960s—long before he became a famous humorist. Steed, a long-time friend to Senator Nunn, was a prominent Atlanta attorney and humorist for *The Atlanta Constitution* whose columns regularly violated all of the Alfalfa restrictions.

Grizzard's career took off when his columns in the Atlanta newspapers became a "must read" for subscribers. The books that followed became best sellers, including my favorite, *Elvis Is Dead, and I Don't Feel So Good Myself.* I'd lost touch with Grizzard, but these were desperate times and I needed help. So, I called. Not surprisingly, he was on tour and unavailable, but, I was told, he would try to return my call. When he called back, he first apologized for the noise. He was calling from a phone booth behind a Wyoming truck stop. For the next hour, I listened and struggled to write down each story and one-liner he offered. The roar of passing eighteen-wheelers made listening difficult and at times impossible. In the end, though, it didn't matter because absolutely none of his material was clean enough to use before a Washington, DC, audience.

Telling Lewis that I couldn't use any material that relied on sex, sexual relations, or use of alcohol rendered him speechless. There was a very long pause before he asked, "Well, what are you going to talk about?"

"Self-deprecating humor is okay," I said, "and political humor is fine so long as it doesn't become personal."

"Oh," he said, "I think we're through. Good luck." He was roaring with laughter as he hung up.

Senator Nunn suggested I call his good friend Bob Steed. He enthusiastically accepted my call, and in a few days, submitted several pages of material, completely ignoring the restrictions I had conveyed in the clearest of language.

In sheer desperation, I enlisted the services of Arnold Punaro, Senator Nunn's director of national security affairs. Punaro had just been tapped to assume new duties as staff director for the minority on the Senate Armed Services Committee. We took our wives to the Shoreham Hotel to see Mark Russell, the piano-playing comedian and satirist. Russell's jokes were great but could hardly be used for anything more than inspiration. Nunn's speech had to be original from first to last joke. Sam Nunn would have to live with the material we created, whatever its merits.

I felt no pressure. None.

Attorney Bob Steed actually provided much material for the Alfalfa speech before the process was over. It was Steed who advised, "Start with your best material. If you can get 'em laughing at the beginning, it will be easier to hold them to the end, especially if they've been drinking."

"They will be," I said.

"Good. You're half way there."

I took a big gulp of coffee and began spreading a couple of hundred jokes and one-liners on index cards across the floor of my office, covering nearly every square inch from corner to corner.

The Alfalfa members were generally familiar with the serious side of Sam Nunn, but most had never seen his sharp wit demonstrated. I'd seen it many times, most often when he was called upon to speak extemporaneously. That devastating deadpan he owns can deliver a piercing one-liner with delicious impact. I encouraged him to use it as often as possible throughout the speech.

The final two weeks were dedicated to organizing material, writing transitions, throwing out jokes, writing new material, polishing, and, most importantly, testing each line on anyone foolish enough to walk into my office. At least once a day, I ran the material by Senator Nunn, who always had suggestions for edits and punch lines.

With five days to go, Nunn began rehearsing the speech, determining where best to pause, when to let his voice rise, when to let it trail off, and how long to wait before the next joke. By Saturday, January 23, 1982, he was ready. I picked him up at his home and drove him to the Capital Hilton on Pennsylvania Avenue, where the event was being held. As we waited in line behind a group of limousines discharging dinner guests, I glanced toward my passenger, who was reviewing his speech.

I've never seen him more nervous. What's going to happen to his timing? His voice? He doesn't look very good to me. This could be a disaster.

Just as he was about to get out of the car, he invited me to come inside and stand near the door so I could hear audience reaction. The dinner was a "members only" affair and I would have been uncomfortable even standing near the back of the room, so I declined. But the true reason for declining Nunn's offer was my renewed concern about the entire evening.

This could be very bad. On the other hand, I do want to know how the whole thing turns out, even if it crashes and burns. I just don't want to be a witness.

"Why don't you call me and let me know how the speech was received," I suggested. He agreed to do that, and a second later, he jumped out of the car.

Washington was experiencing a cold January rain. "Where's your Republican umbrella?" I was hoping he would recall that rainy Election Day morning in 1972 when he remarked, dryly, "Every Republican in Georgia owns an umbrella." But I couldn't get even a hint of a smile. He quickly turned toward the hotel entrance.

"The door! The door!" I shouted. He had jumped out so fast he neglected to shut it.

A moment later, the car door slammed and he dashed inside.

This could be really bad.

As I pulled away, I thought of his high school speech teacher, Florence Harrison, who was first to help him overcome his fear of public speaking. *Where are you now, Mizz Harrison, where are you now?*

Throughout the evening, I kept looking at my watch. No call. I was getting ready to go to bed when the phone finally rang. "Roland, this is Sam."

"How'd it go?" I could barely hear him over the din around him.

"Well, it was not a single," he said, his voice seemed to drop.

"Oh. I'm sor—"

"It was not a double," he interrupted, his pace quickening, his voice rising. "It was not a triple. It was a grand slam homerun!"

I could hear people around him offering congratulations. "I knew you could do it. Congratulations!"

In the final analysis, the best speeches in the world will flop if not delivered well. I read in *The Washington Post* the next morning that one of the attendee's said Nunn's timing was perfect, his delivery impeccable. Someone else said, "Forget President, that guy should head for Vegas to do a show."[1]

In thinking about the speech, the best advice, without a doubt, had been to place the best joke right up front. I loved it, and apparently, the Alfalfa Club agreed. It was a playful poke at former president Jimmy Carter: "We must convince the American people that the time is ripe for another president from the State of Georgia...and it will not be easy. We must convince people of the North that I am a Southerner who can forget the past—and it's about time. I figure that after four years of what Jimmy Carter did FOR YOU, we're just about even for what General Sherman did FOR US."[2] The audience roared—and Nunn owned them to the end.

A few days later, Senator Nunn got a note from Henry Kissinger, who also spoke at the Alfalfa dinner. Kissinger wrote, "Sam, remind me never to appear on the same program with you ever again."

---

[1] Lois Romano, "It Was a Fine Yield for the Alfalfa Club," *The Washington Post* (25 January 1982) B1.

[2] Speech to Alfalfa Club, Washington, DC (23 January 1982).

Commence to Write

Alfalfa was one thing; commencement speeches were altogether different, because each required Nunn to stick to a text. No ad-libbing allowed. He was never more uncomfortable than when he was thrust into such circumstances. An outline was preferred any day. For commencement speeches, however, we spent an inordinate amount of time crafting the prose that he would be forced to follow.

Once, the entire process got terribly off track just as the deadline neared for delivery of the final product. At our first meeting to discuss the forthcoming commencement address, he suggested a particular theme and asked that I flesh it out. A draft was prepared for his review, and another draft, and still another draft, until I had submitted seven drafts. On the day he was to catch a plane for Georgia to deliver the speech, he called me into his office around noon and said, "I know this was my idea [for the theme], but it just doesn't work." There followed a long pause, and he handed the latest draft back to me. "Do you think you can write something else...before I leave today?"

I gulped.

"Didn't you start to work on another topic before this one?"

"Well, yes, I wrote something a while back," I said, "but it's rough, very rough." He was scheduled to depart National Airport around 6:30 P.M. "I'm not sure I can have something for you before six o'clock."

"Well, do what you can in the next five hours, and I'll take it from there."

Five hours to write a fifteen-minute graduation address! "Sure," I said. "I'll have something ready."

Success in Sam Nunn's office often depended upon advance preparation, and I had prepared a draft of another commencement address just in case he made such a last-minute request. It was, indeed, a rough draft, very rough, but it had waited patiently for this day. Back at my desk, I grabbed the draft and headed for a little hideaway office in the basement of the Russell Senate Office Building, where Senator Goldwater, years before, had set up an amateur radio station for the use of ham-radio operators on Capitol Hill. I had permission to use the room anytime. In the quiet of that little room, I massaged my draft with the help of the ham station's IBM Selectric, then pulled out scissors, cut paragraphs, and scotch-taped them into a better organized draft. There was no time to retype a finished product. At 5:30 P.M., I raced back to Nunn's office, slapped the scotch-taped draft on the Xerox machine, and produced one finished copy.

Around 5:45 P.M., I delivered the speech in a three-ring notebook to his secretary, who shoved it into Nunn's briefcase five minutes before he left for the airport. It was not the most polished of speeches but it didn't need to be at that point. He would refine the text with handwritten notes above and below each line while on the plane, and by the time the jet landed, the speech would be his. The following Monday, when he returned the speech to me, he had circled only one paragraph on the third page, and noted, "Move to beginning, not here." I agreed with his improvement. It *was* much better.

In subsequent years, I never had a client who made similarly urgent time-sensitive demands. Most of my clients marveled at my fast turnaround on requests for speeches or op-eds. I smiled every time I heard their amazement and was grateful for the time I spent with Senator Nunn. Working with him made every other career assignment a cakewalk.

Chapter 13

Consistent, Cautious, Exhaustive

In the spring of 1973, not long after arriving in Washington, Senator Nunn answered a reporter's question about his approach to solving the nation's problems this way: "I'm not idealistic enough to think [political expediency] is going to be eliminated by me or anybody else completely, but that's what we need today."[1] Nunn then proceeded to tick off a laundry list of national problems that demand the attention of elected officials "who are capable of long-range thinking, people who are not just looking at the next election, people who are interested in what kind of country we're going to leave for our grandchildren, if I have any."[2] He chuckled because his own children were in elementary school at the time.

And then he added something to his answer that I'd not heard from him previously. "I'm taking it six years at a time and trying to do the very best job I can, and if the chips fall where I don't get re-elected, so be it...if [getting reelected] becomes my aim, then I've lost the whole perspective of why I ran."[3]

The cynical nature of the reporter probably thought Nunn was giving him a politically expedient answer, but if so, he was wrong. Senator Nunn's words were a true reflection of his commitment to the oath he took on the first day in office and had been demonstrated by consistent votes for twenty-four years.

Sam Nunn's belief in fair and equal treatment under the law for all citizens was evident in his vote to approve the extension of the Voting Rights Act in 1975.

---

[1] Ibid.; Maurice Fliess, "A Day in Life of Freshman Sen. Nunn," *The Atlanta Journal and Constitution* (25 March 1973): 18A.

[2] Ibid.

[3] Ibid.

His belief in nonpartisan consideration of critical national security issues persuaded him to vote in favor of the Panama Canal treaties in 1978.

His strict adherence to the highest ethical standards led him to vote against the confirmation of his former colleague, John Tower, nominated for secretary of defense in 1989.

His belief in the exploration of all plausible solutions *before* sending American soldiers into harm's way led him to oppose the Persian Gulf Resolution in 1991.

Extension of Voting Rights Act of 1965

The Voting Rights Act of 1965 was up for renewal in the summer of 1975. In the decade since its enactment, the law remained controversial in Georgia, and the debate surrounding it, often heated, had cooled very little. According to old hands around the Congress, the forthcoming debate on extending the Act would be as difficult as the debate on passage of the original bill. They were not wrong.

When the House approved an extension in June, only two Georgians voted in favor of the bill: Elliot Levitas of Decatur and Andrew Young of Atlanta.

Gordon Giffin, legislative director from 1975 to 1979, has reminded me many times that he was the only member of the Nunn staff in favor of the extension. Giffin, who spent his formative years in Canada, was fortunate to be able to approach the voting rights issue without the weight of Old South experiences on his back. That kind of start will give one clearer eyes with which to consider and discuss the evolution of race relations in the South.

Nunn knew that he would have to be an active participant in the debate if he was to develop a rationale for voting in favor of the extension. As he sat down to discuss a legislative strategy, he asked Giffin to research the history of the Voting Rights Act and develop options for extending the application of the Act to areas of the country currently exempted from its provisions. There was more than anecdotal evidence that voting rights were being abridged in areas beyond the eight states explicitly covered by the Act.

Senator Talmadge said he was willing to support an extension but only if the law could be made to cover all parts of the nation. For six months, Nunn and Giffin worked on amendments. Preparation was intense, but one thing was certain: Nunn's participation would be based on substance, not rhetoric.

In the months leading up to the debate, I fielded an increasing number of calls from Georgians worried that their new senator was about to cast a vote contrary to their wishes. If there was even a hint in my voice that he might be considering a vote in favor of the extension, some callers became outraged and promised a one-way ticket home for Nunn and any Southerner, for that matter, who committed such a traitorous act.

"Senator Nunn prepared for the debate by spending an enormous amount of time reflecting on the positive consequences of civil rights improvements in Georgia,"[4] Giffin recalled. "Atlanta and the rest of the state had clearly developed beyond many of the other Southern states due, in some degree, to the progressive actions of its civil rights leadership. The record of the past decade demonstrated that Georgia had made great strides in minority voter registration and participation."[5]

By the time debate got underway, Nunn was armed with enough data to show that Georgia's minority voting participation exceeded that of many states in the North. Nunn offered two amendments: one to extend the protections of the Act to other regions of the nation, and a second amendment to permit states that could demonstrate minority voting now exceeded national standards to revert to the voting rules applicable elsewhere.

During debate on his amendments, Nunn argued in favor of voting rights for all Americans and for all states to be treated equally. "These two principles were in conflict in the Act," Nunn said, in a statement released to the press after the vote. "I can be more effective in working for both principles—voting equality and equity among the states—by an affirmative vote than I could have with a negative vote."[6]

---

[4] Gordon Giffin, interview with the author (7 November 2015).

[5] Ibid.

[6] "Voting Rights," editorial, *The Atlanta Constitution* (26 July 1975): 4A.

Regrettably, both of his amendments were defeated, although not by wide margins. When his amendments went down, many Georgians expected Nunn to vote with his colleague, Talmadge, against passage of the extension.

"In the end, I think it was the sanctity of the fundamental right to vote in a democracy that carried the day with Nunn," Giffin said. "Plus, I think he felt it truly was the best way to position himself to make improvements in the Act at a later time."[7]

Giffin sat next to Nunn in the Senate chamber in one of the smaller chairs reserved for staff. "As the roll call proceeded, Nunn got up from his desk, walked to the well of the Senate where he stood in quiet reflection," Giffin said, "and when his name was called by the clerk, Senator Nunn responded, 'aye,' and thereby became the first Senator from Georgia to vote in favor of civil rights legislation."[8]

Georgia's two senators split their vote that day. Only eleven Southerners in the Senate supported final passage of the extension.

Nunn told the Associated Press he would continue to work toward the day "when all minorities and all sections of our nation are afforded equal treatment under federal law."[9] He knew his vote in favor of the extension was the right vote, but he was also aware that many Georgians would immediately disavow their support for him, including many he counted among his closest supporters.

"Sam is the grandson of a 'War between the States' veteran," one caller said to me when he heard that Nunn voted "aye" on renewal of the law.

"I'm well aware of that," I replied.

"Well," the caller continued, "has Sam forgotten who he is?"

Suddenly, images from my youth came to me: placing flowers on Confederate graves with fourth grade friends on Confederate Memorial Day, writing essays about Civil War heroes, listening to adults refer to black citizens as "darkies," watching voters file into the courthouse with

---

[7] Ibid.; Giffin interview.

[8] Ibid.

[9] "Southerners Break Ranks on Voting Act," Journal Washington Bureau, *The Atlanta Journal* (25 July 1975): 6A.

hardly a black citizen among them even though the county was nearly 50 percent black.

"Forget who he is?" I finally said to the caller. "No, he knows very well who he is, sir, and that's why he voted the way he did today. He knows who he is and where he came from, and today, sir, he's attempting to lead Georgia out of its past."

The caller slammed the phone down. I could almost feel the receiver bounce on the other end.

It would have been much easier to allow sentiments deeply ingrained in Georgia's culture to guide his vote. The more courageous decision, however, was an "aye" vote that let the world know Georgia was, indeed, moving beyond its past—beyond the heated rhetoric of demagogues.

Senator Nunn was well aware that a "yes" vote would likely guarantee a serious opponent for his 1978 reelection campaign but a "no" vote would close a heavy door on any opportunity he might have to make the current law fairer for all citizens. Knowing how Nunn prepares for every challenge, I'm confident he was making a list of potential opponents who might run against him by the time he returned to his office that day.

For a freshman senator, the pressure to reflect popular opinion was, and is, strong. Every time a senator casts a vote on a controversial issue that does not follow longstanding and accepted views, votes will be lost. Some voters, angry at first, will cool off in time and realize that the senator in whom they placed their trust initially is a thoughtful and moral person who will always put his country first. Thankfully, there were still a good many of those voters around when Nunn was up for reelection in 1978.

Twenty years later, I found Senator Nunn in a reflective mood as we talked in his Washington office. At one point in the conversation, the subject turned to race relations and, in particular, the voting rights debate of 1975. "I think Georgia has come a long way since 1975." Looking up, Nunn added, "Don't you?"

I raised an eyebrow. "You sound like Carter and Sanders, and even Vandiver before them. All three made similar statements when they delivered their inaugural addresses as newly elected governors in the '50s, '60s and '70s. They declared racism was in the past."

I paused and Nunn looked expectantly in my direction.

"Racism still exists, Senator. A simple declaration in a speech doesn't make it go away...but now, I would say, it's mostly *sub rosa*." I shook my head. "Insidiously...*sub rosa*."

He didn't offer further comment on the subject, and neither did I.

Panama Canal and Neutrality Treaties of 1978

In March 1978, the US Senate was asked by President Carter to ratify the Panama Canal treaties that had been negotiated by several previous administrations. The treaties granted control of the canal to Panama in 1999, thereby providing a full twenty years for a transition period.

Approval of the treaties was not a sure thing, and President Carter needed Senator Nunn's help. To say the vote was controversial in Georgia is putting it mildly. If passed, the treaties would represent a major foreign policy victory for Carter, but a defeat is what many Georgians had in mind. "We built it. We own it. It's ours!" was the rallying cry of those who opposed the treaties. It didn't help that Carter had campaigned for president in 1976 promising to oppose the treaties, and now he urged acceptance by Congress. Many viewed a vote for the treaties as a betrayal of the trust they had placed in the president *and* their new senator. To complicate matters, the vote was scheduled to occur less than six months before the Georgia Democratic primary in which Sam Nunn would be seeking nomination to a second term in the Senate.

As the debate progressed in the Senate and a final vote approached, some Georgians sensed their first-term senator was about to support a "giveaway" of the canal, so they plastered bumper stickers on their vehicles to convey a decidedly negative sentiment: "Once we had a Canal, Now we have Nunn." In one community, a rally against the treaties ended with a group of protestors parading a coffin through town with a sign attached: "The Political Careers of Talmadge and Nunn." Very few Georgians were in the "undecided" category on this issue.

When Senator Nunn made his decision to support the treaties, he spoke directly to his constituents through a statement on his weekly videotaped *Report to Georgia*: "I believe that if anyone looks at my record, on an objective basis, considering foreign policy and national security issues during the terms of Presidents Nixon, Ford, and Carter, I believe this record demonstrates that I approach these critical issues for our nation in a nonpartisan manner. If the Senate rejects these treaties, which have been negotiated by four presidents, I believe that a dangerous erosion of Executive Branch effectiveness in foreign affairs would inevitably result and, thus, adversely affect our foreign policy long after the Carter presidency."[10]

Approval of treaties requires concurrence of two-thirds of the senators present. The final vote, March 16, 1978, approved the treaties, 68 to 32.

Everywhere Senator Nunn campaigned in the summer of 1978, he was greeted by hecklers unhappy with his vote. At one stop, a man stood up and shouted, "Because of your vote, we're going to send you home!" Senator Nunn looked at the man and, in a quiet but clear voice, said, "One thing you need to understand is that the threat of going home is no threat at all to me."[11]

We fielded telephone calls regarding Nunn's vote for many weeks. Some voters were reluctant to let this one go. At first, I thought we might lose as much as 5 percent of the vote permanently, but as time went by, the number became no more than about 3 percent. If a serious challenger had emerged, that lost 3 percent would have loomed large. Nunn was convinced it was the right vote, but ten years later he was still receiving heated letters criticizing it. For twenty years or more, opponents continued to urge Congress to declare the treaties null and void. Some voters hold fast to their views even when their views are proven wrong—and that is their right. But they don't have the right to insist on their views to the exclusion of all others.

Senator Nunn has always believed Georgians to be eminently fair people. If he offered a rational explanation on controversial votes, most voters would understand, and, more importantly, he would be able to retain their trust. In the end, his rational, dispassionate approach to issues was a part of his nature that people admired most. In the fall of

---

[10] Sam Nunn, videotaped interview with the author, "Report to Georgia" (March 1978).

[11] Ibid.; McDonald, "Explain It Sam."

1978, the voters gave Senator Nunn an overwhelming vote of confidence with a renewal of his tenure in the Senate for another six years.

The passing years have proven the vote correct and in the best interest of the nation. The peaceful transition of control to Panama accrued to the benefit of the entire free world.

Issues May Change; Sam Nunn Does Not

I was not a member of Senator Nunn's staff when the Tower nomination was considered. Nor was I present when the controversial vote on the Gulf War Resolution took place. I would be remiss, however, if I did not include these two examples of his disciplined constancy on all serious issues.

John Tower Nomination in 1989

Shortly after his election, President George H. W. Bush wanted to make former senator John Tower (R-TX) his secretary of defense. The nomination came to the Senate for consideration soon after Bush took office. Sam Nunn believed a president should expect the Senate to confirm his cabinet picks *unless* testimony presented in the confirmation process proved overwhelmingly negative. As chairman of the Armed Services Committee, Senator Nunn was responsible for the floor debate surrounding the nomination, but first, he had to preside over hearings to examine the nominee. The testimony revealed that John Tower had a number of problems, among them possible conflicts of interest in his business dealings as well as a reputation as a womanizer and abuser of alcohol.

Near the end of the committee's deliberations, I was in Senator Nunn's office to discuss a separate matter. His secretary, Rose, asked me to wait in an outer office and speak with him when he arrived.

"You'll be surprised when he comes through that door," Rose Johnson said, pointing in the direction of the senator's private entrance.

A couple of minutes later, Nunn walked through the door and stumbled briefly as his shoe caught on the carpet. I was surprised—actually, shocked. "You've lost too much weight," I said, without thinking. "What's going on?"

He looked absolutely haggard. I hadn't seen him this far under his optimal weight since that period in the 1972 campaign when he was forced to drive himself and wasn't eating regularly. He had become very thin in '72, but never like this.

"Not getting much sleep these days." He pulled out his daily schedule for a quick scan and didn't even look up. I thought he was in a hurry and might walk straight into his office, where a group of Georgia teachers waited. He certainly didn't have time for me. He stopped and looked toward Rose, who was just getting off the phone. "Rose, this schedule stops at three o'clock; where's the rest of it?"

He still hadn't looked my way. "Sleep? You look like you're not getting *any*," I said. "I heard Dole has a name for anyone who opposes Tower—I think he calls them 'Nunn-Partisan.'"

Nunn didn't smile and he still didn't look up.

"I heard someone in the Senate chamber this morning suggesting that you want the job for yourself, that your opposition is that of a jealous man."

That did it. Nunn looked up. His baleful glare made me wish I could take back that comment. For a second, it appeared he had something to say on that one, but whatever it was, he thought better of it.

I didn't learn until Bob Schieffer's book, *This Just In.* was published in 2003 that President Bush had offered the job of secretary of defense to Nunn *before* it was offered to Tower. Nunn turned it down, preferring to stay in the Senate. The offer had been made in confidence, and Nunn, not known to break a confidence, wasn't about to start that particular day in 1989.

Rose handed him the missing schedule card. He took it without a word and put it in his vest pocket. "Let's see the phone list."

She handed him a clipboard with the names and numbers of people who had tried to reach him earlier in the day. After a quick scan, he checked the ones he wanted to return when he finished his meeting with the teachers in his office. The rest he would call later, perhaps from home.

As he checked off names on the clipboard, I decided to start over. "Why does Dole think you are playing politics with the nomination? You're not running for president. Surely, he knows that."

"He's trying to help his president," Nunn said, now shuffling through Rose's inbox. "Playing politics is not something I do. Nothing could be farther from my mind."

"I know that." *Dole has touched a nerve.* "We all know that."

"I don't have any major problems with Tower," Nunn said. "In fact, I wanted to support him, but now this." He held up papers he had been carrying when he came in. "It's an accumulation of facts. What people don't realize is that most of this stuff [stories of Tower's drinking and womanizing] came out before we got the FBI file."

Nunn and Tower had worked closely on a bipartisan basis on a number of issues, including setting up the Tower Commission in the fall of 1986 to investigate the Iran-Contra scandal. Their close working relationship went back to the Reagan years of increased defense spending. This had to be an awful time for Sam Nunn.

What else should I say? I don't think I'm helping a bit. And the more he talks, the more irritated he seems.

"And a lot of that has been in the press many times," I said.

"That's right," Nunn said, "and the other thing people don't realize is that many people come up and tell me firsthand experiences who can't testify—or won't testify. What do you do with that?" He turned and walked toward his office.

"I don't know," I said, but he didn't hear. He wasn't looking for an answer. All the questions raised he had asked himself many times.

And now he was shaking hands with the teachers in his office as if everything was fine in his world, and they were asking if they could take a picture with him. For the first time that day, I saw him smile, but it quickly disappeared when the camera was put away.

By that time, I had forgotten the purpose of my visit.

In March 1989, the Senate rejected Tower's nomination pretty much along party lines. The Senate was swayed by the FBI report with its damning material on alcohol abuse, concerns about Tower's conduct toward women, and possible conflicts of interest stemming from his consulting services.

"It was a very, very hard—a tough call," Senator Nunn told his staff after the vote. "Other than John Tower himself and his immediate family and very close friends, I think that whole episode was more painful to me than to anyone else in America."

Persian Gulf Resolution in 1991

Two years after the Tower nomination was settled, Senator Nunn created a whirlwind of controversy in Georgia when he chose not to support a Senate resolution declaring war against Iraq. He thought the allies should give economic sanctions against Iraq more time to work in order to break Iraq's will and prevent a costly conflict.

Some said he was being overly cautious and would pay dearly at the ballot box. Others, such as John Stuckey, chairman of the Georgia Republican Party at the time, claimed Nunn's vote was "calculated to make himself more attractive to the national Democratic Party"[12] in 1992 and beyond. Stuckey added, "It was...an unprincipled, liberal establishment vote [that] can't be explained away."[13]

In my view, it was none of that and easily explained. Actually, Sam Nunn was being typical Sam Nunn, practicing a philosophy that has always been a part of him: "You should only use military force when it is vital to your own interest and when there is no other reasonable alternative."[14] Nunn's "reasonable alternative" was to let sanctions work a while longer. "The secret," Nunn said, "is to find ways to settle international disputes and force rogues into a corner without wars."[15]

In the case of the 1991 Gulf conflict, Nunn worried about the number of casualties America might suffer, whether the alliance President Bush had put together would hold, and, importantly, he wondered if President Bush's team had given enough thought to what they would do when the conflict was over. "We would need to be as skillful in handling the aftermath as our military was skillful in fighting the war."[16]

---

[12] Ibid.; McDonald, "Explain It Sam."

[13] Ibid.

[14] Sam Nunn, transcript of interview, *Face the Nation*, CBS (17 March 1991).

[15] Ibid.; McDonald, "Explain It Sam."

[16] Ibid.

He had no doubt about the outcome of the conflict and said so. Even as he voted against the resolution, Senator Nunn warned Iraq's leader, Saddam Hussein, "not to misinterpret the debate or underestimate American resolve."[17]

As a former member of his staff, I was not surprised by his vote. The only thing that surprised me was why anyone who followed national security issues—from the president down—did not understand the rationale behind his vote. In my view, it was Sam Nunn being Sam Nunn: consistent, cautious, and exhaustive in his analysis while searching for a decision that would be in the long-term best interest of the United States.

The ruckus the vote raised in Georgia reminded me of a phone conversation I had with James Brady, press secretary to Ronald Reagan, shortly after Reagan's inauguration in 1981. I knew Brady well from his days as press secretary to Sen. Bill Roth (R-DE). "The President," Brady explained when I picked up the phone, "has just read that background paper on arms control that Senator Nunn sent over, and when he finished, Reagan's only comment was 'Damn, I wish he was one of us.'"

"Jim, don't look for a partisan view from Senator Nunn when it comes to defense and foreign policy issues," I said. "Not gonna' happen. He'll be with the president some of the time and against him the rest. Best that relationship remain as is."

---

[17] Statement to media following vote, 12 January 1991.

Chapter 14

A Legacy of Landmark Accomplishments

Many have tried for years to pigeonhole Sam Nunn under one ideology or another, and, generally, they've come away frustrated, because their efforts never succeed. An editorial writer at the *Rome News Tribune* got it right when, near the end of Senator Nunn's twenty-four years in the Senate, he wrote: "*Public events shift and change, but Sam Nunn keeps right on being Sam Nunn.*"[1] Nunn stands, as he always has, at the high point in the middle of the road, searching for like-minded individuals on his right or left who are willing to put their nation's interests above party.

Several legislative landmarks resulted from his desire to work with like-minded senators. All are notable; several are absolutely prescient in their success.

Goldwater-Nichols Defense Reorganization Act of 1986

In Barry Goldwater, Sam Nunn certainly found a kindred spirit. Ideologically, they were not even close, but they shared two common traits: a strong sense of personal integrity and a passion for placing the defense of their nation above all other priorities. They needed both qualities to succeed in their effort to reorganize the defense department in the early 1980s.

It is worth noting that Senator Nunn's grand-uncle, Rep. Carl Vinson, strongly opposed reorganizing DoD in the 1940s and 1950s, first, as ranking member, and later, as chairman of the House Armed Services Committee. He was certainly instrumental in the defeat of all reform initiatives. Even President Dwight D. Eisenhower was unable to punch through the Vinson barricade to implement reform. Thus, for

[1] "Nunn Being Nunn," editorial in *Rome-News Tribune* (2 June 1995) 3.

more than a generation, the Pentagon successfully defeated every attempt to seriously address meaningful reform of its operational and administrative functions.

Why was it so urgent for someone to try yet again? Wasn't the sheer might of American forces a sufficient deterrent to ill-considered aggression by our adversaries? Perhaps not. Consider the failed Bay of Pigs attempt to overthrow Castro in 1961, the failed rescue attempt of American diplomats held hostage in Iran in 1979, the Soviet invasion of Afghanistan in 1979, or the terrorist bombing in 1983 that killed 241 Marines in their Lebanon barracks. The need for some type of major reform was apparent to many, but few in Congress understood what reorganizing the Pentagon meant. It certainly was not going to be politically rewarding in the way building weapons systems and adding another military base were rewarding. Besides, the whole question was boring. Really boring. It was, therefore, the perfect task for Senator Nunn to embrace.

As for Vinson's position on defense reorganization, by the mid-1980s it might have evolved, but we'll never know for sure. I do know that Carl Vinson would have listened closely to his grand-nephew. Vinson taught Sam Nunn that no representative of America should ever put the defense of his country below any other priority. Vinson's view became Nunn's view on the first day he arrived in the Senate. And I believe Nunn's view on reorganizing the DoD would have become Vinson's view by 1986, when the reform legislation finally became law.

Goldwater and Nunn struggled mightily against entrenched bureaucratic self-interests in the military services, and it took them four and a half years of close hand-to-hand legislative combat to craft a bill that could pass both House and Senate and be accepted by the president. Nunn and Goldwater had a clear vision of how a unified military establishment would work, and they had the passion to bring it to fruition despite the considerable obstacles in their way. Some are surprised that Senator Nunn's name is nowhere in the title. While that is true, make no mistake; Senator Nunn was the Act's principal architect. Goldwater was chairman of the Senate Armed Services Committee and became a close working partner with Nunn on the bill's details. "While Goldwater kept the legislation on course and protected the project, the ranking Democrat

[Sam Nunn] zeroed in on more detailed analyses and solutions," Jim Locher wrote in *Victory on the Potomac,* the complete account of the defense reorganization initiative. Locher was the Armed Services Committee staff member who helped write the legislation. "Nunn's work would give full expression to the organization principles that he and Goldwater were formulating."[2]

Senator Nunn insisted that the bill carry the name of his colleague from Arizona. "Nunn's magnanimous gesture so pleased Goldwater that the crusty old man cried," Locher wrote. "Nunn set aside his own interest to ensure that Goldwater got the credit he deserved."[3]

Alabama Democrat Rep. William F. "Bill" Nichols was credited as coauthor of the bill and managed its passage in the House of Representatives. President Ronald Reagan signed the bill into law October 1, 1986, even as elements of the Pentagon refused to give up the fight and urged a presidential veto.

Here's what the Act changed: The Act stripped away multiple layers of military bureaucracy and laid the foundation for better interservice cooperation. The chairman of the Joint Chiefs of Staff became the principal military adviser to the president, and a vice-chairmanship of the Joint Chiefs of Staff was created. Most importantly, the Act gave more autonomy to the ten theater commanders based from Europe to the Pacific.

Pentagon resistance melted away when the Act proved its worth in the 1991 Persian Gulf War.

"It was a good-government issue with great upsides for the nation if successful and great downsides for the two senators if defeated,"[4] said Locher. But the Act was so successful that, according to Locher, "it became the 'gold standard' for all subsequent government reorganizations." Locher pointed out on several occasions that the 9/11 Commission recommended a Goldwater-Nichols Act for the entire intelligence community.

---

[2] James R. Locher III, *Victory on the Potomac: The Goldwater-Nichols Act Unifies the Pentagon* (College Station: Texas A&M University Press, 2002) 233.

[3] Ibid., 421.

[4] James R. Locher III, interview with author (9 November 2014).

Legislation initially reviled by the Pentagon was soon revered for its insightful analysis, and today it is considered to be the most comprehensive reorganization of the Department of Defense since the department was established by the National Security Act of 1947. The Act may well be the single most visionary contribution Sam Nunn made to America's national security during his entire Senate career.

Senator Nunn understood that to get things done in Washington, one needs only the desire to work closely with colleagues across the aisle and not worry about who gets the credit. That sentiment, perhaps, should be carved in stone near the entrance to the Capitol for all freshmen members of Congress to read before being sworn into office.

National and Community Service Act of 1990

Throughout his career, Senator Nunn talked about the need for young Americans to find ways to give back to their nation in voluntary or perhaps involuntary service. Ideas began to pop into his head as soon as the military draft was abandoned in favor of an All-Volunteer Force (AVF) in 1973. Nunn was opposed to the AVF, primarily because he wondered how young Americans, in the absence of military service, would understand the costs that had been paid by others for the freedoms they took for granted. If there was to be no draft, he wanted men and women to be given the opportunity to participate in preserving their freedom, and he began championing the idea of voluntary national service.

Nunn's idea, developed at the Democratic Leadership Council in the late 1980s, became the National Community Service Act of 1990, signed into law by President George H. W. Bush. First to be created were state pilot programs that operated under the name "Learn and Serve America." Participants received education grants in exchange for their service. President Clinton adopted the idea in his 1992 presidential campaign and urged the creation of the National Civilian Community Corps when he became president. Clinton's program was based on the Civilian Conservation Corps created during the Depression. In 1993, the program morphed into the National and Community Service Trust Act, which ultimately created AmeriCorps. President George W. Bush enhanced the program yet again in 2002 when he created the USA Freedom Corps, a program broad enough to help all Americans find opportunities to serve. President Obama took the program to the next level in 2009 by signing the Serve America Act, which reauthorized and expanded national service programs administered by the Corporation for National and Community Service.

The Cooperative Threat Reduction Act of 1991

Senator Nunn watched with the rest of the world as the former Soviet Union began to unravel in the summer of 1991. He knew better than most that the worst danger in a period of instability lay with control of the Soviet nuclear arsenal.

By August, hardliners staged a coup against President Mikhail Gorbachev and put him under house arrest. After several anxious days, a revolt led by Boris Yeltsin brought an end to the coup. Gorbachev was released and returned to the Kremlin. Nunn, in Moscow on an official trip at the time, met with Gorbachev in his Kremlin office and asked him directly if he had retained command and control of the Soviet nuclear forces during the coup attempt. "President Gorbachev did not answer, and that was answer enough for me," Nunn said. "It was unclear who held the nuclear launch codes to the Soviet nuclear arsenal during the period of his house arrest."[5]

Nunn returned home convinced that Congress had to do something quickly to help Soviet authorities maintain control over their nuclear weapons. He found an enthusiastic supporter in Richard Lugar (R-IN), who shared Nunn's commitment to reducing the threat from nuclear weapons.

But the hour was late on the legislative calendar—too late, their staffs said, to get anything done before adjournment for the year. Both defense authorization and appropriation bills had been passed and sent to conference to resolve their differences by September 1991. To get something passed so late seemed an impossible task. However, Les Aspin, chairman of the House Armed Services Committee, asked conferees to

[5] Sam Nunn, speech, "Moving Away from Doomsday and Other Dangers," National Press Club, 29 March 2001.

consider a humanitarian-aid package for the Soviet Union. Senator Nunn, chairman of the Senate Armed Services Committee, saw an opportunity to link Aspin's humanitarian-aid package with his concerns about weapons of mass destruction. Nunn and Lugar offered their proposal, bold as it was, only to see it rejected amid angry protests from some committee members. The Pentagon and the White House also let it be known they were cool to the idea. Nunn and Lugar were forced to withdraw the measure.

Undaunted, the duo organized a breakfast meeting and invited fifteen or twenty senators to hear Dr. Ash Carter of Harvard's Center for Science and International Affairs talk about a study he had just concluded on the Soviet Union's nuclear weapons. The study outlined in an analytical, scholarly format the dangers inherent in the command, control, and safety of nuclear weapons in an unstable Soviet Union.

Within a few weeks, legislation passed in the Senate and House that addressed concerns of Nunn, Lugar, and Aspin. Passed with little opposition, the measure provided $400 million for control of nuclear weapons and $100 million for humanitarian aid. The initiative, attached as an amendment to an unrelated bill, also contained language to provide help in finding employment for unemployed Soviet scientists and engineers.

President George H. W. Bush signed the bill in December 1991 and the Cooperative Threat Reduction Act became the law of the land. More than $10 billion was spent in the ensuing fifteen years to reduce the number of nuclear warheads in the world. Although very few Americans have heard of the Nunn-Lugar program, it is considered by many experts in the field to be the most important national security legislation to pass Congress in the past half century.

The Nunn-Lugar-Domenici Domestic Preparedness Initiative

Five years later, Senators Nunn and Lugar joined with Sen. Pete Domenici to put additional funding in the defense authorization bill to strengthen and expand the effort to prevent terrorist use of weapons of mass destruction on American soil. "Nunn-Lugar II," as some called it, provided $150 million to the Pentagon to begin coordinating a domestic defense against nuclear, chemical, and biological weapons that might be deployed by terrorists against American cities.

Two decades after Senator Nunn left the Senate, the Nunn-Lugar program had deactivated "more than 7,000 nuclear warheads, hundreds of missiles and bombers, and numerous elements of the former Soviet Union's WMD programs."[6]

Senator Nunn is fond of quoting from Gen. Omar Bradley's famous Armistice Day address of 1948. When Nunn addressed the graduating class of 1996 at Georgia Tech, he shared Bradley's warning with the graduates: "Ours is a world of nuclear giants and ethical infants. We know more about war than we know about peace, more about killing than we know about living."[7] The Bradley comment was not an idle insert in Senator Nunn's speech. Nunn followed the Bradley quote with his own conviction: "Science does not ensure that we will use our technology with wisdom and prudence. It does not address matters of the heart and soul. For those matters, men and women of the highest moral fiber and intellectual honesty are needed."[8]

---

[6] Sam Nunn and Richard Lugar, "There Are No Perfect Nuclear Deals," *Politico Magazine* (30 August 2015) is an op-ed column.

[7] General Omar N. Bradley, "An Armistice Day Address," delivered 10 November 1948. *The Collected Writings of General Omar N. Bradley: Articles, Broadcasts, and Statements, 1945–1967*, vol. 3 (GPO: 1967) 193.

[8] Sam Nunn, spring commencement, Georgia Institute of Technology (22 March 1996).

Chapter 15

That Vision Thing

The gift of being able to see beyond the horizon is just that, a gift, not a skill that can be developed or learned from another person. It is a gift outside the realm of human influence. Visionaries in public life are rare, even rarer than the obvious ones who appear periodically in science and technology. Steve Jobs and Ted Turner are modern examples of visionaries among us. I would count several of our Founding Fathers among them, including Benjamin Franklin, one of the first to perceive that the colonies did not have enough gunpowder to defeat the British. The colonists needed more—much more. As every student of the Revolutionary War learns, Franklin persuaded the French to supply the bulk of the gunpowder the Americans needed. For his efforts, he received little thanks, but that is often the case for visionaries who see a critical problem and commit to finding a solution, often before ordinary citizens become aware they even have a problem.

In the late 1970s, an excited Ted Turner stopped by Senator Nunn's office in Washington to discuss two issues: the FCC's "must carry" rule and his most passionate idea, a 24/7 news channel that would originate in Atlanta from the studios of his UHF television station.

He wanted to get the "must-carry" rule altered to allow cable systems nationwide to add his Atlanta "Super Station" to their systems. He had already persuaded a cable system in Montana to carry the baseball games of his Atlanta Braves. "The Braves have more fans in Montana than they do in Atlanta," Turner said, and slapped me on the back. "In time, we'll reverse that."

My ears really perked up when Turner turned to his idea for an all-news channel. I listened as he talked about leasing transponders on commercial satellites that could bounce his news channel from satellites to local cable systems around the country, and, eventually, the world. Major television networks were dependent in those days on hard-wired copper cable to distribute their evening news to affiliated stations. Turner's idea was to skip all currently accepted technology and go straight to satellites for news distribution. He had researched "subject specific" channels already on the air and discovered there was no all-news network. "The networks do a little news in the middle of the day and a few minutes more at six and eleven local time in the evening," he said. He thought there was a market for more information and said he was surprised the three major networks did not see the opportunity, too.

Turner readily admitted that most of the people who heard him describe his idea thought he was crazy, but he was not deterred. As he spoke that day in Senator Nunn's office, he became ever more animated. Periodically, he jumped up, threw his arms out, began pacing, and asked his attorney to take over with more details. While his attorney talked, Turner walked around the room, stopping abruptly to read every word on the twenty-three plaques on one wall, before moving on to the diplomas and other framed documents. Finally, there was a glass display cabinet filled with an assortment of mementoes and recognition gifts. Turner read every word on all of them. He was filled with so much energy he couldn't stop. Finally, he walked behind Senator Nunn's desk and began reading every word on every sheet of paper on his desk.

I'm sure there is nothing classified there but still....

I glanced at Senator Nunn. He tilted his head to one side and raised an eyebrow, as if to say, "Don't worry; that's Ted."

As his attorney continued, Turner turned to a wall of photos. There were individual pictures of Senator Nunn with Dean Rusk, Moshe Dayan, Anwar Sadat, and Menachem Begin, as well as Presidents Carter and Ford.

I was trying to listen to his attorney while all this was going on, and the closer I listened, the more farfetched the idea of a 24-hour news channel sounded. When Turner left, I told Senator Nunn I didn't think an all-news channel could succeed because, among other reasons, there wasn't enough news to occupy more than an hour or two of any day, much less a full twenty-four hours. It didn't occur to me that CNN would repeat the same news story over and over. "There would be no way to hold an audience that way," I said. "Surely, they'd soon become bored and switch to another channel."

Senator Nunn was not so quick to dismiss the idea.

When a visionary advances an idea for addressing a problem or issue, the worth of which can only be determined with the passage of time, the idea is often given short shrift by ordinary mortals. A short-term resolution of a problem is relatively easy to understand, even accept, but an idea to address an opportunity that is hidden itself is something else altogether. Consider the Panama Canal treaties, submitted for approval to the US Senate in early 1978. A short-term solution would have been to reject the treaties and appease constituents who opposed "giving it away." A long-term solution was more difficult to accept, especially if one could not see that its approval might free up American resources for other purposes in Latin America. In order to see that possibility, one must have the ability to see over the horizon and discern broader objectives. That is, indeed, a gift that few possess.

In the decade preceding World War II, Rep. Carl Vinson could see the need for a two-ocean Navy by a United States fast becoming a world leader on all fronts. From 1931 to 1947, Vinson was chair of the House Naval Affairs Committee, and from his leadership position, he pushed an ambitious program of shipbuilding that strengthened the US fleet in the years before anyone was imagining war with Japan. Vinson saw the need when others could not.

In Nunn's office, several of us laughed when Turner launched his news network in June 1980 proclaiming that CNN would be around until the world ends. I thought people would soon tire of continuous news, repeated over and over, but they did not. Indeed, each day brought increasing numbers of curious people to Turner's channel. When he hired seasoned journalist Daniel Schorr away from CBS, it suddenly became clear even to the most dubious observers that the new network was here to stay. "I have a sense that television news reporting will never be the same," Nunn said, "and I think that's exactly what Ted has in mind."

Vinson had vision. Ted Turner had it as well. And so did Carl Vinson's grand-nephew, Sam Nunn. His vision for improving national defense began with lessons learned as a young lawyer on the staff of the

House Armed Services Committee, a full decade before his election to the Senate.

From Senator Nunn's experience in Europe during the 1962 Cuban Missile Crisis, he could see a world in increasing danger from a growing arsenal of nuclear weapons kept on hair-trigger alert. One mistake, one errant blip on radar, could mark the end of our planet. Nunn had hard questions: "Under what conditions would it be likely to happen? What can we do to prevent such a cataclysmic human disaster?" His focus was always on tomorrow.

In examining Senator Nunn's full Senate record, one is struck by his consistent and unwavering labors to address the proliferation of nuclear weapons as well as chemical and biological weapons of mass destruction. From the start, the visionary in him began thinking of ways governments in the nuclear club around the world could reduce and ultimately eliminate the need to protect their homelands with weapons of such vast destruction.

In a 1982 Senate debate centered on cruise missile deployment, Senator Nunn proposed the establishment of a crisis control center to prevent the accidental exchange of nuclear missiles between America and the Soviet Union. Such a facility would have the capability "to address the question of how to prevent terrorists or third-world rogue nations from using nuclear weapons."[1]

Unfortunately, the idea for a crisis control center did not survive a final vote on the bill under consideration that year. But Nunn did not give up. In his view, the first priority of every president should be to make sure that nuclear, chemical, and biological weapons are safe, secure, and accounted for.

Senator Nunn's boldest step in reducing the spread of nuclear weapons was yet to come: establishment of the Nuclear Threat Initiative in 2001.

---

[1] Sam Nunn, videotaped remarks to network correspondents (23 March 1982).

Nuclear Threat Initiative (NTI)

Senator Nunn's visionary sense may have been the reason Ted Turner felt comfortable turning to him to discuss mutual concerns about national security. Turner was a keen observer of the work begun in 1991 by Senators Nunn and Lugar under the Cooperative Threat Reduction Act. The Nunn-Lugar program, as it was generally known, provided assistance for more than twenty years to Russia and the former Soviet republics for securing and destroying their excess nuclear, biological, and chemical weapons. The Nunn-Lugar program was also responsible for removing all strategic warheads from Kazakhstan, Ukraine, and Belarus.

In early 2000, Turner was shocked to learn from a *60 Minutes* report that both the United States and Russia still had thousands of nuclear weapons aimed at each other. He invited Senator Nunn to join him for breakfast in Atlanta and asked, "Sam, what can we do?" They spent six months exploring whether a nonprofit organization could be effective in reducing nuclear dangers.

Turner pledged $250 million in AOL-Time Warner stock to help Senators Nunn and Lugar create an organization dedicated to stopping the spread of nuclear weapons and related materials around the globe.

On January 8, 2001, Senator Nunn announced the creation of the Nuclear Threat Initiative (NTI) at a press conference at the National Press Club. On that January day, only eight months prior to the attack on Washington and the World Trade Center, Senator Nunn used words that had been a staple in his speeches on the floor of the Senate for years and in conversations with heads of state as well as national-security experts at every level: "As a nation, we have just begun to come to terms with the full scope of the terrorism threat."[2]

The announcement would have appeared on the front pages of major newspapers across America if the press conference had taken place nine months later, *after* September 11, 2001. At the January news conference, Nunn patiently explained that the terrorism threat was part of the larger danger that accompanies nuclear proliferation. He worried for

[2] Sam Nunn, speech to the Senate, *Congressional Record*, 142:238 (28 September 1996).

years that weapons of mass destruction might fall into the hands of foreign zealots who, "filled with hate for civil society," would use those weapons against us, "believing their conduct is justified or divinely inspired."[3]

When terrorists used hi-jacked airliners to attack America, the world began to pay attention to every word Nunn uttered on the threat of terrorists using weapons of mass destruction. In their first op-ed for *The Wall Street Journal*, Senator Nunn, Henry Kissinger, George Shultz, and William Perry penned a persuasive argument against the proliferation of nuclear weapons. "The peacekeeping value of nuclear weapons is more and more outweighed by the risk of their possible use."[4]

Americans should be grateful for the work the United States did to eliminate nuclear weapons from eastern Ukraine before the Russian invasion of 2014. Who knows what that part of the world would look like today if those weapons had been in place? Indeed, a complete reading of Sam Nunn's record in the Senate brings one sobering question to mind: how many wars have been avoided by the quiet but powerful impact of Sam Nunn's presence in the US Senate? There is no award or special recognition given for wars avoided, but there should be.

International Fuel Bank

One of NTI's key initiatives is its support for an international fuel bank that would allow nations to generate nuclear power without developing an independent nuclear weapons capability. Warren Buffett backed NTI's effort with a pledge of $50 million, and the International Atomic Energy Agency (IAEA) received an additional $100 million in two-to-one matching funds provided by the European Union, Kazakhstan, Kuwait, Norway, the United Arab Emirates, and the United States.

The nuclear fuel bank, owned and operated by the IAEA and located in Kazakhstan, will assure that countries with a need for nuclear fuel

---

[3] Ibid.

[4] Sam Nunn, Henry Kissinger, George Shultz, and William Perry, "A World Free of Nuclear Weapons," *The Wall Street Journal*, an op-ed column (4 January 2007).

to generate electricity will have a source for that fuel should there be an interruption in their supply.

In other words, countries generating power at nuclear power plants would have no need to develop an independent capability to produce low-enriched uranium. In an op-ed for the *The New York Times*, Senator Nunn wrote, "A world where more and more countries make their own nuclear fuel—and thus can also produce nuclear weapons materials—is a far more dangerous world, as we have seen from North Korea."[5] According to Nunn, more than thirty countries are exploring whether to build their first nuclear power plant. "These countries will import their fuel or make it themselves."[6]

The IAEA and Kazakhstan recently signed a Host State Agreement establishing the fuel bank in Kazakhstan. The agreement calls for the fuel bank to be operational in 2017.

The Vision and the Steps

NTI is the coordinating entity behind the work of Nunn, Shultz, Perry, and Kissinger as they seek to realize their vision of a world without nuclear weapons. The four statesmen have written a groundbreaking series of op-eds on this subject and have outlined ten steps to reduce nuclear dangers. In their first op-ed, they called for a "solid consensus for reversing reliance on nuclear weapons globally...and ultimately ending them as a threat to the world."[7]

"I believe the vision and the steps go together," Nunn said. "The way I like to express it is that we ought to make nuclear weapons less relevant and less important, prevent nuclear weapons or materials from getting into the hands of dangerous people, and eventually eliminate nuclear weapons as a threat to the world."[8]

---

[5] "Open a Nuclear Fuel Bank," op-ed by Sam Nunn, *The New York Times* (11 July 2014).

[6] Ibid.

[7] Ibid.; Nunn et al., "A World Free of Nuclear Weapons."

[8] Daryl G. Kimball and Miles A. Pomper, "A World Free of Nuclear Weapons: An Interview with Nuclear Threat initiative Co-Chairman Sam Nunn," *Arms Control Today*, Arms Control Association, Washington, DC (March 2008).

In the fall of 2015, Nunn quantified the progress that has been made in reducing the supply of nuclear fuel available for making weapons. "Twenty years ago there were fifty countries that had weapons-grade nuclear material and now there are twenty-five, so you can say we've made progress, but you can also say we have a long, long way to go."[9] Nunn shows no signs of giving up his pursuit of a world free of nuclear weapons and seems committed to that goal, no matter how long it takes. His experience in Europe in the middle of the Cuban Missile Crisis so long ago is writ large and indelibly in his memory.

[9] Michael Coleman, "Ex-Senator Continues Dogged Pursuit to Rid World of Nuclear Weapons," *Washington Diplomat* (30 September 2015).

Chapter 16

Running for President?

Someone, it seems, has always been talking about Senator Nunn running for president of the United States. As early as 1977, his Senate office began hearing from voters who wrote, "The wrong Georgian was elected president," a clear reference from unhappy constituents to President Carter's election in the fall of 1976. Nunn attempted to dismiss such talk but often added that he would never run for the presidency unless—and here's where he opened the door a bit—he concluded that he possessed the particular skills the nation needed at that moment in time and the constructive ideas needed to keep the Republic moving forward and secure.

The presidential bug didn't bite him at any time in his career in the same way the senatorial bug bit him in Perry, Georgia, in 1971. In other words, he had a raging bonfire in the belly for the Senate seat of Richard Russell, but there has never been even a flicker of warm flame taunting him to pursue the presidency. Nevertheless, it was tempting. I remember an instance in 1983 when a constituent caught Senator Nunn's appearance on Paul Duke's public television program, *The Lawmakers*. He called the next day to urge Senator Nunn to "run for president immediately." I sent Senator Nunn a memo to that effect, and he sent it back with a note at the bottom: "Raise the $20 million and then see me for further discussion."[1] I could imagine him smiling as he wrote the note.

The time was not right, and, I thought, there is a distinct possibility that time may never come.

In the fall of 1984, I had lunch at the 116 Club on Capitol Hill with my Georgia friend Powell Moore of Milledgeville. Powell was a former

---

[1] Personal memo in possession of the author (28 February 1983).

member of the Nixon legislative liaison team. Years before, he had been press secretary to Senator Russell, but that was before his "conversion" and gradual drift to the other side of the aisle.

The 116 Club, full of Southern ambience, has been described as a holdover tradition from the days when Southerners controlled the Senate through their chairmanships at the head of major committees. When Nunn arrived in Washington in the fall of 1972, Russell Long of Louisiana was chairman of the Finance Committee and John McClellan of Arkansas chaired Government Operations. Alabama's John Sparkman chaired the Banking Committee. Sam Ervin of North Carolina became a household name when he was named to chair the Senate Watergate Committee. Georgia's own Herman Talmadge led the Agriculture Committee, and the genteel Southern gentleman John Stennis chaired the Armed Services Committee. That's just a partial list of Senate leadership from the old Confederacy. Hardly anything got done in Washington that wasn't approved first by a Southern chairman. Maybe that's why the private 116 Club served the best Southern cuisine in town.

Powell and I were just getting into the banana pudding when he startled me with an outrageous comment: "Republicans are likely to hold the White House for the rest of this century and well into the next."

I put down my spoon. *He's not just seeking my reaction; he really believes that.*

Reagan had not completed his first term, and here was a former Democrat turned Republican proudly predicting the near permanent banishment of Democrats from national leadership. "Why do you say that?"

The waiter stopped by at that moment and Powell asked for another glass of tea. He didn't have to ask for sugar; they served only sweet tea, as anyone from the South would expect.

"Well, you saw what they did in San Francisco, didn't you? Mondale—of all people! Do you know anyone in Georgia who is going to vote for Mondale?"

"I am. I'm still registered there." I pushed the pudding around the bowl. "I don't think the pudding tastes the same as it used to."

"What have you got against Reagan?" he asked.

"Look, he's an affable fellow, and I'm sure I would enjoy meeting him. But when someone says I want you to vote for me because I believe in a smaller government and a balanced budget, I expect to see some movement on those issues." I motioned for the waiter to come over. "Ronald Reagan has not proposed one balanced budget since he arrived and doesn't seem likely to do so in the future. He has not cut the size of government by one excess federal employee. In fact, government has grown considerably since he arrived and is still growing. Anybody can talk it; Republicans never walk it, and that's my problem with them. I don't care what one's political leanings might be, but please stand for something besides empty rhetoric. One day, Republican loyalists are going to see through those empty promises, and they're going to vote Democrat or bolt their party."

Powell smiled. "They love Ronald Reagan and always will," he said.

"Are you saying all it takes to keep Republicans happy is a Hollywood actor willing to play the role of president? God help us if presidential politics ever becomes a contest between entertainers."

He ignored the question. "Not everybody is like your boss." Powell had heard me compare Reagan to Nunn before and was probably afraid I was about to launch into another lecture about the call to public service. "It's not as simple as you may think."

I raised my hand to get the waiter's attention. "Bring us some of Johnny's homemade peach ice cream, will you?" The waiter nodded.

"And two coffees," Powell said.

I waved off the offer of cream and sugar. "Look, we can talk about something else, if you like, but let me just say, I think you're wrong about Republican control of the White House for the rest of this century." I pretended to be stirring something in my coffee even though I hadn't added anything to it and didn't plan to. "But if your prediction comes true, America will be in a heap of trouble." I took a sip of Johnny's finest Sumatra coffee just as the peach ice cream arrived. "Everyone needs a partner at the dance. The two sides will always need each other."

When Senator Nunn and his three friends, Sen. Lawton Chiles, Gov. Chuck Robb, and Rep. Dick Gephardt, founded the Democratic Leadership Council (DLC) in 1985, they thought one of them surely would use the new organization to launch his own candidacy for president. But first they had to find a way to move the party closer to the middle of the ideological spectrum, or Powell Moore might turn out to be right. No Democrat was going to see the inside of the White House for a very long time if they were unsuccessful. That elusive political center was the goal of the DLC.

While Senator Nunn's energy was focused on making the DLC a success, others continued to hope he would join the race for president in 1988. By 1987, the stage was being readied for him. Some of the nation's best known political observers wrote flattering articles about him. James Barnes of *National Journal* polled twenty-two state Democratic Party chairs on their preferences. Twelve of them said someone not in the race would be more acceptable in their state: seven of them chose New York governor Mario Cuomo, six chose Georgia senator Sam Nunn, and two selected New Jersey senator Bill Bradley.[2] Nunn read all of the articles, usually smiled as he handed them to me, and went back to work at his day job.

I had many conversations with Senator Nunn about running for the presidency, most of them on the little tram that runs between the Senate office buildings and the Capitol. It was a good place to talk. The noise of the tram kept conversations confidential. Near the end of one of those brief discussions, he turned to me with the look of one who often finds his own thoughts amusing. "Can you see me in the East Room, dancing with Colleen?" He gave a sideways glance out of the corner of his eye to check my reaction. "Can you? Can you see us dancing after some state dinner?"

I thought about his question, frivolous, no doubt, but with a serious element in it. *What's the right answer here?* Honesty is best even though I wanted to say, "Yes, I can."

"No, I guess not," I said.

Senator Nunn stepped off the tram. "Neither can I," he said, smiling. "Neither can I."

---

[2] James A. Barnes, "Reluctant Bridegrooms," *National Journal* (20 June 1987): 1581.

Nunn's good friend, Sen. Lawton Chiles, walked up about that time, slapped him on the back, and the two of them walked into the Capitol. A few seconds later, they were laughing heartily.

He must have asked Chiles to imagine the dancing scene in the East Room.

I stayed on the tram for the return ride to the Dirksen building.

But the talk of his running never ceased as long as there was the slightest chance he might change his mind. Meanwhile, state legislatures in the South were doing their best to prepare the way for a Southerner to make a serious run. A single Tuesday in the spring was selected—a "Super Tuesday," they called it—when Southern states would hold simultaneous presidential primaries. It was designed to reduce the influence of the Iowa caucuses on the nominating process. In all, twenty-four states agreed to hold a Super Tuesday primary that year, the first ever in US history. It seemed custom-made for a moderate-to-centrist candidate such as Senator Nunn, who also had demonstrated appeal to the most conservative of the Democratic base. They liked his "tell it like it is" candor.

I entered the private sector in late summer of 1986 and was not around when the pressure for Senator Nunn to run was greatest, but I was constantly hearing from present and former staff who wanted him to run. Even Walter Mondale, the defeated 1984 nominee, was encouraging him to run in 1988. Mondale told friends that "the Democratic Party has drifted too far left and needs a 'good Southern component' to win in '88."[3] He was pushing Georgia's Sam Nunn. When it appeared Senator Nunn was beginning to waffle on the decision, I got a call from anxious staff members. Senator Nunn was home in Georgia at the time, and they wanted me to call him to find out what it would take to get him into the race. Nothing I could say would do that, I told them, but I reluctantly agreed to call him.

As I was walking to meet some of the staff prior to making the call, I ran into Sen. Chuck Robb of Virginia, who was also chairman of the Democratic Leadership Council. When I told him about my assignment, he said, "Go ahead and make the call. I've told Sam he's uniquely quali-

[3] "Periscope—Personal Factors," *Newsweek* (3 August 1987): 6.

fied to lead the country right now. You want me to go with you and tell him again?"

"No, not necessary," I said. "Any other advice?"

"Yes, tell him if he can't make a decision now, at least keep the door open."

Senator Robb was really no help that day. He was repeating the same advice close friends were giving Senator Nunn in face-to-face conversations. I resisted making the call as long as I could because I knew he didn't need another call on the subject, least of all from me. He knew my view, and I understood his; there was no need for us to talk about this subject. But I made the call anyway. He picked up right away. I didn't call often, and when I did, it usually meant, "We have a problem." On that day, we talked briefly, and his words reaffirmed the conclusion I had reached by the time I left his staff more than a year earlier: he was happy in the Senate and felt he had more work to do before he closed that chapter. That was the sum of it. And I was fine with that.

"This is the opposite of '72, isn't it?" I said into a quiet phone.

More silence.

"Yes," he said at last, with no energy in his voice.

He knew I was one of only a handful who understood what that meant. In 1972, hardly anyone was advising him to run for the US Senate. But *he* burned for the job. He wanted the Senate seat more than anything. In 1987, it seemed *everyone* was clamoring for him to run for president, but he did not have the requisite burning drive for the race.

Why are we having this conversation? I wondered.

I tried to lighten up the conversation before closing. "Probably feels more like heartburn than ambition, doesn't it?"

He chuckled, and that was the end of our discussion. The staff was totally deflated when I related the conversation to them.

A few days later, he called a press conference in Atlanta to announce his decision not to run. I stood in the back of the room, listening first to his announcement, then as he answered a few questions.

"The window and door are closed," Senator Nunn said, in response to one question. "The chance of winning was there. I do believe it was possible for someone of my philosophy to win, and that made the decision not to run that much harder."[4]

In a best-case scenario, he might have been able to run the table in the South on Super Tuesday, or nearly so, but the question remained, what about the other thirty-nine states. He had addressed that question carefully, exhaustively, in his own mind, and his conclusion was the same as it had been that day we talked on the tram. America will never see an image of President Nunn dancing with First Lady Colleen Nunn in the East Room. And we will all be the poorer.

When the press conference was over, the two of us got into his car and began a two-hour drive from Atlanta to the small house on Lake Burton that he and Colleen had recently purchased. He needed some time to decompress, and the house on Lake Burton was the ideal spot. Several current and former staff members were invited to join us that night for dinner and a review of the day's events.

Since we were the first to depart Atlanta, Nunn and I agreed to pick up something along the way for all to share at dinner. For a while, neither of us said a word as we drove up I-85 toward Gainesville. When we passed the infamous "spaghetti junction," I decided to break the silence. "Well," I said, "maybe another time, a better time."

A long silence followed. At least five miles later, he said, in a quiet, even tone with a note of finality in it, "No...this was my time. There will be no better time."

More silence.

Neither of us said another word until we pulled into a Golden Pantry about 60 miles down the road. Inside, a man in overalls, flannel shirt, and John Deere baseball cap spied Senator Nunn poking around the freezer section. He stepped back a moment until he was sure he had identified his US Senator, then took a step forward and stuck out his hand. "Hey, I'm with you, man!"

Senator Nunn smiled and shook his hand. "Thanks." Nunn looked at me as we walked out. "Guess he hasn't seen the news tonight."

---

[4] Michelle Cohen, "Nunn Won't Seek Presidency," *Sun Sentinel* (28 August 1987).

Later that evening, as all of us sat on the dock overlooking Lake Burton, I thought about the town of Burton, once the second largest in Rabun County, now located at the bottom of the lake where it's been since Georgia Power flooded the little town in 1919. None of us said much because we all felt lower than the town of Burton that night.

I've always thought there was another factor that had a powerful influence on Nunn's decision not to run for president, one that most people failed to see even though it should have been obvious to any who knew him very long. Control of the Senate had changed hands in the fall elections of 1986. Democrats were now in control after a six-year hiatus, and Senator Nunn was the new chairman of the Senate Armed Services Committee. In 1972, while campaigning for the Russell seat, he promised Georgia voters that he hoped the day would come when he could step into Russell's role as chairman of this committee. He was completely enamored of the legislative process, and he was exactly where he said he wanted to be from the beginning.

Political cartoons on the wall of his Capitol office were a reminder to his guests of the many times pundits thought he might run for president or join someone's ticket. Many of the cartoons were drawn by Clifford Baldowski, or "Baldy," as he was known to readers of the Atlanta newspapers. One depicted Senator Nunn in a bathing suit standing near a pool with a single toe in the water as if testing the political waters. Another showed him lolling around a starting line while other candidates were already in position for the race.

"To speculate about the presidency with Sam Nunn is to miss the point of his career," said Dr. Thomas Mann, senior fellow at the Brookings Institution. "He's made a choice...a choice to stay out of presidential politics. It was probably a good choice. It was good for him. It was certainly good for the Senate."[5]

And, in my view, his choice was certainly good for Georgia.

But as long as Sam Nunn was in the Senate, the speculation never stopped. Again, the pressure to run was keenly felt in 1991. And in 1999, observers thought he'd make a good running mate for Al Gore. By 2007,

---

[5] Ibid., McDonald, "Explain It, Sam."

the drums were beating yet again, but this time, they urged him to run as an independent.

Consensus in Oklahoma

At a pre-legislative forum in 1974, a Statesboro voter asked Senator Nunn to explain why the parties did not get along and why they couldn't seem to work with the president. It's a question that could have been asked yesterday. "The purpose of the two parties and the government in general is to serve the people—all of the people," Nunn said. "Congress needs to display the kind of compromising attitude and constructive criticism that will help us work together, and with the president. He cannot solve all our problems alone. Cooperation is absolutely essential."[6] Sam Nunn talked about the need for bipartisanship on his first day in the Senate and whenever he had the opportunity. He talked about the need for a bipartisan approach to issues almost as much as his fellow Georgian Newt Gingrich talked about never compromising.

Thirty-four years after his appearance at that pre-legislative forum, former senators Nunn and David Boren (R-OK) hosted a bipartisan forum on the campus of the University of Oklahoma. Boren was president of OU in 2008. I tagged along to provide whatever assistance might be needed in crafting a statement for the media. Fifteen participants were invited to attend—mostly current or former members of Congress. There were six Republicans, four Democrats, and the rest were mostly unelected officials from the private sector or academia. They gathered for a two-day forum to "exchange ideas in the spirit of bipartisanship, and challenge the major contenders for president in 2008 to spell out their plans for forming a government of national unity, a government that will end the gridlock in Washington that has polarized our nation."[7] To say the least, it was an ambitious goal.

The group convened as soon as all participants arrived at President Boren's home, Sunday afternoon, January 6, 2008. It was a members-only meeting, so I went to dinner with a small group of OU staff, return-

[6] Pre-Legislative Forum, Statesboro, GA, transcribed audio recording (August 1974).

[7] Sam Nunn, public statement to media (7 January 2008).

ing around 11 P.M. The principals were still at it. Senator Nunn stepped out briefly and motioned to me. "Come in," he said. "We're wordsmithing the final statement."

As I entered the room, I heard one of the group say, "I believe many members [of Congress] don't work together because they're afraid something good might come from it and their political opponents will get the credit." The others chuckled in acknowledgement of the truth. I don't remember who made the statement, but I wrote it down because it captured perfectly one of the reasons why Washington is so rigidly dysfunctional. I thought about Senator Nunn's successes. You can, indeed, get a lot done if you don't care who gets the credit.[8]

The hour was late. Most of the participants soon excused themselves and departed for their overnight accommodations. David Boren, Sam Nunn, Susan Eisenhower, former governor Angus King of Maine, and I were the only participants still working on the draft statement. As we were about to move to Boren's small upstairs office, somewhere in the house, Westminster chimes marked 12:30 A.M.

I am absolutely too old to do this anymore.

"Bipartisanship shouldn't be so hard," Senator Nunn said to Governor King as we walked up the stairs. "I can't think of a single major legislative accomplishment in my twenty-four Senate years that didn't include working with a member from the other side of the aisle."

I smiled and remembered how much his nonpartisan approach to drafting legislation perturbed and sometimes frustrated his Democratic colleagues. The only ingredient in the legislative process today that was not there years ago is the unceasing echo of opinion from conservative and liberal media, usually expressing extreme views, feeding the idea that government is not working when both sides of an issue can't get on one page—*their* page. As a result, the American people have difficulty sorting through all the voices and tend to believe only what they hear loudest and most often. Unfortunately, this leads to further polarization of the electorate, which, in turn, is reflected in their representatives. The result: Senators and Representatives become increasingly intractable in their

---

[8] See appendix for a partial list of legislation passed by Senator Nunn with bipartisan assistance of Republican colleagues.

positions and unwilling to consider other points of view. Senator Nunn and his Oklahoma forum participants were trying to find a way to stimulate needed change.

Did the hall clock just strike one o'clock? I wasn't expecting that sound so soon. One political forum will not be enough. The American people will have to help if they expect a change—ever.

Participants in the Oklahoma forum also wondered if any one of them might have what it took in 2008 to win the presidency as an independent candidate. If the time was right for an independent, who among them should pick up the independent standard? Body language seemed to suggest that mutual assessments were taking place among the participants over the course of the entire two-day meeting. But there were no takers.

Later that year, Jonathan Alter wrote one of the last pieces about a potential Nunn candidacy when he suggested Nunn would make a perfect vice president on Barack Obama's ticket. "A foreign policy heavyweight," wrote Alter, in describing Nunn's credentials. "Nunn's foreign policy experience, unquestioned intelligence, and big thinking assure that he does qualify under Obama's criteria for a 'plausible president.'"[9] Despite Alter's glowing recommendation, Obama never asked. Perhaps he was aware of the scope of Senator Nunn's considerable influence and did not want to diminish it by forcing him into an unacceptably narrow partisan position.

[9] Jonathan Alter, "Why Obama Should Pick Sam Nunn for Veep," *Newsweek* web exclusive, 3 July 2008.

Chapter 17

A Confiscated Label

Prior to the 1960s, the Georgia Democratic Party had always been neatly divided into two general governing philosophies: the conservative side of the party supported the county-unit system and white supremacy; the other was more racially moderate and economically progressive. This bifactional arrangement made the Democratic Party a stable political force for generations and made a two-party system unnecessary in the view of governing leaders, who were mostly conservative and white.

Georgia functions under a similar system today but governs under a Republican banner. It doesn't take a genius to figure out that there has been no dramatic change in political philosophy in the state, but Georgia has experienced a dramatic shift in political affiliation.

Why would conservative Democrats become conservative Republicans? The Republican Party in Georgia had been ignored, and, indeed, held in contempt, since the Civil War—and for good reason, according to the "Hell, no, we ain't fergettin'" crowd. There would be no reason to switch allegiance unless some external force was responsible for moving the political pendulum.

Impact of External Forces

Political scientists have suggested that the passage of the Civil Rights Act of 1964 initiated movement to the Republican Party. In my view, it is more likely that the shifting began two years earlier when a federal court ruled the county-unit system unconstitutional. Reapportionment would be based, henceforth, on population—the one person-one vote principle. Prior to the court's decision, disproportionate weight was given to the rural counties in the state, a political condition that kept white segregationists securely in charge of state government.

The court's ruling came just months before the Georgia gubernatorial primary in 1962. When the first statewide primary under the new rules was held that year, Atlanta attorney Carl Sanders, who favored racial moderation and economic progress, emerged the victor, defeating Marvin Griffin of Bainbridge. Segregationist Griffin had little chance for a statewide win once the county-unit system was abolished.

Democrat Sanders won in 1962 with a mix of urban white and statewide black support, and a new day in Georgia politics was born. Many conservatives decided it was time to learn how to spell "Republican."

The Civil Rights Act of 1964 and the Voting Rights Act of 1965 provided additional impetus for switching party affiliation. For conservative Democrats who still needed a reason to change parties, Sen. Barry Goldwater's race for the presidency in 1964 came at the best possible time. His staunchly conservative approach was just what they were looking for, and, thus, Goldwater became the first Republican presidential nominee to carry the state. Georgians loved his states' rights position. Incredibly, Goldwater's 9-point victory in Georgia came just four years after John F. Kennedy had carried the state handily. The established political order had been dealt a body blow in the four years that transpired between 1960 and 1964.

Howard "Bo" Callaway of Pine Mountain, a converted Democrat, was elected to Congress as a Republican the same year that Barry Goldwater carried the state in the presidential race. The next morning, voters in rural areas smiled and winked at each other. Maybe this change was going to be all right.

The fortunes of both parties continued to modulate up and down for a while. In the presidential race of 1968, Gov. George Wallace carried Georgia, as rural, small-town whites flexed their political muscle. Former vice president Richard Nixon came in second, and Vice President Hubert Humphrey, third. Hard-core Yellow Dog Democrats had a right to be nervous.

By 1972, rural white voters joined suburban whites to help Richard Nixon carry the state with a whopping 75 percent of the vote. Indeed, Georgia was second only to Mississippi in the percent of the vote given to the Republican president for his reelection.

Many Democrats voted against their own nominee, Sen. George McGovern. As they left the voting booth, they hoped the Hubert Humphrey, George McGovern days were behind their party. Rural whites were glad that Sam Nunn had not "thrown in with those liberals" and felt comfortable supporting him in 1972.

Georgia Democratic leaders were convinced there was no reason to panic because Democrats occupied both seats in the US Senate as well as nine of the ten congressional seats. Deniers of the political shift were quick to point out that Republicans recorded no gains in the Georgia General Assembly in 1972. Democratic control of state government appeared safe.

And it was safe—for a short while, a very short while.

Democratic governor Jimmy Carter carried Georgia twice in his campaigns for president, 1976 and 1980. I remember concluding that Georgia was moving beyond its days of racially divisive politics when Jimmy Carter invited the Reverend Martin Luther King Sr. to close the 1976 Democratic Convention with a benediction. In so doing, the senior King bestowed his blessing on the first white Democratic presidential nominee from the Old South. Political life will be different, I thought, but at least it will be a Democrat leading the way. I was wrong.

President Carter's election only accelerated white migration from the blue to the red side of the ballot. If it hadn't been for Georgia pride in having a native son at the top of the ticket in 1976 and 1980, the Republican nominee for president no doubt would have carried the state both years. In 1976 and 1980, old-fashioned pride trumped Carter's low-to-moderate popularity in the state.

But why become a Republican? Why not just declare yourself an Independent? Why associate yourself with a political party that agreed with Richard Nixon's liberal idea of creating a new agency of government to protect the environment (the EPA) or Nelson Rockefeller's idea of raising taxes if necessary to balance the federal budget? Or the socially liberal views of New York Republican Jacob Javits? Surely their ideas were anathema to those switching their allegiance in Georgia. But it was too late to ask such questions. There was a party label to be confiscated in the name of preserving, if possible, "the way things were, the way things had always been, the way God meant for things to be."

And Then There Was Newt

A little background is in order. I knew very little about the future speaker of the US House of Representatives in early 1972 when he invited Sam Nunn to West Georgia College in Carrollton to meet some of his political-science students. Nunn's race had not officially begun when the invitation came. We were still feeling our way and exposure to a classroom of college students sounded like a good idea. My memory of that event is that Gingrich—in favor of legalizing marijuana in his liberal days—got a reporter from the school newspaper to stop Nunn as he was leaving the campus to ask if he believed marijuana should be legalized. Nunn did not bite.

Nice try, professor, I thought. *Nice try, but no hashish.*

A number of thoughts ran through my mind as we got into the car for the return drive to Perry. *This guy is persuasive, yes, and manipulative...not for us.* Over the years, I never had a reason to change my initial assessment.

The unsettled state of political affairs in Georgia in the 1970s became a springboard to the Congress for the college history professor.

Gingrich was sworn in January 3, 1979, and at that moment, the National Republican Party began an inexorable descent into political expediency that weakened the national party (as seen in the government shut-down of 1995) and opened the door for extremists within its ranks to push it farther and farther to the right over succeeding years. Gingrich preached an ideology that called for political purity. "We will not compromise," he shouted on the western steps of the US Capitol as he introduced his "Contract with America" in 1995. His was welcome rhetoric to the ears of a growing number of former Democrats, now Republicans, in Georgia and throughout the South. Emboldened by his proclamations, many of his right-leaning supporters evolved into the Tea Party. They became partisans willing to ride over the leadership of their own party, if necessary, to achieve their ends.

By 1980, Georgians could admit openly to voting for Republican candidates without fear of being ostracized from Thanksgiving and Christmas family gatherings. In other words, "Republican" was no longer "the name which shall not be spoken," to borrow author J. K. Rowling's phrase to describe Harry Potter's nemesis.

Two years later, one of my six South Georgia sisters called as the 1980 general election approached. Talmadge was up for reelection but was feeling the heat from his opponent, an office-supply salesman from St. Simons. "I'm not going to vote for Herman Talmadge," she said. "Even though you say I ought to, I just can't; I don't agree with the way he's conducted himself of late. By the way, what do you know about this fellow Mattingly? I'm definitely going to vote for him—but I don't know anything about him."

I called Gordon Roberts, press secretary to Senator Talmadge, and informed him that based on my unofficial political barometer (my sister), voter sentiment was turning anti-Talmadge. "If good Democrats like my sister are switching long-held allegiances," I told him, "anything can happen in the voting booth this year, and it's not going to be pretty."

Roberts waved me off with, "Don't worry; Talmadge has this."

He didn't.

If my sister, a longtime Democrat, had made the switch, I was convinced 1980 was going to be a bad year for Democrats.

It was.

The result of the Mattingly-Talmadge race was so close the outcome wasn't known until the following morning. Mack Mattingly defeated one of the oldest names in Georgia politics. And with Talmadge's defeat, Democrats had lost control of the US Senate.

Along came the 1984 Democratic National Convention in San Francisco. Walter Mondale and Geraldine Ferraro were nominated, and almost immediately, even more conservative Georgia Democrats switched to the GOP.

The Democratic Leadership Council (DLC) was conceived during that convention when Senator Nunn, sitting in the back of the convention hall with his friends Sen. Lawton Chiles of Florida, Gov. Chuck Robb of Virginia, and Rep. Dick Gephardt of Missouri decided their party had swung too far to the left and a course correction was in order. Democrats went on to lose forty-nine of fifty states to Ronald Reagan that year. A course correction suddenly became critical for Democrats.

A few weeks after the decision was made to establish the DLC, Democratic National Committee chairman Paul Kirk visited Senator Nunn. I sat in on part of their luncheon discussion in Senator Nunn's Capitol office and heard Kirk plead with him not to go forward with the DLC idea. Kirk never smiled during the entire meeting. He was there to convince Nunn that he was already working to bring the national party back to the center. "I just need a little more time," Kirk assured Nunn. His assurances weren't good enough to dissuade Senator Nunn, and the DLC was established in 1985. Al From, for many years a close adviser to Rep. Dick Gephardt, was chosen to lead the new organization. The first national candidate to benefit from the DLC's work turned out to be not one of the DLC's founders, but Arkansas governor Bill Clinton, who successfully ran in 1992 on many of the centrist positions advanced by the DLC.

Meanwhile, Georgians continued their drift toward the Republican Party. Over a period of twenty years at the end of the twentieth century, Republican voting percentages grew with each passing election. Some political observers believe the chaotic Democratic Convention of 1968 marked the beginning of the national shift of Southern Democrats and Democratic leaning independents to the Republican side of the aisle. Bill Moyers, former press secretary to President Lyndon Johnson, wrote that Johnson, after signing the Civil Rights Act of 1964, "had more or less given up on the South."[1]

Johnson hastened the Southern political shift with his signing of civil rights legislation, but other factors were at work as well. McGovern's anti-war stance in 1972 and Mondale's left-leaning agenda in 1984 certainly played key roles. By the time Tennessee's Al Gore ran for president in 2000, the Democrat label was so tarnished in the South that he couldn't even carry his home state.

Nunn and his campaign staff witnessed the beginnings of a Southern political shift from front-row seats in 1972. Republican congressman

[1] Bill Moyers, *Moyers on Democracy* (New York: Doubleday, 2008) 117. (Note: President Johnson, upon signing the Civil Rights Act, was reported to have said, "I think we have just lost the South," but that is not the quote Moyers remembers and the correct quote is reflected here.)

Fletcher Thompson got 48 percent of the vote on Election Day. No Republican had previously done as well statewide since Reconstruction. Thompson, a weak candidate, had done better than many expected. That should have been a credible harbinger of things to come.

Save the Last Dance for Me

At first, Republican victories in Georgia statewide races were few and far between. As a lifelong Democrat, I found it hard to believe Georgians would abandon the party that brought them to the dance. If they were unhappy, I assumed they would work within their party to make changes. Abandon the party that brought them Social Security, rural electrification, the GI bill, tobacco subsidies, and Medicare—all of which were important to the Georgia electorate? It seemed unlikely to a Yellow Dog Democrat like me.

While Democrats pondered the question, Republicans continued their gains, gradually picking up more seats in the state legislature. As a party, they were becoming increasingly more partisan, much of that due to the "no compromise" stance of their new hero, Newt Gingrich. And there was one new factor: Fox News Channel went on the air in October 1996. Conservative voters now had a "home" where they could find news and opinion that reinforced their views. I didn't realize how partisan the average Republican had become until one Sunday in late 1997. We welcomed several new members in church that Sunday morning. One of them was identified to me as a person who liked to "talk politics." I introduced myself and asked, "So, do you consider yourself a Democrat or a Republican?"

He glared at me, grabbed his lapel, and pushed his lapel pin into my face. "Republican, of course," he said, his face fast turning crimson. "Don't you see my flag?!" He was wearing one of those American flag lapel pins that politicians have worn for at least a hundred years.

"Sorry," I said, "I didn't know Republicans had bought the flag, too."

He turned and walked away as soon as he concluded I was—you know—"one of those moderates." I confess I saw plenty of people wearing an American flag stickpin in their lapels in those days but never concluded that little pin had become a secret way for Republicans to recognize each other.

And why is he so angry? I saw him at church several times after that day but he never spoke or even made eye contact.

In Georgia, Republicans were flexing their muscle. Republican US Senator Paul Coverdell ran unopposed in 1998. Democratic fortunes were, indeed, in the tank. That same year, Republicans captured several statewide offices: state school superintendent, insurance commissioner, and public service commissioner.

Republican momentum hit one speed bump in the gubernatorial race of 1998 when Democrat Roy Barnes, a lawyer from Cobb County, won the race by 52 to 44 percent. Barnes previously served in the state Senate and House and had run for governor unsuccessfully in the 1990 Democratic primary. There was enough evidence of Democratic life in the election of 1998 to allow some to speculate the dance wasn't completely finished.

The Dance Is Definitely Over

The total swing from Democrat to Republican control of Georgia government took twenty-five years to complete, plus two transition years, 2003 to 2004. Since 2004, Republicans have held a majority in both chambers of the state legislature and occupied the governor's office.

By 2013, Democrats were down to eighteen seats in the state Senate while Republicans enjoyed a majority of thirty-eight seats. In the statehouse, Republicans held 119 seats and Democrats, sixty. The political strength of the two parties had been completely reversed in less than a generation. Bi-factionalism was back. Its name was Republican.

In the forty years since Sam Nunn's first election to the United States Senate, both senators, once Democrats, were now Republicans, and of the fourteen congressional seats, only five remained in Democratic hands. After the 2014 mid-term elections, only four of Georgia's fourteen congressional seats were held by Democrats.

I watched the votes being counted in 2014 from my Northern Virginia home and recalled a brief conversation I had with the Speaker of the Georgia House, Tom Murphy, thirty-three years earlier. The 1980 census numbers had been released a few weeks before I walked into his office in the state capitol. Speaker Murphy was chewing the end of a cigar and studying a large map he had spread across his desk.

"I think we'll just carve out a safe district for Newt," he said, turning his cigar over and over. "That should keep him happy." Gingrich had just won reelection to his second term in Congress. "What do you think?"

I shook my head. "It'll be like giving a shot of whiskey to an alcoholic, Mr. Speaker, and expecting the alcoholic not to want another. He'll be back. Newt wants more. Make no mistake about it, much more."

"Well, he won't get it, not so long as I'm the Speaker, that's for damn sure."

"But a safe seat—forever?" I said. "I don't think it's supposed to work that way, Mr. Speaker."

He gave me a look that said, "Son, did you just fall off a turnip truck?"

Someone appeared at the entrance to his office and the Speaker waved him in. "Come on in; we're through."

The Speaker seemed glad for the interruption. Nevertheless, I tried again. "Mr. Speaker, Newt won't be happy with that arrangement, but more importantly, it's not democratic." The Speaker was tired of the conversation and just shook his head. He was an intensely loyal man and simply trying to find a way to protect as many Democratic members of the delegation as he could. I don't think he realized he was already too late.

"You'll be the last Democrat in the state of Georgia"

In 1987, less than a year after I left Senator Nunn's office, Reagan advisor Haley Barbour, just out of the White House political affairs office, joined two former Hill staffers and me, already ensconced in the Watergate office complex, to offer public affairs counseling to clients. Our informal group consisted of two Republicans and two Democrats. Each had his own client base, but we also joined forces for a couple of clients.

I remember distinctly the day Haley walked into my office and encouraged me to renounce my Democratic ties and join the Republican

Party. "Everybody in the South is doing it," he said. "It's where you belong."

"No, I don't," I told him. "Democrats are not Republicans. I've seen the two parties in action, up close. Democrats propose solutions to problems; Republicans repeat the same empty ideas they have repeated over and over for decades, the only occasional changes occurring when they nuance their stale positions in order to win elections. Why would I want to go there?"

Haley didn't hear what I said about the difference between the two major parties. He focused only on my first three words. "Well, you'll be the last Democrat left in the state of Georgia," he said and abruptly walked away.

"There might be something else at play, Haley." I called after him. "Any idea what that might be?" But he was out of earshot.

Just as well. We don't need to get into that today.

Haley went on to lead the Republican Party as its national chair and, still later, he served as governor of Mississippi. He was a brilliant political strategist, indeed, as good as any I ever met. Haley had more to do with shaping the "new" Republican Party in the South than anyone I know. Not even Newt Gingrich had more influence, in spite of his influential position as Speaker in the US House of Representatives.

It took a while, but Haley Barbour's late 1980s prediction was not far off base. By the end of the millennium, I was feeling pretty lonely walking around in my New Deal shoes, believing government has a legitimate and wide-ranging role to play in serving the people who established it and sent their hard-earned tax money to support it.

Georgia voters had learned the world would not come to an end if they voted Republican, so they did—again—in the 2014 US Senate race that pitted Republican businessman David Perdue against Democrat Michelle Nunn, the senator's daughter and CEO of the nonprofit Points of Light organization. Remaining Democrats—no matter how passionate their support for Michelle Nunn—were too few to overcome the red tide. That was regrettable. Voters who met Michelle Nunn during her Senate campaign understood after a few minutes that she was made of the same tough mettle, and possessed the same skills for bringing people together, as her father.

But it was too late. Georgians were satisfied with their new party affiliation, for the most part, and didn't care to give Michelle a good look. As I listened to Republicans on my occasional visits to Georgia, I realized that many didn't know anything about Michelle and didn't care to learn out of fear that they might be persuaded she was a better choice. It is my fervent hope that Georgians will not miss the next opportunity to choose someone of Michelle Nunn's caliber to represent them. For if there is a servant leader in our state today in the mold of Rep. Carl Vinson and Sen. Sam Nunn, it is surely Michelle Nunn.

Very Much Like Today—Only Better

People often ask me why our political system is so messy. Why can't elected officials just get along and work together? It's the same question asked of Senator Nunn at the Statesboro pre-legislative forum in 1974, and mentioned earlier here. My response: dictatorships can be unbending and quite orderly in their efficiency even as they suppress the basic freedoms of the people. Democracies are, by definition, messy, especially when their leaders work to reach consensus while attempting to serve the best interests of the electorate. "Messy" doesn't make them weak. On the contrary, diverse points of view at every level make democracies strong. Majorities rule and minority interests are protected, and both sides work collaboratively to arrive at consensus to move the country forward. In a representative democracy, not everyone is going to be happy with every outcome. And when citizens are unhappy, they complain. Congress was made to be a target for those complaints—and it serves that purpose very well. Senate Majority Leader Mike Mansfield made that point in a conversation with Sam Nunn not long after we arrived in Washington. I can personally attest to the fact that unhappy people write more letters and make more phone calls than people who are satisfied with the way their government is functioning. If I worked on the Hill today, I'm sure I would be adding social media to the list of means voters employ to lodge their dissatisfaction with government.

I enjoy talking politics with my Democrat-turned-Republican friends in Georgia. Our conversations, however, come to a cold stop when I say something like, "You do realize we will soon have a Hispanic president, don't you?" Or "In the near future, Georgia is likely to elect a governor who is female and Latino." My Republican friends usually fall silent for a long time because, in spite of their public denials, they understand the trends in census data. There will be no going back in time no matter how hard they wish for it. The number of Hispanic residents in Georgia has nearly doubled in the past decade while the number of whites, as a percentage of the vote, has declined. These new Republicans know that the growing number of minorities in Georgia tend to lean progressive. The very suggestion that Georgia may become a "purple" state that could vote either way is enough to threaten cardiac arrest in many of my Republican friends. They refuse to allow themselves to imagine what the world will be like under those conditions. "Chances are," I tell them, "the world will be very much like today—only better."

Epilogue

When Sam Nunn is asked what he would change about America, he's likely to give a list, starting with expecting elected officials to abide by principles of honesty and integrity. "And there's one more thing," he is likely to say. "I would like to see our president convene meetings between Muslims and Jews and Christians in the White House, and work to inspire those meetings around the world in order to turn the moderate Muslims against the violent extremists." Nunn acknowledges the limits of a president's power and influence but believes the president is uniquely positioned to bring about some measure of tolerance and reconciliation among religions. Once again, that's Sam Nunn being Sam Nunn: always working to develop a long-term strategy that no one else has the will, or political courage, to undertake. Perhaps, some day, American voters will put such a person in their White House.

When Senator Nunn made his retirement official at the state capitol in Atlanta, October 9, 1995, I listened from the back of the room and thought about the political career we were closing that began in a cow pasture on the outskirts of Perry nearly twenty-five years before.

"I look forward to more time to read, write, and think," he said.

I smiled and recalled the instructions he gave me at the start of the 1972 campaign: "Make sure there is time in my schedule to read, write, and think." Through the years, every staffer called upon to handle his schedule has heard the same words. I'm confident, however, that not one of them succeeded in providing as much time as Sam Nunn thought he needed for those highly coveted activities. Now that he was leaving the Senate, I'm sure he thought he would finally have the time he had sought to "read, write, and think." But it was not to be.

A year after he left the Senate, I asked how he was enjoying his retirement. Nunn gave me a smirk and shook his head. "I thought it was not possible to be busier than I was when I was in the Senate." He paused as if mentally reviewing the breadth of his new life obligations. "But I am. What happened?"

"You just need more hours in the day."

He chuckled. "Look into that, will you?"

I thought he might miss the Senate when he retired. He was one of the few senators who seemed to really enjoyed hearings— the probing for information and evidence, the constant milling for ideas, and processing it all through a prism of keen analysis to produce well-defined lines of practical policy options. It is not an understatement to say he had a passion for such pursuits. Where would he find a similarly stimulating experience outside the US Senate? It turns out that the Nuclear Threat Initiative enabled him to continue his involvement in public policy, and, specifically, continue his focus on securing and dismantling nuclear weapons around the world. It was, after all, the issue that brought him to the dance way back in October of 1962.

Is there any wonder that no fewer than three presidents asked him to serve as secretary of defense, that his name came up as a potential nominee for president or vice president every four years starting in 1988, or that he was pressured to run as an independent candidate for president in 2008?

When Senator Byrd told his colleagues "Sam Nunn could have been an outstanding US Senator at any time in the history of this Republic,"[1] he may have been exercising a bit of senatorial hyperbole. Perhaps Byrd exaggerated even more when he professed his belief that Senator Nunn would have been "comfortable in the gallery of delegates to the Constitutional Convention in 1787, and in the company of the first Congress, serving with William Few, the first senator from Georgia in 1789."[2] But if, indeed, Senator Nunn could have served at that time in our nation's history, surcly his casc with such early colleagues and his success would have been attributed to his rigid adherence to an ethical standard grounded in integrity, discipline, and courage. Such a standard never goes out of style.

[1] Ibid.; Byrd, "Tribute to Senator Sam Nunn."

[2] Ibid.

A Final Word

Sam Nunn never made a decision on major legislative issues without a thoughtful, sometimes extended analysis that was absolutely never based on political expediency. The idea that a public opinion poll should dictate how one should vote on a controversial issue was anathema to him. So, what should guide a Member's vote? The correct answer boils down to a fundamental principle of representative democracy: members of Congress are not elected to vote the weight of public opinion but to read, study, debate, and then, with the considered advice and counsel of constituents, vote the best interests of the nation. If one is not capable of such an exercise, he or she should not run for office. It's as simple as that. The role of constituents is critical, of course, but limited, and purposely so. I am dismayed by the number of voters I encounter who believe their Member's vote should "reflect the mail they receive" or "reflect the latest opinion polls." Congressional mail generally reflects a disproportionately negative view on nearly every issue, and polls change frequently, sometimes dramatically, as voters become better informed. Of course, if enough voters disagree with the way a Member is voting, they can make a change at the ballot box. They have the freedom to do so; indeed, that is their duty in a representative democracy.

Appendix

Bipartisan Victories: Essential to Governance

In 1986, journalist Steve Coll conducted a lengthy interview with Senator Nunn in preparation for a story he was writing for *The Washington Post*. His editors sensed the possibility that Nunn might be one of the serious contenders for the Democratic presidential nomination in 1988, and the interview was a journalistic exercise in due diligence as preparation for that possibility. The interview was lengthy and wide-ranging. Toward the end of the interview, Coll asked Senator Nunn to comment on the changes he had seen in the Senate and their impact on government. Senator Nunn's words are as applicable today as they were in 1986:

> The changes we've seen in the Senate are not in the best interest of the country. You get a senator mad on the floor of the US Senate and they can gum up this place for a week. Some of them do it even when they aren't mad. If comity breaks down in the Senate, the institution itself would change. We would become more like the House. We would have to impose rules on the amount of debate allowed, and I think we would lose an important protection for minority views in the country.
>
> A lot of people misread the role of Congress; they believe they should be able to measure the institution against efficiency. Is it efficient? Is it effective? How many bills did you pass? That is not what the founding fathers intended. This place wasn't designed constitutionally to be efficient. It was designed to be a place where the frustrations of the people could be voiced on the floor of either chamber. In those times when I think the whole process is for naught—and occasionally, I come to that conclusion—I back off a bit and ask, "Now, what do they really mean by this? What is the role of Congress?" If either body breaks down, we'll lose an important part of what the Congress is all about. Sometimes, groups visit my office, thirty at a time, and all are on one side of an issue. Another group follows them, all on the other side of the same issue. As frustrating as it can be to sit and listen, pulled between the two sides and trying to arbitrate the differing views—I am

> reminded in such moments of how great a system our founders created. What would happen if we didn't have such a system? What would happen if those people were going at each other all of the time? What would happen in the communities and states? This [Congress] is an outlet for citizen frustration. If we forget that, we've forgotten an important part of our mission.[1]

From Senator Nunn's point of view, voters should strive to elect a critical mass of moderate, moderate-to-conservative, and moderate-to-liberal members of Congress who are close enough philosophically to develop substantive proposals that preserve and strengthen our Republic and keep it moving forward.

In the Senate and his post-Senate years, Senator Sam Nunn left a significant record of achievement that proves his point: bipartisan cooperation works.

Senate Career

Cosponsored the landmark Department of Defense Reorganization Act (also known as Goldwater-Nichols), which increased the department's efficiency and gave more authority to the chairman of the Joint Chiefs of Staff and to commanders in the field. *Cosponsored by Senator Nunn and Sen. Barry Goldwater (R-AZ).*

Conceived of and cosponsored legislation creating the Nunn-Lugar Cooperative Threat Reduction Program, which provided assistance for more than twenty years to Russia and the former Soviet republics for securing and destroying their excess nuclear, biological, and chemical weapons. *Cosponsored by Senator Nunn and Sen. Richard Lugar (R-IN).*

Cosponsored legislation creating the combatant command for Special Operations, with unique budget and acquisition authorities, and reenergizing this critical national-security asset. *Cosponsored by Senator Nunn and Sen. Bill Cohen (R-ME)*

---

[1] Ibid.; Steve Coll, interview of 22 January 1986, transcribed for "Sam Nunn, Insider from the Deep Southland," *The Washington Post* (19 February 1986).

Restructured military pay and benefits to put the All-Volunteer Force on sound footing. *Cosponsored by Senator Nunn and Sen. John Warner (R-VA).*

Sponsored legislation that led to the complete overhaul of the government's procurement system. The law eliminated numerous paperwork requirements and greatly increased the government's ability to purchase less expensive commercial products. *Worked with the bipartisan leadership of the Senate Armed Services, Governmental Affairs, and Small Business Committees.*

Cochaired the "Strengthening of America" Commission, which proposed a $2 trillion plan to balance the federal budget over ten years. The key to the deficit-reduction plan was a cap on the growth of entitlement spending and a proposed legal ratio of $1 in revenue increases to every $2.75 in spending reductions. *Cochaired by Senator Nunn and Sen. Pete Domenici (R-NM).*

Cosponsored the Unlimited Savings Allowance (USA) Tax proposal that, if enacted, would have replaced the current income tax code with a progressive individual tax that would allow a deduction for personal savings and a flat-rate business tax that would allow a deduction for capital investment. *Cosponsored by Senator Nunn and Sen. Pete Domenici (R-NM).*

Post-Senate Career

Senator Nunn has continued bipartisan cooperation through his work with the Nuclear Threat Initiative, the Center for Strategic and International Studies, and the Concord Coalition.

1972 Election Results

Results of August 8, 1972, Democratic Primary

David Gambrell	*31.4%*
Sam Nunn	*23.17%*
Ernest Vandiver	20.5%
Hosea Williams	6.44%
J. B. Stoner	5.68%
Bill Burson	3.99%
Jack Dorsey	2.08%
Lloyd Russell	1.21%
Wyman C. Lowe	1.21%
William I. (Bill) Aynes	.99%
W. M. (Don) Wheeler	.97%
Thomas J. Irwin	.74%
Austin D. Graham	.57%
Darrell W. Runyan	.53%
Gerry Dokka	.43%

Results of August 8, 1972, Republican Primary

Fletcher Thompson	*92.7%*
Darrell W. Runyan	2.8% [Runyan ran as Republican and Democrat]
Clarence Porter	2.4%
Howard Tucker	2.2%

Results of August 29, 1972, Democratic Primary Runoff

Sam Nunn	*53.8%*
David Gambrell	46.2%

Results of November 7, 1972, General Election

Unexpired Term of Richard Russell
(November 8, 1972 to January 3, 1973)[1]

Sam Nunn	*52%*
Fletcher Thompson	48%

Full Six-Year Term
(January 3, 1973 to January 3, 1979)

Sam Nunn	*54%*
Fletcher Thompson	46%

[1] Voters were required to vote twice, once to fill Senator Russell's brief unexpired term, and a second time for their choice to serve a full six-year term. Many voters reported they did not understand that requirement or missed it entirely on the ballot. Thus, the discrepancy in percentages reported.

1972 Campaign Staff

Political staffs never get the credit they deserve. They work quietly, mostly in the background, and, usually, in total anonymity. What the Nunn campaign staff accomplished in 1972 with their obscure candidate in a relatively short period of time was nothing short of miraculous. They are named here to record their efforts and to express the thanks of all Georgians for the support they gave Senator Nunn every hour of every day during the campaign of 1972.

My role in the 1972 campaign was multifaceted. I had a broad portfolio by virtue of my early arrival and my familiarity with the candidate. By November, I had been involved in nearly every aspect of the campaign except fundraising. Because my responsibilities did not fit a traditional campaign definition, I was never given a specific title, but press relations and scheduling were foremost among my duties. I responded to all statewide radio and television inquiries and coordinated the daily schedule of campaign events. I was also the resident expert on Nunn's life and accomplishments. As a result, media quickly found me their "go to" contact for information on the candidate.

In the early days of the campaign, there wasn't enough money to hire one of the big names in polling, but we found Dr. Tim Ryles, a political-science professor at Georgia State University. Ryles was experienced in polling and statistical analysis, skills the campaign sorely lacked. His work helped staff gain some understanding of the difficult political environment in which they were working.

Although the campaign actually began in a small apartment in the Landmark building in downtown Atlanta, the headquarters was officially established in a two-room suite in a Travel Lodge Motel located just off I-85 on the northeast side of Atlanta. We were shoehorned into two rooms—a laughable space even then—but somehow we made it work.

Sue Bishop was the campaign secretary through the early, tough days of getting started, setting up the office, and smoothing out administrative wrinkles. Later in the campaign, Bishop's duties were assumed by Chris Berry.

Bill Pope, one of the few campaign veterans willing to risk his professional reputation with political amateurs, came aboard in late February 1972 to help with writing assignments and handle Atlanta print media. I'd never met anyone who liked to drink his beer warm until Pope came along. In spite of that little idiosyncrasy (he would say, "Because of it"), he was a good writer, excellent at turning a phrase and particularly good when condensing an issue into a few plain-spoken words any layman could understand. He once wrote, "When a citizen gets mugged, he doesn't need a federal program, he needs a cop." It was perfect for a law-and-order speech.

Connell Stafford was a young history teacher in Macon when Nunn asked him to become his youth coordinator. Stafford later became a key member of Nunn's Washington staff, where he served until he was asked to return to Georgia to manage Nunn's 1978 reelection effort. Unlike the first campaign, the campaign of 1978 ran like a well-oiled machine, and much of the credit goes to Stafford.

The person who provided wordsmith discipline after the August 30 runoff for the Democratic nomination was Norman Underwood, an attorney from Troutman Sanders law firm. Underwood was known for his writing skills, but he possessed one critically important intellectual quality: the analytical skills Nunn needed on a broad range of issues. When Underwood stepped into the campaign, he said it felt like being sucked into a tornado. That may be how it felt to Underwood, but from my perspective, his arrival had an immediate calming effect on the entire staff. Maybe it was the result of his having been involved in the 1970 Carl Sanders campaign for governor. Maybe it was his wise-beyond-his-years confidence. Whatever it was, his demeanor telegraphed to the staff that we really did have a chance to win. Every day he helped refine the campaign's underlying theme. "There was a 'message' but we didn't call it that," said Underwood. "Sam's message basically was kind of a common-sense conservatism that later became the record and the career."[1]

---

[1] Norman Underwood, Sam Nunn Oral History, Washington, DC (30 September 1996).

Joe Brannen was working at a bookstore on the Georgia Southern campus in Statesboro when he was hired to be Nunn's driver. He drove Nunn through the most frenetic weeks of the campaign—from early August through the general election. After the campaign, he came to Washington with Nunn and worked in constituent services. In 1974, Senator Nunn tapped him to head the Atlanta field office. For six years, Brannen built a staff and established one of the more effective field operations in the Senate.

We added Bill Robinson to the press operation toward the end of the campaign. Robinson, a former reporter for the Atlanta newspapers, was another good writer whose presence added significant strength. Robinson didn't care if his beer was warm or cold, so long as it didn't run out.

For a short time, the campaign benefited from the part-time services of public relations executive George C. "Buddy" Creal. Creal's mother, Gladys, had served as executive secretary to Herman Talmadge while he was governor. Perhaps that's the connection that brought him to our attention. He was with the campaign for only a few weeks, long enough for me to discern an innate sense of what makes good public relations. His handicap was having to work in a campaign with never enough resources to bring his ideas to reality.

Rick Wood worked with Connell Stafford to build a youth organization. Ned Young and Bill Gray came in to make sure Lester Maddox voters went to the polls. Tom Forbes, a college student from Texas, literally walked in off the street and worked wherever he was needed. Not everyone had a seat in the campaign office, including Bill Adams, Kip Klein, Paul Powell, Susan Wells, Tricia Rogers, Tommy Fulford, Bonnie Shiver, Shirley Nowacki, Marcia Wade, John Gerson, Laura Barre, Ernest Lee, Tony Scarwid, Sally Paris, Alice Fitzgerald, Sue Kilgore, Carroll Hawkins, Grace Flowers, and Jeanne Kromer. Kromer worked with me and actually sat in a chair next to my desk and took notes with a pad on her lap.

There was another group we jokingly referred to as the "Second Fiddle Corps." These were the courageous individuals who traveled the state as surrogates for the candidate whenever there was a need for a speaker at a civic club, barbecue, political rally, or school government class. Bill Arndt, Chuck Stapleton, Avon Buice, Mary Hitt, Macky

Mulherin, Jean Mori, and Charles Crawford filled these duties admirably.

Never on the official campaign staff but always available were two young teachers from Augusta, Mary Jane Langford and Jane Hart, both of whom later moved to Washington to join Senator Nunn's US Senate staff.

Jim Brown of Perry and Ralph Sark of Macon were loyal campaign pilots throughout the campaign. Working with the Nunn campaign was a part-time job for both of them, but happily they were always available when I called.

Campaign staff, Atlanta headquarters, November 7, 1972, General Election Day.

There was never a moment in the campaign when we had time for an official photo of the entire staff. On Election Day, most of the staff assembled briefly in Atlanta, and I realized if we were to capture such a scene, we would have to snap it that day or lose the opportunity forever. I gathered all of the staff present on the driveway in front of the Travel Lodge for a two o'clock photo. Two o'clock marked the beginning of that campaign twilight zone between the final instructions issued to Get-Out-the-Vote managers in every county in the morning and that stomach-churning time in late afternoon when campaigns begin to steel themselves for whatever decision the voters have made.

(L-R, Back Row): Ned Young, Bill Robinson, Connell Stafford, Tim Ryles, Tommy Fulford, Tom Forbes, Ed Sieb, Bill Pope, Bill Gray, Avon Buice, Rick Wood, Norman Underwood. (L-R, Front Row): Roland McElroy, Tony Scarwid, Sue Bishop, Dot Wood, Chris Berry, and Jeanne Kromer.

Photo courtesy: Roland McElroy

Bibliography

Books and Reports

Barone, Michael, and Grant Ujifusa. *The Almanac of American Politics 1986.* Washington, DC: National Journal, 1985.

Coleman, Kenneth. *A History of Georgia.* Athens: University of Georgia Press, 1977.

Cook, James F. *Carl Vinson, Patriarch of the Armed Forces.* Macon, GA: Mercer University Press, 2004.

Fite, Gilbert C. *Richard B. Russell, Jr., Senator from Georgia.* Chapel Hill: University of North Carolina Press, 1991.

Henderson, Harold Paulk. *Ernest Vandiver, Governor of Georgia.* Athens: University of Georgia Press, 2008.

Locher, James R. III. *Victory on the Potomac: The Goldwater-Nichols Act Unifies the Pentagon.* College Station: Texas A&M University Press, 2002.

Moyers, Bill. *Moyers on Democracy.* New York: Doubleday, 2008.

Nunn, Sam. "Policy, Troops, and the NATO Alliance." Report of Senator Sam Nunn to the Committee on Armed Services, United States Senate, 93rd Congress, 2nd Session, 2 April 1974.

Scheiffer, Bob. *This Just In.* New York: Berkley Publishing Group, 2003.

Schlesinger, Arthur M. Jr. *The Almanac of American History.* New York: G. P. Putnam's Sons, 1983.

Shipp, Bill. *Murder at Broad River Bridge.* Atlanta: Peachtree Publishers, 1981.

Cited Works

Magazines and Periodicals

Alter, Jonathan. "Why Obama Should Pick Sam Nunn for Veep." *Newsweek* Web Exclusive (3 July 2008).

Barnes, James A. "Reluctant Bridegrooms." *National Journal* 19/25 (20 June 1987).

"Best and Worst of Congress." Annual Survey. *Washingtonian* 31/12 (September 1996).

Coleman, Michael. "Ex-Senator Continues Dogged Pursuit to Rid World of Nuclear Weapons." *Washington Diplomat* 22/10 (October 2015).

Kimball, Daryl G., and Miles A. Pomper. "A World Free of Nuclear Weapons: An Interview with Nuclear Threat Initiative Co-Chairman Sam Nunn." *Arms Control Today* 38/9 (March 2008).

Kramer, Michael. "Smart, Dull and Very Powerful." *Time* 133/11 (13 March 1989).

McDonald, R. Robin. "Explain It Sam." *Atlanta Magazine* 31/4 (July 1992).

Methvin, Eugene H. "Sam Nunn: Senator for the Defense." *Reader's Digest* (October 1981).

Nunn, Sam. "Q&A Interview." *Arms Control Today* 38/9 (March 2008).

Nunn, Sam, and Richard Lugar. "There Are No Perfect Nuclear Deals." *Politico Magazine* (30 August 2015) www.politico.com/magazine/story/2015/08/there-are-no-perfect-nuclear-deals-121810.

"Periscope—Personal Factors." *Newsweek* 87/31 (3 August 1987).

Towell, Pat. "Sam Nunn: The Careful Exercise of Power." *Congressional Quarterly* 44/24 (14 June 1986).

Newspapers

"4,000 Attend Kick-Off Here Saturday." *Houston Home Journal* (1 June 1978).

"Mrs. Nunn Kills Snake at Home." *The Atlanta Journal* (7 October 1972).

"Nunn Being Nunn," *The Rome-News Tribune*. Editorial (2 June 1995).

"Perry Welcomes Senator George." *Houston Home Journal* (13 August 1938).

"Southerners Break Ranks on Voting Act." *The Atlanta Journal* (25 July 1975).

"Thompson says he's leading." *The Augusta Chronicle* (21 September 1972).

"U.S. Senate." *The Atlanta Constitution*. Editorial (7 August 1972).

"Voting Rights." *The Atlanta Constitution*. Editorial (26 July 1975).

Branch, Bobby. "Out on a Branch." *Houston Home Journal* (1 May 1969).

Cohen, Michelle. "Nunn Won't Seek Presidency." *Sun Sentinel* (28 August 1987).

Fliess, Maurice. "A Day in Life of Freshman Sen. Nunn." *The Atlanta Journal and Constitution* (25 March 1973).

Fort, Bob. "Carter Warns Nunn on Charges." *The Atlanta Constitution* (11 August 1972).

———. "Mrs. Nunn and Shotgun Take Care of Copperhead." *Atlanta Constitution* (6 October 1972).

———. "Nunn Rolls Over Gambrell." *The Atlanta Constitution* (30 August 1972).

———. "Nunn-Wallace Visit Fake, Says Thompson in Debate." *The Atlanta Constitution* (30 September 1972).

———. "Thompson Admits He Knew about Controversial Ads." *The Atlanta Constitution* (27 September 1972).

Gailey, Phil. "Sam Nunn's Rising Star." *The New York Times* (4 January 1987).

Hunt, Albert R. "Little Giant: In the SALT Debate, Sen. Sam Nunn's Role Could Prove Decisive." *The Wall Street Journal* (22 March 1979).

Linthicum, Tom. "Carter Hits Nunn on Ad." *The Atlanta Constitution* (20 May 1972).

Meaders, Homer. "10,000 Grads Crowd Campus for Tech Homecoming Game." *The Atlanta Journal and Constitution* (28 October 1956).

Murphy, Reg. "The Race Nobody Can Possibly Win." *The Atlanta Constitution* (24 June 1972).

Nesmith, Jeff. "Endorsement Put Bond on the Spot." *The Atlanta Constitution* (1 September 1972).

Nordan, David. "Fletcher Thompson Denies Using Racist Digs." *The Atlanta Constitution* (10 September 1972).

Nunn, Sam. "Open a Nuclear Fuel Bank." Op-ed column. *The New York Times* (11 July 2014).

Nunn, Sam, George P. Shultz, William J. Perry, and Henry A. Kissinger. "A World Free of Nuclear Weapons." Op-ed column. *The Wall Street Journal* (4 January 2007).

Riner, Duane. "Georgians Saying Ho-Hum to Senate Race." *The Atlanta Constitution* (27 April 1972).

Shepard, Scott. "Nunn Not a One-Issue Senator Despite Defense Work, He Says." *The Atlanta Constitution* (9 December 1986).

———. "Nunn Sets the Standard with His Ethics Code." *The Atlanta Journal and Constitution* (3 July 1988).

Shipp, Bill. "'71 Big on Little News." *The Atlanta Constitution* (1 January 1972).

Will, George. "Best President We've Never Had." *The Washington Post* (22 June 1998).

Oral Histories

Carter, Jimmy. Manuscript. Sam Nunn Oral History Collection, 1996–1997. Archives and Rare Book Library, Emory University, 16 July 1997.

Nunn, Colleen. Sam Nunn Oral History. In possession of the author. Washington, DC, 30 September 1996.

Nunn, Sam. Sam Nunn Oral History. In possession of the author. Washington, DC, 30 September 1996.

Ray, Richard. Sam Nunn Oral History. In possession of the author. Washington, DC, 30 September 1996.

Talmadge, Herman, to journalist Jack Nelson. Interview for Southern Oral History Program Collection, A-0331-1, Washington, DC, 15 July 1975.

Talmadge, Herman E. Manuscript. Sam Nunn Oral History Collection, 1996–1997. Archives and Rare Book Library, Emory University, 17 July 1996.

Thompson, Fletcher S. Manuscript. Sam Nunn Oral History Collection, 1996–1997. Archives and Rare Book Library, Emory University, 10 July 1996.

Underwood, Norman. Sam Nunn Oral History. In possession of the author. Washington, DC, 30 September 1996.

Vandiver, Ernest. Manuscript. Sam Nunn Oral History Collection, 1996–1997. Archives and Rare Book Library, Emory University, 29 May 29 1996.

Speeches

Bradley, General Omar N. "An Armistice Day Address." 10 November 1948. In *The Collected Writings of General Omar N. Bradley: Articles, Broadcasts, and Statements, 1945–1967*. Vol. 3 (GPO: 1967).

Byrd, Robert. "Tribute to Senator Sam Nunn." 27 September 1996. *Congressional Record*: 142:136.

Carter, Jimmy. Governor's Inaugural Address, 12 January 1971. Atlanta: Jimmy Carter Library.

Nunn, Sam. Alfalfa Club Speech, 23 January 1982. Washington, DC: In possession of the author.

———. Cunningham Center for Leadership Development Speech. 29 August 2006. Columbus, GA.

———. Dedication of Houston County Board of Education Complex and Senator Sam Nunn Exhibit. 8 September 1996. Perry, GA. In possession of the author.

———. First Robert S. McNamara Lecture on War and Peace. Delivered at John F. Kennedy Jr. Forum of the Institute of Politics, Harvard University: 17 October 2008.

———. Spring Commencement. 22 March 1996. Atlanta: Georgia Institute of Technology.

———. Retirement Speech. 9 October 1995. Atlanta: Georgia State Capitol.

Roosevelt, Franklin D. Opening of nation's first electric membership cooperative, Lamar EMC. March 11, 1938. Barnesville, GA.

Transcript of Media Interviews

Coll, Steve, excerpt from interview of 22 January 1986, as transcribed for "Sam Nunn, Insider from the Deep Southland," *The Washington Post* (18 February 1986).

About the Author

I have always been a Democrat.

My father didn't talk much about politics, but when he did, I listened. "Franklin Roosevelt was a great president," my father often said. "During the Depression, no one around Quitman had any money; all the money was in the hands of rich Republicans up North. Roosevelt got it circulating again and the country recovered."

How was I to be anything other than a Democrat?

Dad was the pastor at the only Presbyterian church in town. He read Frank Gilbreth's book *Cheaper by the Dozen* and got the idea that having a large family was a fine goal to pursue. "Twelve seems like a worthy ambition," he would say, as mother rolled her eyes. I think it disappointed him that he and mother ran out of biological time shortly after number nine was born.

Of the nine, I was sixth in the lineup. By the time all nine were old enough to sit at the table, Dad began scheduling regular deliveries of fresh produce via an eighteen-wheeler from the warehouse of W. J. Powell Produce Company in nearby Thomasville. As far as I know, ours was the only family in town that bought toilet paper in the forty-eight-count economy size.

In high school, I participated in Boy's State, helped my school's debate team win a state championship, won a couple of essay contests, three speaking contests, and waited for college days to arrive. At the University of Georgia, I earned a bachelor's degree in economics and later a master's degree in journalism.

In Washington, I worked a total of seventeen years for two US Senators: Sam Nunn of Georgia and Chuck Robb of Virginia. With Senator Robb, I served two years as his chief of staff and helped prepare his staff for a tough reelection in 1994. In the mid-1990s, I established McElroy & Associates, a public relations consultancy.

Oral history recording session with US Senator Sam Nunn, Atlanta, 2005.

Clockwise: Roland McElroy, Joe Brannen, Norman Underwood, Connell Stafford, Colleen Nunn, Hal Gulliver, Gordon Giffin, Senator Sam Nunn.

Photo courtesy: Roland McElroy

Acknowledgments

My thanks to Connell Stafford, Joe Brannen, and Norman Underwood, veterans of the 1972 campaign, who graciously took my calls and kept me from straying too far from the truth. And my special gratitude to Arnold Punaro and Gordon Giffin, valued members of Nunn's Washington staff, whose early and late review of drafts preserved the integrity of my recollections.

Many professionals at Emory University helped, including Lauran Whitworth, doctoral fellow at the George Woodruff Library; Kathleen Shoemaker, reference coordinator, Research Services; and Heather Oswald, Public Services And Outreach coordinator. They patiently searched and found every campaign note, memo, and clipping requested by the author, no matter how deeply hidden in Emory's Sam Nunn Archives.

Deep appreciation is extended to Emory University's Dr. Tom Chaffin, who conducted two-dozen interviews from 1996 to 1997 with major political figures of the period. Several of the interviews focused exclusively on Sam Nunn's 1972 campaign, and all of them enriched this manuscript with their honesty and candor.

Cathy Gwin, Senator Nunn's longest serving press secretary and communications director at the National Threat Initiative, put her critical eye on every page, with emphasis on issues addressed in the final decade of Senator Nunn's service. Her personal knowledge of those years limited the number of mistakes the author might have made otherwise. Any mistakes that may still exist are the fault of the author alone.

Thanks also to editor Amy McElroy (no relation) for her gentle critique of early drafts and her strong suggestions throughout the process for making the narrative arc more compelling.

And to my wife, Bettie, I reserve the deepest appreciation for her partnership in this entire endeavor. She read every draft several times, and her suggested edits never failed to improve the manuscript.

Index

Adams, Bill, 228
Adams, Charlie, 35
Agnew, Spiro T., 116, 133-34
Alter, Jonathan, 204
Arndt, Bill, 228
Aspin, Les, 183-84
Aynes, William I. (Bill), 224
Baldowski, Clifford "Baldy", 201
Barbour, Haley, 213-14
Barnes, James, 197
Barnes, Roy, 212
Barre, Laura, 228
Barron, Bud, 97
Bartlett, Dewey, 126
Beckham, Ed, 7-9, 13, 33, 147
Beckham, Jane, 73
Begin, Menachem, 187
Berry, Chris, 227, 230
Berry, Chuck, 16
Biden, Joe, 116
Bishop, Sue, 226-27, 230
Blum, Deborah, 127
Bodenhamer, Bill, 16-18
Bond, Julian, xii, 96-98
Boren, David, 126, 202-3
Bork, Robert, 133
Bradley, Omar, 185
Bradley, Bill, 197
Brady, James, 124-25, 178
Bramlett, Gail, 132
Branch, Bobby, 25-26, 33
Brannen, Joe, 73, 105-6, 114, 228, 237
Brinkley, David, 133
Brinkley, Jack, 32, 41
Brown, Jim, 229
Bryan, William Jennings, 7
Buffett, Warren, 191
Buice, Avon, 108, 138, 228, 230
Burson, Bill, 76, 224
Bush, George H.W., 174, 177, 182, 184
Bush, George W., 182
Byrd, Robert C., x, 218
Calhoun, John C., 133
Callaway, Howard "Bo", 206
Camp, Billy Joe, 97
Camp, Lawrence, 2-3, 103
Carter, Ash, 184
Carter, Jimmy, xi, 26-27, 29, 31-33, 38, 43, 75, 79-81, 91, 95-96, 101, 126, 134, 164, 171-73, 187, 194, 207
Carter, Rosalind, 157
Castro, Fidel, 180
Chaffin, Tom, 237
Cheney, Dick, 124, 149
Chew, Emerson, 106
Chiles, Lawton, 76, 126, 196, 198, 209
Clinton, Bill, 182, 210
Cochran, Leonard, 154
Cohen, Bill, 126, 222
Coll, Steve, 221
Courtney, John J., 19
Coverdell, Paul, 212
Cox, Archibald, 133
Crawford, Charles, 229
Creal, George C. "Buddy", 228
Creal, Gladys, 228
Cuomo, Mario, 197
Dayan, Moshe, 187
Dokka, Gerry, 224
Dole, Bob, 175-76
Domenici, Pete, 126, 184, 223
Dorsey, Jack, 224
Duke, Paul, 194
Eastland, James, 119
Eisenhower, Dwight D., 179
Eisenhower, Susan, 203
Ellender, Allen, 119
Ervin, Sam, 195
Evans, Martha, 71
Fanning, J.W., 27

Faubus, Orval, 18
Feldman, Joel, 108, 128
Ferraro, Geraldine, 209
Few, William, 218
Fitzgerald, Alice, 228
Flowers, Grace, 228
Flynt, Jack, 157
Forbes, Tom, 228, 230
Ford, Gerald R., 134, 173, 187
Forest, Nathan Bedford, 16
Fortson, Ben, 154
Franklin, Benjamin, 108, 156, 186
From, Al, 210
Fulford, Tommy, 228, 230
Galloway, Jim, 127
Gambrell, David, 29-31, 44, 75, 79-80, 85-87, 89-92, 96, 101, 107, 110, 114, 224-25
Gambrell, Luck, 92
George, Walter, 1-3, 14, 154
Gephardt, Dick, 196, 209-10
Gerson, John, 228
Giffin, Gordon, 127, 153, 168-70, 237
Gingrich, Newt, 157, 202, 208, 211, 213-14
Goldwater, Barry, xii, 102, 165, 179-81, 206, 222
Gorbachev, Mikhail, 183
Gore, Al, 201, 210
Graham, Austin D., 224
Gray, Bill, 97, 228, 230
Griffin, Marvin, 76, 83-85, 123, 139, 206
Grizzard, Lewis, 161-62
Gulliver, Hal, 38
Gwinn, Cathy, 28, 237
Hammock, Jimmy, 71
Hardman, Lamartine G., 9
Hargett, Gil, 72
Harman, Charlie, 54-55
Harper, Clyde, 21-23
Harrison, Florence, 6, 59, 164
Hart, Jane, 229
Haskell, Floyd, 116-17
Hathaway, Jim, 73
Hawkins, Carroll, 228
Hébert, Eddie, 12
Hewett, Harriet, 15-16
Hitt, Mary, 228
Hodges, Courtney H., 6
Holmes, Hamilton, 18
Hope, Bob, 159-60
Horner, Dick, 76
Humphrey, Hubert, 206-7
Hunt, Al, 149
Hunter, Charlayne, 18
Hussein, Saddam, 178
Irwin, Thomas J., 224
Jackson, Henry "Scoop", 126, 158-60
Javits, Jacob, 207
Jennings, Henry, 86
Jennings, Robert, 86
Jobs, Steve, 186
Johnson, Leroy, xii, 96-97
Johnson, Lyndon B., 107, 210
Johnson, Rose, 174-75
Johnston, Bennett, 126
Kennedy, John F., 206
Kennedy, Robert, 113
Khrushchev, Nikita, 20
Kilgore, Sue, 228
King, Angus, 203
King, Coretta Scott, 96
King, Martin Luther Sr., 207
Kirk, Paul, 210
Kissinger, Henry, 40, 161, 164, 191-92
Klein, Kip, 228
Kramer, Michael, 149
Kromer, Jeanne, 228, 230
Laird, Melvin, 131
Landrum, Phil, 11, 102
Langford, Mary Jane, 229
Laroe, Joie, 42
Lee, Ernest, 228
Levin, Carl, 150
Levitas, Elliot, 168
Lewis, Jerry Lee, 62-63
Lincoln, Abraham, 114
Little, Tom, 42, 82, 86-88
Locher, Jim, 181

Long, Russell, 124, 126
Lowe, Wyman C., 224
Lowery, J.E., 96
Lugar, Dick, 126, 136, 183-84, 190, 222
Maddox, Lester, xii, 31, 36, 40-41, 44, 76, 83-85, 96-97, 154-55, 228
Mann, Thomas, 201
Mansfield, Mike, 117, 126, 135, 215
Mason, Jimmy, 32
Mathis, Dawson, 41
Mattingly, Mack, 157, 209
McClellan, John, 195
McClure, James, 116-17
McDonald, Mike, 42
McElroy, Amy, 237
McElroy, Frank H., vii, 4-5, 10-11, 39, 235
McElroy, Frank H. Jr., 39, 65
McElroy, Ginny Sears, 21, 69, 71-72, 93, 114
McGovern, George, 51, 93, 95, 97, 102, 104, 207, 210
McKinley, James, 154
McLuhan, Marshall, 82-83
Methvin, Eugene, 149
Mondale, Walter, 134, 195, 198, 209-10
Moore, Powell, 194-97
Mori, Jean, 229
Moyers, Bill, 210
Mulherin, Macky, 229
Murphy, Reg, 75
Murphy, Tom, 212-13
Nelson, Bobbe, 5
Nelson, Jack, viii
Nichols, William F. "Bill", 181
Nixon, Richard, xii, 11, 40, 43, 93, 103, 121-22, 124, 131-34, 173, 195, 206-7
Norwood, Jack, 49
Nowacki, Shirley, 228
Nunn, Betty, 73
Nunn, Brian, 74, 104, 117-18
Nunn, Colleen Ann O'Brien, 20, 38-39, 54, 56, 58, 60, 73-74, 104, 117-18, 197, 200
Nunn, Mary Elizabeth Cannon, 2-3, 8, 10, 14, 73, 80, 94, 117
Nunn, Michelle, 104, 117-18, 214-15
Nunn, Samuel Augustus, Sr., 1-3, 9, 13, 64
O'Conner, Sandra Day, 158
Obama, Barack, 183, 204
Orben, Bob, 161
Oswald, Heather, 237
Pace, Stephen, 5
Paris, Sally, 228
Pastore, John, 34
Patterson, Rudolph, 35
Perdue, David, 214
Perry, William, 191-92
Pettys, Dick, 44
Pinkston, Frank, 32
Pope, Bill, 45, 72, 89, 93-94, 105, 120, 227, 230
Porter, Ben, 35-37
Porter, Clarence, 224
Porter, Dubose, 127
Powell, Jody. 26-28
Powell, Paul, 228
Punaro, Arnold, 127, 144-45, 162, 237
Quitman, John A., vii
Ralston, David, 127
Ray, Richard, 23-25, 35, 60-61, 72, 107-8, 115
Reagan, Ronald, 14, 149, 176, 178, 181, 195-96, 209
Reese, Malcolm, 35
Richardson, Elliot, 121-22, 133
Riner, Duane, 67
Robb, Chuck, 196, 198-99, 209
Robb, Lynda Bird, 107
Roberts, Gordon, 123, 209
Robinson, Bill, 228, 230
Rockefeller, Nelson, 134, 207
Rogers, Tricia, 228
Roosevelt, Franklin D., viii, 2-3, 9, 103, 154

Roosevelt, Theodore, 42
Roth, Bill, 124-25, 178
Rowling, J.K, 209
Ruckelshaus, William, 133
Runyan, Darrell W., 224
Rusk, Dean, 187
Russell, Lloyd, 224
Russell, Mark, 162
Russell, Richard B., xi, 103, 106-7, 110, 119-21, 134, 194-95
Ryles, Tim, 226, 230
Sadat, Anwar, 187
Sanders, Carl, 20-21, 23, 31, 36, 40-41, 44, 83-84, 91, 95-96, 171, 206, 227
Sark, Ralph, 229
Scarwid, Tony, 228, 230
Schieffer, Bob, 175
Schorr, Daniel, 188
Schultz, George, 191-92
Scott, Hugh D., 117
Shapard, Virginia, 157
Sheehan, Joe, 42, 44, 59-60
Sherman, William T., 164
Shipp, Bill, xi-xii, 38
Shiver, Bonnie, 228
Shoemaker, Kathleen, 237
Sieb, Ed, 59-60, 230
Simpkins, John, 68, 97
Smith, George L., 96
Smith, Jeff, 144
Sparkman, John, 195
Stafford, Connell, 61, 93-95, 105-6, 227-28, 230, 237
Staples, Eric, 8
Stapleton, Chuck, 228
Steed, Bob, 161-62
Stennis, John, 126, 134-35, 195
Stevenson, Adlai, 35
Stokes, John W., 156
Stoner, J.B., 76, 224
Stuckey, Bill, 31, 41
Stuckey, John, 177
Sullivan, Frank, 134-35
Talmadge, Eugene, viii, 2, 155
Talmadge, Herman, 92, 101-2, 111, 117-19, 136, 154-56, 169-70, 172, 195, 209, 228
Talmadge, Robert, 118
Tate, Martha, 121
Taylor, Henry, 108
Thompson, Bill, 35-36, 42, 60, 87-89
Thompson, Fletcher, 75, 81, 93, 95, 97, 100, 102-5, 107, 116, 211, 224-25
Thompson, M.E., 154
Thompson, Spencer, 81
Till, Christine, 110-12
Tolleson, J.M. "Buddy", 3, 45
Tower, John, 168, 174-77
Trudeau, Elliott, 82
Tucker, Howard, 224
Tucker, Malissa, 6
Turner, Ted, 186, 188, 190
Underwood, Norman, 91, 93, 95, 97, 99-100, 227, 230, 237
Vandiver, Ernest, 17-18, 20-21, 44, 76, 87, 89, 101-2, 171, 224
Vinson, Carl, ix, 11-12, 19, 47, 103, 134, 154, 179-80, 188, 215
Wade, Marcia, 228
Walker, Larry, 40-41
Wall, Anita, 71
Wallace, Cornelia, 99
Wallace, George, xii, 18, 40, 42, 96-97, 99-100, 206
Warner, John, 126, 223
Wells, Susan, 228
Wheeler, W. M. (Don), 224
Whitworth, Lauran, 237
Wild, Claude C. Jr., 137
Will, George, 150
Williams, Hosea, 76, 224
Wood, Dot, 89, 230
Wood, Rick, 228, 230
Yeltsin, Boris, 183
Young, Andrew, 168
Young, Ned, 228, 230